THE CIVIL RIGHTS MOVEMENT

Studies in Contemporary History
Series Editors: T. G. Fraser and J. O. Springhall

PUBLISHED

T. G. Fraser   *The Arab-Israeli Conflict*

Raymond Pearson   *The Rise and Fall of the Soviet Empire*

William T. Martin Riches   *The Civil Rights Movement: struggle and resistance*

Dennis B. Smith   *Japan since 1945: the rise of an economic superpower*

FORTHCOMING

James Loughlin   *The Ulster Question Since 1945*

Stephen Ryan   *The United Nations and International Politics*

The Civil Rights Movement

Struggle and Resistance

William T. Martin Riches

St. Martin's Press
New York

St. Martin's Press, Scholarly and Reference Division,
175 Fifth Avenue, New York, N.Y. 10010

First published in the United States of America in 1997

This book is printed on paper suitable for recycling and
made from fully managed and sustained forest sources.

Printed in Hong Kong

ISBN 0–312–17403–9
ISBN 0–312–17404–7

Library of Congress Cataloging-in-Publication Data
Riches, William Terence Martin, 1939–
The civil rights movement : struggle and resistance / William T.
Martin Riches.
p.   cm. — (Studies in contemporary history)
Includes bibliographical references and index.
ISBN 0–312–17403–9. — ISBN 0–312–17404–7 (pbk.)
1. Afro-Americans—Civil rights—History—20th century.   2. Civil
rights movements—United States—History—20th century.   I. Title.
II. Series: Studies in contemporary history (New York, N.Y.)
E185.61.R514 1997
973'.0496073—dc21   96–40415
                                                                      CIP

To Judy

CONTENTS

SERIES EDITORS' PREFACE

There are those, politicians among them, who feel that historians should not teach or write about contemporary events and people – many of whom are still living – because of the difficulty of treating such matters with historical perspective, that it is right to draw some distinction between the study of history and the study of current affairs. Proponents of this view seem to be unaware of the concept of contemporary history to which this series is devoted, that the history of the recent past can and should be written with a degree of objectivity. As memories of the Second World War recede, it is surely time to place in perspective the postwar history that has shaped all our lives, whether we were born in the 1940s or the 1970s.

Many countries – Britain, the United States and Germany among them – allow access to their public records under a thirty-year rule, opening up much of the postwar period to archival research. For more recent events, diaries, memoirs, and the investigations of newspapers and television, confirm the view of the famous historian Sir Lewis Namier that all secrets are in print provided you know where to look for them. Contemporary historians also have the opportunity, denied to historians of earlier periods, of interviewing participants in the events they are analysing. The problem facing the contemporary historian is, if anything, the embarrassment of riches.

In any case, the nature and extent of world changes since the late 1980s have clearly signalled the need for concise discussion of major themes in post-1945 history. For many of us the difficult thing to grasp is how dramatically the world has changed over recent years: the collapse of the Soviet Union and Russian communism; the end of Soviet hegemony over eastern Europe; the unification of Germany; the end of the Cold War; America's sense of a 'new world order'; the pace of integration in the European Union; the disintegration of Yugoslavia; the Middle East peace settlement; the continuing economic strength of Japan. Writing in a structured and cogent way about these seismic changes is what makes contemporary history so challenging, and we hope that the end result will convey some of this excitement and interest to our readers.

The general objective of this series, written entirely by members of the School of History, Philosophy and Politics of the University of Ulster, is to offer concise and up-to-date treatments of postwar themes considered of historical and political significance, and to stimulate critical thought about the theoretical assumptions and conceptual apparatus underlying interpretation of the topics under discussion. The series should bring some of the central themes and problems confronting students and teachers of recent history, politics and international affairs into sharper focus than the textbook writer alone could provide. The blend required to write contemporary history that is both readable and easily understood but also accurate and scholarly is not easy to achieve, but we hope that this series will prove worthwhile for both students and teachers interested in world affairs since 1945.

University of Ulster

T. G. Fraser
J. O. Springhall

PREFACE

A friend at Harvard University in 1964 enquired about the places that my wife and I would visit during our travels in the United States from our home in Canada. When we informed him that we were going to visit the southern states, including Alabama and Mississippi, he was very concerned about our safety and pressed us to buy a flag and put it in the front of the car. He warned us that we would be mistaken for civil rights 'outside agitators' and the locals would not know that our Ontario licence plate proved we were from Canada but would assume it was just another northern state. We assured him that we would take the necessary precautions.

As foreigners we were naive about the dangers we faced and, more important, equally unaware of the 'etiquette of segregation'. This became apparent as we approached the town of Biloxi, Mississippi. We were thirsty and just after crossing the city limits we stopped at a restaurant for a drink. It was crowded and we sat at the counter and I ordered two coffees. The woman did not respond. I asked for a second time and still no acknowledgement. I assumed it must be my accent and, with a slightly raised voice, I spoke slowly and distinctly and repeated my order. The woman turned and fled. Before we could leave a man appeared and asked politely what we wanted and I repeated my order. Looking at the woman he told her to give us the cups of coffee. Throughout this almost surrealistic exchange we were aware that the conversations of the other customers had stopped and there was just an oppressive silence. Looking around the restaurant we realised why. We were the only white couple in the place. With my long hair and beard it must have seemed that I was one of those civil rights 'trouble makers' and by integrating that cafe we had endangered the man, his wife and even his customers. Inadvertently we had defied segregation etiquette. In later years as graduate students at the University of Tennessee, Knoxville, our defiance of the South and its custom was never accidental.

The challenge in writing contemporary history is that the writer has lived through the events and some would argue that this makes considered judgement impossible. In my case it is even more difficult in that I was also a participant in a very small way in some of these events. However, this is not a participant's history, but rather seeks objectively to analyse the struggle of African Americans and other minorities, such as Native Americans, women and gays, to achieve equality in the years after World War II and those who sought to resist that change. I believe the intervening years and my views as an outsider living in Ireland have ensured some objectivity. I can only agree with Alan Dawley that 'the destiny of modern America was in the hands of the meek as well as the mighty'. As he points out, the struggles for racial justice and sexual equality were not simply a matter of the good versus the bad guys but 'there is no doubt that good and evil hung in the balance. In comprehending what happened, I have aspired to objectivity. But objectivity does not mean indifference. It matters very much how things turned out' (Dawley, 1991).

I am aware of the vital role played by Martin Luther King Jr in the civil rights movement and very conscious of the tragic consequences of his assassination in Memphis. However, in this study I have stressed the role of the civil rights movement as a mass movement and its interaction with those who held political power at the state, federal and local levels. It was the extraordinary courage and sacrifice of hundreds of thousands of the 'meek' that achieved the successes of the movement. I am very conscious that the movement had a profound influence on the ideology and tactics of those who participated in the anti-Vietnam War campaign. I have alluded frequently to the connections between the two but it has not been possible within the current text to elaborate on the anti-war movement. In addition, in chapter six, 'A New South?', it may be argued that I have neglected the resurgence of racism and the role of the modern Ku Klux Klan. In my defence, I have pointed out in every chapter the resistance to the movement, but what has not been sufficiently acknowledged is the change in the attitudes of a

significant number of southerners. Having lived in the South for
many years, having studied at a southern university with students
from all over the South, I believe that it is time that their voices
were heard because they played a vital part in the struggle and many
continue to do so today. I consider myself fortunate to include many
of these people as my friends.

With the election of Richard Nixon in 1968 and with the
Democratic party deeply divided, it seemed that the gains of the
civil rights movement would be wiped out. A white friend who was a
doctor in Tennessee, whose father was an illiterate sharecropper in
Alabama, invited me and my wife to a dinner with friends, black and
white, who were active in the civil rights movement and the anti-
Vietnam War movement. We reminisced about the years that had
passed and were fearful about the years ahead. Before we left he
insisted that we all sit, listen and in the years ahead, when we were
separated, to remember these words and try to live by them. He left
the room and returned shortly. On that very late hot summer night
in East Tennessee the small group of southerners – academics,
ministers, atheists and the couple from the United Kingdom – sat
and listened to the speech given by Martin Luther King Jr at the
Washington rally of 1963.

So I say to you, my friends, that even though we must face the
difficulties of today and tomorrow, I still have a dream. It is a
dream deeply rooted in the American dream that one day this
nation will rise up and live out the true meaning of its creed –
we hold these truths to be self-evident, that all men are
created equal.

ACKNOWLEDGEMENTS

I would like to thank the editors of the series, Tom Fraser and John Springhall, for their advice, criticism and support. I owe Professor Fraser a special debt of gratitude for his support of the American Studies programme at the University of Ulster at Jordanstown, at both the undergraduate and postgraduate level. I would also like to thank the University for its support for my teaching and research for the last 20 years. In addition, I appreciate the criticism and advice given by my daughter, Julia Riches, who is currently studying at Georgetown University, and my son, Theo, who, despite his interest in medieval studies, has also read and commented on the manuscript. All lecturers owe great debts to their students who have helped in so many ways. It is invidious to single out individuals but I must thank Jacqueline Tine Nichols for persuading me to take a closer interest in the role of Native Americans, Leonora Campbell for introducing me to the struggle of Oglala women on the Pine Ridge Reservation (especially the poetry of Beth Brant), Simon Topping for a copy of his interview with James Meredith and David McAree for use of his taped interviews with African American women who worked with the Student Nonviolent Coordinating Committee. This book also owes much to friends from the South such as David Bowen, John Thomas, Tom Wilson, O. C. Richardson and Dan Pomeroy, to name just a few of my fellow graduate students from the University of Tennessee, Knoxville. Apart from my colleagues in England and Ireland who have provided constructive criticism, I would like especially to mention friends and members of the Milan Group for the Study of American History. This book is dedicated to my wife Judith, who made my academic career possible and who is my sternest critic and supporter.

GLOSSARY

Baby boom
This is an expression commonly used to describe the generation born in the late 1940s and 1950s, a period which saw a dramatic increase in childbirth in the United States.

Bossism
The corruption of democratic government primarily in the urban centres of the United States enabled parties to control local government with the corrupt use of patronage. The most notorious city Boss in the nineteenth century was Boss Tweed of New York City and in the twentieth Mayor Richard Daley of Chicago.

Bussing
After World War II southern states used bussing to consolidated schools, thereby eliminating many inferior rural institutions, in an effort to raise academic quality of the school system. However, the bus was also used to guarantee the segregation of white and black school children. In *Swann v Carlotte-Mecklenburg* (1974) the Supreme Court ordered the use of bussing to achieve racial integration.

Carpetbagger
An allegedly corrupt, white or black, Republican politician from the North who had moved to the South after the Civil War and who was active in southern politics. Carpetbaggers were seen by southerners as coming to rob the South because the only belongings they had with them were capable of being carried in a carpetbag.

Filibustering
A method of delaying or preventing legislation in Congress or in the state legislatures by prolonging the debate or using parliamentary procedures to prevent the passage of legislation.

Governor
The title of the leading executive officer of a state.

Great Society
The 1964–68 liberal social and economic reform programme of President Lyndon Baines Johnson who hoped to resolve the problem of poverty in the United States and thereby to complete the New Deal begun by Johnson's hero, Franklin Delano Roosevelt.

Interposition
The argument of southerners before the Civil War and during the civil rights movement that a state was sovereign and should interpose its authority between the people of the state and the federal government and protect the citizens of the state from the enforcement of a federal law which the people of the state deemed unconstitutional.

Jim Crow Laws
The system of segregation of the races imposed after the Civil War in southern and some border states. The origin of the term Jim Crow is not known but may have its origins in a minstrel song.

Ku Klux Klan (KKK)
A paramilitary terrorist organisation founded in Pulaski, Tennessee, after the Civil War. Despite the protestations of some southerners, the Invisible Empire of the Ku Klux Klan was the paramilitary wing of the Democratic party and was instrumental in the overthrow of the Reconstruction governments in the South. The modern KKK was launched in Georgia and claimed five million members by 1925. It not only emphasised issues of race but also gained popularity throughout the United States with its anti-Semitism and anti-Catholicism. It still exists and it is not confined to the South.

New Deal   The title given by President Franklin Delano
                       Roosevelt to the wide-ranging social and econ-
                       omic legislation which he introduced after his
                       election in 1932, which was designed to regu-
                       late the capitalist economy and introduce a
                       welfare state.

Nullification   The southern argument that every state was
                       sovereign and had the right to declare null
                       and void federal legislation that the people of
                       the state deemed unconstitutional.

Ole Miss   The popular title of the University of Missi-
                       ssippi.

Peculiar institution This was a euphemism that was used by
                       southerners before the Civil War to describe
                       the institution of slavery. In the North it was
                       used to indicate that slavery was an institution
                       peculiar (i.e. belonged exclusively) to the
                       South.

Sharecropper   A tenant farmer in the South who paid for
                       rent and supplies by giving a share of the crop
                       to the landowner.

Solid South   Following its defeat in the Civil War, the South
                       was governed by Republican state governments
                       which were defeated with the end of Recon-
                       struction. Following 1876, the South voted for
                       one-party rule – by the Democratic party.

Territories   Land acquired by the United States was held
                       by the federal government and organised into
                       territories governed by four judges until the
                       population reached 5000 eligible voters. After
                       that they could elect a territorial legislature
                       and send a nonvoting delegate to Congress.
                       When the population reached 60 000, the land
                       was subdivided into congressional districts and
                       a republican constitution was adopted; when
                       Congress had approved these measures, the
                       state was allowed to enter the Union with its
                       own members of the House of Representatives,
                       the number of whom was based on its popu-
                       lation, and with two senators.

Acronyms

ACHR	Alabama Council on Human Relations
ACLU	American Civil Liberties Union
ACMHR	Alabama Christian Movement for Human Rights
ADA	Americans for Democratic Action
AFL–CIO	American Federation of Labor–Congress of Industrial Organizations
AIM	American Indian Movement
AME	African Methodist Episcopal
BIA	Bureau of Indian Affairs
CEEO	Commission on Equal Employment Opportunity
CIA	Central Intelligence Agency
COFO	Council of Federated Organizations
CORE	Congress of Racial Equality
ERA	Equal Rights Amendment
FBI	Federal Bureau of Investigation
FDR	Franklin Delano Roosevelt
FEPC	Fair Employment Practices Commission
FOR	Fellowship of Reconciliation
FSC	Friends Service Committee
HEW	(Department of) Health, Education and Welfare
HUAC	House Un-American Activities Committee
IRS	Internal Revenue Service
KKK	Ku Klux Klan
MFDP	Mississippi Freedom Democratic Party
MIA	Montgomery Improvement Association
NAACP	National Association for the Advancement of Colored People

NCAI	National Congress of American Indians
NOW	National Organization for Women
LBJ	Lyndon Baines Johnson
ROAR	Restore Our Alienated Rights
SCEF	Southern Conference Education Fund
SCLC	Southern Christian Leadership Conference
SDS	Students for a Democratic Society
SNCC	Student Nonviolent (in 1965 changed to National) Coordinating Committee
UCMI	United Christian Movement Incorporated
UT	The University of Tennessee, Knoxville
WPC	Women's Political Council

Basic Chronology

1945	Harry S. Truman becomes President on the death of FDR
1947	Truman is the first President to address the annual conference of the NAACP
1948	Both parties support civil rights, but the Democrats split over the issue and Strom Thurmond, governor of South Carolina, leads the resistance, forming the Dixiecrat party
	Truman uses executive orders to set up Fair Employment Board and to begin the integration of the armed forces
1954	*Brown v Board of Education, Topeka Kansas*
	First White Citizens' Council, Mississippi
1955	*Brown II*
	Segregation on interstate transport banned
	Montgomery bus boycott begins
1956	Martin Luther King Jr's home is bombed
	Southern Manifesto published
	Eisenhower re-elected President
	Supreme Court orders bus desegregation
	Bus boycott ends
1957	SCLC established
	Little Rock Central High School integration stopped by riots
	First Civil Rights Act since 1875
	Ghana wins its independence
1959	Massive resistance to school integration starts in Virginia
1960	Sit-in movement starts in Greensboro, North Carolina
	SNCC set up

	Civil Rights Act becomes law
	Eleven colonies in Africa gain independence
	John F. Kennedy elected President
1961	CORE organises 'Freedom Rides'
	Kennedy appoints his brother Robert Attorney General and voter registration drive is started
	Albany protest starts
1962	Kennedy signs executive order on integration of federal housing
	Riots as students resist integration of the University of Mississippi
1963	Albany protest ends
	Birmingham, Alabama, demonstrations
	George Wallace tries to stop integration of University of Alabama
	March on Washington
	John F. Kennedy and Medgar Evers killed
1964	LBJ elected President
	Martin Luther King Jr wins Nobel Peace Prize
	Civil Rights Bill passed
	Mississippi Freedom Democratic party established
	Rioting in New York, Chicago and Philadelphia
1965	Selma demonstrations
	Voting Rights Act becomes law
	Malcolm X is murdered
	Rioting in Watts, Los Angeles
	King's first anti-Vietnam War speech
	SNCC advocates black power
1966	Civil rights campaign meets fierce resistance in Chicago
1967	Civil rights demonstrations extended to Cleveland
	King attacks Vietnam War
	National Organization of Women set up
1968	Poor People's Campaign plans march on Washington
	Martin Luther King Jr assassinated in Memphis
	Civil Rights Bill enacted
	Robert Kennedy assassinated in California
	AIM established
	LBJ does not seek re-election
	Richard Nixon is elected President
1969	Nixon greatly extends the use of affirmative action

	Stonewall gay bar raided in New York City, Gay Liberation Front set up
1970	Nominations of Haynesworth and Carswell defeated
1971	Supreme Court orders desegregation by bussing
1972	Richard Nixon re-elected
	Watergate scandal begins to emerge
	Equal Rights Amendment campaign begins
1973	Supreme Court legalises abortions in *Roe v Wade*
	Second Battle of Wounded Knee
1974	Richard Nixon is the first President to be forced to resign
1976	Jimmy Carter of Georgia elected President; he appoints two black women to his cabinet and extends affirmative action
1980	Ronald Reagan elected President
	Reagan's opposition to Voting Rights Act defeated
1981	First cases of AIDS reported
1988	Reagan's veto of the Civil Rights Restoration Act fails
	George Bush elected President
1990	George Bush first President to veto civil rights law successfully
	Civil rights law extended to include the disabled
1991	Bush nominates black conservative, Clarence Thomas, to Supreme Court
1992	William Clinton elected President
1993	Clinton extends Voting Rights Act with Motor Voter Bill
	Clinton fails to keep his promise to gays in the military

INTRODUCTION

John Rolfe, one of the first settlers in Virginia, described the arrival of the first Africans in what is now the United States of America. They came by accident. A Dutch ship seeking supplies visited the new English colony and exchanged '19 and odd Negroes' for food. Historians have argued ever since about the status of these first Africans in North America. Virtually all are agreed that *de facto* slavery did not emerge until 1640 and this was not codified into law to become *de jure* slavery until 1660. From then on, Africans in the British colonies were overwhelmingly classified as property and, even after American independence, nine out of ten were held as slaves by 1860 (Jordan, 1968).

White American colonists may have fought against the 'slavery' and 'tyranny' of George III but the vast majority of African Americans remained slaves, something which the British were quick to point out and sought to exploit to their advantage (Quarles, 1961). Although virtually all northern states by the early nineteenth century had granted African Americans their freedom (Zilversmitt, 1967) the situation for most black Americans declined rapidly in the South, with emancipation made virtually impossible and the American Colonization Society seeking to return the few free blacks to Africa (Eaton, 1966).

The Constitution drawn up by the leading intellectuals in America avoided the use of the word 'slave'; instead African Americans held in slavery were deemed to be three-fifths of a white man. According to Article 1, Section 2, representatives and direct taxes in each state were 'determined by adding to the whole number of free persons, including those bound to service for a term

1

of years and excluding Indians not taxed, three fifths of all other persons'. These 'other persons' were in fact African American slaves. For many American historians this compromise between representatives of the North and the South personified the wisdom of the Founding Fathers in their search for stable government. What they ignore is that it was achieved at the expense of African Americans and only delayed the confrontation which would lead to four years of civil war which would destroy *de jure* slavery.

Slavery and the Civil War

The growing dispute between North and South over the issue of slavery was about it as an institution rather than about the freedom of the slave – free labour, northerners argued, was superior to slave labour (Foner, 1970). For most northerners who wanted to limit the expansion of slavery it was not about the plight of the slave, but the corrupting nature of slavery. Even some abolitionists, led by William Lloyd Garrison, argued that the North should secede from the South to prevent the corruption of the North and its democratic institutions by slaveholders. As the former slave and leading abolitionist Frederick Douglass was quick to point out, such a programme might save northern institutions but did nothing to help the slave (Douglass, 1962).

With these attacks on slavery, southerners saw themselves as a beleaguered minority in the Union in which their 'peculiar institution' of slavery was in danger of being swept away by the tyranny of the majority. Under the leadership of John C. Calhoun, former Vice President and senator from South Carolina, they claimed that the Union was a compact of sovereign states, not of people, and it was the duty of state governments to protect the people of the state from overbearing federal authority. It was argued that if a state convention deemed a federal law to be unconstitutional, the state had the right to nullify the law and it was the duty of the state officers to raise troops to interpose their authority between the state and federal government. The first attempt to practise this theory of nullification and interposition was by South Carolina during the dispute over tariffs in 1832. These arguments in favour of state sovereignty, interposition and nullification were defeated when the

Southern Confederacy was overwhelmed by Union forces. This did not stop southerners from trying to breathe life into these arguments when they opposed the civil rights movement of the 1950s and 1960s.

Lincoln and the Republicans argued that they were only in favour of barring slavery from the territories and did not endorse abolition. With the outbreak of the Civil War, and as late as August 1862, Lincoln assured Horace Greeley, a leading Republican and the editor of the New York *Tribune*, in a letter that was made public, that he was only interested in saving the Union. Even if the majority of whites in the North opposed emancipation, African Americans in the North and the slaves of the South knew that the war was about abolition. Southerners, who had lulled themselves into the belief that their slaves would be loyal, were shocked and then angered as more and more of their 'happy darkies' fled the plantations and sought to join the Union army. Despite the frequently hostile reception by Union officers, slaves continued to flood past the Union lines in search of freedom. Emancipation of the slaves was inevitable and Lincoln knew it. Even as he was writing to Greeley, the Emancipation Proclamation, which freed slaves in Confederate-held territory, had already been drawn up. The President, in part responding to pressures from black abolitionists, agreed that African Americans could volunteer for the Union army. The long tradition of black Americans fighting in America's wars was continued and this time they had even greater incentive because they were not fighting for the freedom of white Americans but for all Americans (Parish, 1975).

The willingness of African Americans to take up arms to defend the Union, as well as ensuring emancipation, had a dramatic effect on northern attitudes. This was reflected in the cover of the most popular journal in the North, *Harper's Weekly*, which in 1863 had a cover of three dead Union soldiers on top of a hill. They had fallen with their arms around each other and the Stars and Stripes streams in the sky above. What was unusual about the picture was that two of the men are white but the central soldier is an African American. As Peter Parish has written: 'Millions of white Americans, who in 1861 regarded emancipation or the use of black troops as a fantasy or a nightmare, had four years later learned to live with both. Millions of black Americans gained pride and self-respect from the knowledge that their own menfolk had shared in the fight for freedom'

(Parish, 1975). And the South which had gone to war to defend slavery ensured its abolition with the Thirteenth Amendment, adopted in 1865.

The assassination of Lincoln, the first President to be murdered, horrified the North. The anger and dismay at the murder were expressed not only by Lincoln's friends and members of the Republican party, but even by those who had opposed him and his policies. A Union soldier in Tennessee on hearing the news of the President's death wrote in his diary 'that the black flag of extermination' should be raised over the South. Lincoln's place was taken by his Vice President, Andrew Johnson, who, like his fellow Unionists of Tennessee, believed that 'the government of the United States and the governments of the states erected under the Constitution thereof are governments of free white men, to be controlled and administered by him and the negro must assume that status which the laws of an enlightened, moral and high-toned civilization shall assign him' (*Nashville Daily Union*, 1 June 1864). Unlike the northern members of the Unionist party, Johnson before the war had defended slavery consistently as a positive good for blacks and whites and necessary for the maintenance of civilisation.

Reconstruction

Many northern Unionists were conservative, even racist, but none of them had ever argued along these lines and it was this very difference in the nature of their racism that would lead to the conflict between moderates and radicals in the Union party. The southerners' willingness to allow the former Confederate states to pass 'Black Codes', which virtually returned the freed slaves to servitude, alienated Johnson from the northern Unionist party he was supposed to represent. The extent of this alienation is seen in Johnson's veto of the Freedmen's Bureau Bill and the Civil Rights Bill. In the latter veto Johnson used an argument that would be used in the 1990s, ironically by Republicans in their assault on affirmative action. Andrew Johnson argued that the Civil Rights Bill established 'for the security of the colored race safeguards which go infinitely beyond any that the General Government has ever provided for the white race. In fact, the distinction of race and color is by the bill made to operate in favor of the colored and against the white race.' What Johnson sought to forget was that African Americans had been subjected to laws for over 200 years which not only provided safeguards for the white race but had held slaves as chattel with no rights in law.

Johnson's obduracy benefited the freedmen in the long term. By alienating northern sentiment and the Republican party with attacks on the leadership as traitors, Johnson ensured a majority in favour of the Fourteenth Amendment, ratified in 1868, which made all the former chattel slaves citizens of the United States. In addition, Section 1 gave the country its first national law of due process, stipulating that 'nor shall any State deprive any person of life, liberty, or property, without due process of law; nor deny any person within its jurisdiction the equal protection of the laws.' In 1870, with the aid of radical Republican governments in the South, the Fifteenth Amendment declared that a citizen's right to vote 'shall not be denied or abridged by the United States or by any State on account of race, color, or any previous condition of servitude'. It is important to remember that the modern civil rights movement and the vital legislative victories in the 1960s – the Civil Rights Acts of 1964 and 1968 and the Voting Rights Act of 1965 – would not have been possible without these amendments.

Although Reconstruction was not the unmitigated disaster that some historians have portrayed, the legacy of the radical Republican governments was to unify the white South in opposition to what they believed was corrupt carpetbagger rule, which was only made possible by the votes of freedmen. Not only had the South lost the war and its system of slavery but now they were expected to acquiesce to 'Negro domination'. African Americans did not dominate the white South; the highest state office held by a black man was lieutenant governor of Louisiana. All the governors were white, as were the majority of politicians representing the South at state and federal level. But the legend of black rule had disastrous consequences for black southerners until well into the twentieth century. Whites of all classes turned to violence and paramilitary organisations such as the Ku Klux Klan (KKK), which in effect became the armed wing of the Democratic party. Radical Republicans were driven from office, and despite the assurances of the Fifteenth Amendment African Americans were virtually stripped of the right to vote, first through violence and then, starting in 1890 in

Mississippi, through a series of devices such as literacy tests and poll taxes. These did not deny many poor white illiterates their right to vote. According to white southerners the South was redeemed. Ironically it was this very Christian language of redemption that would be used by African Americans in their struggle for justice 80 years later.

Freedmen Abandoned

Increasingly the Republican party became unwilling to oblige the South to obey the Constitution. In order to ensure one-party control of the South the Democrats virtually conceded the federal executive power to the Republican party. In return the Republicans turned a blind eye to the maltreatment of African Americans in the South and the denial of civil liberties. With the power in the hands of the Democratic party, most African Americans sought accommodation with the dominant whites and they were prepared to follow the advice of Booker T. Washington, who told a large white audience in Atlanta in 1895, 'In all things that are purely social we can be as separate as the fingers yet one as the hand in all things essential to mutual progress'. And he assured his listeners that he would advise fellow Negroes to 'cast down your bucket where you are.... Cast it down in agriculture, mechanics, in commerce, in domestic service, and in the professions.' It was the black man who had worked, without strikes, in the fields, had built railways and cities and worked in the mines. If the white man supported the education of blacks then the white man could live with 'the most patient, faithful, law-abiding, and unresentful people that the world has seen' (Spencer, 1955). One year later the Supreme Court accepted Washington's view of social relations between the races. In 1896 the Supreme Court by a vote of eight to one in the case of *Plessy v Ferguson* upheld the right of the South to segregate its facilities, transport and education on the basis of race so long as they were separate but equal. As Justice Harlan, a man from the border state of Kentucky, pointed out, the very act of segregation was a denial of equality. But the Jim Crow system would become to southerners the touchstone of their way of life and it would not be seriously challenged until the 1950s.

It was the widespread use of lynching that forced Washington in his speech in Atlanta to seek reassurance from the business leaders of the South. From 1885 to 1917 inclusively there were 3740 lynchings in the United States. Although 997 of the victims were white, 2734 were black. But as the National Association for the Advancement of Colored People (NAACP) pointed out in its 1918 report, whereas the number of white victims declined sharply in the years 1900 to 1917 (186, or 13.3 per cent of all those over the entire period) the number of coloured people murdered by the lynch mobs did not show a similar decline, with 1241 (or 86.7 per cent) being victims. According to the Association, while African Americans were serving their country in the armed services in 1918, there were a further 63 black victims. The worst states were Georgia, Texas and Mississippi. Fourteen were murdered because they either were alleged to have attacked white women or, as in one case, were 'guilty' of 'living with a white woman'. Four whites were lynched for 'disloyal utterances' and two for murder. It is important to understand the barbarity of some of these acts because it helps us to understand the violence that so often has marred the South well into this century. Those involved in the civil rights movement of the 1950s and 1960s were always aware of this violent past and that they could easily be the next victims. The NAACP report briefly outlines what it considers to be the 'special features' of the lynchings of 1918.

> Five of the Negro victims have been women. Two colored men were burned at the stake before death; four Negroes were burned after death; three Negroes, aside from those burned at the stake, were tortured before death. (Bracey *et al.*, 1972)

However, civil rights workers did not have to rely on their collective memory of white violence against black Americans because such violence would remain a characteristic of the southern way of life throughout the 1950s and 1960s and even into the 1990s. For example, in August 1955 Emmett Till's mutilated body was dragged out of a Mississippi river. The young man was accused of whistling at a white woman. It was alleged by the defence in the subsequent trial that it was all an NAACP plot and that Till was alive and well in Chicago. John Whitten, the defence counsel, was chairman of the county Democratic party and his brother was a member of Congress, and in his appeal to the jurors he stated that he was 'sure that every last Anglo-Saxon one of you has the courage to free these men' (Whitfield, 1988). They did after two hours – most of which was spent chatting and drinking Coke. Nearly 40 years later a Mississippi Democrat would defend the violent attacks on a women's commune, Camp Sister Spirit, by citing the Till case. Till, he suggested, was killed because he failed to obey the customs of the South and the women had brought the attacks on themselves with what he believed was an assault on the southern way of life.

Millions of African Americans, from 1890 onwards, responded to the violence by seeking a better place in the North. Despite the pleas of Booker T. Washington 'to cast down your bucket where you are', many sought freedom from segregation and poverty in the cities of the North. Although not free from racial prejudice, at least there was no *de jure* segregation and although only free to compete for the most menial of jobs, earnings in the stockyards of Chicago were far in excess of anything they could have earned as share-croppers in the South. This was especially so when the price of cotton plummeted after World War I. The United States entered the war as an associated power in 1917. White workers who were drafted into the army were replaced on many occasions by black workers from the South. Black industrial labour was important also because of the cessation of European immigration. The competition for jobs and housing with northern white Americans led to serious racial violence in cities such as East St Louis, in 1917 (Rudwick, 1964). During the Red Scare of 1919, which saw an attack on communists in the USA, more northern and southern cities were racked by racial violence – white Americans attacking their black citizens. One of the worst riots was in Chicago, where Irish and Polish workers attacked the black ghetto. During these riots white workers with the support of the police and military attacked African Americans in their communities and carried out appalling atrocities (Tuttle, 1980).

Another explanation for this white rage is political. African Americans simply by moving from the South were no longer denied the franchise because of devices such as poll taxes and literacy tests. As William Tuttle points out, during World War I the black vote decided two mayoralty elections and had even seen three African Americans elected as aldermen. 'Black people paid a high price for their victories, however, for in several significant ways politics was instrumental in precipitating and sustaining the Chicago race riot. The blacks' voting behavior,' according to Tuttle, 'aroused and reinforced the hostility and racial hatred of numerous groups, certain of which reacted violently' (Tuttle, 1980). While the President of the United States, Woodrow Wilson, campaigned under the slogan 'The World Must be Made Safe for Democracy', for African Americans it was the United States that lacked democracy. Wilson, who had introduced segregation into the federal government, and who had praised the Ku Klux Klan for its part in redeeming the South from Carpetbag and Negro rule, did nothing about the revival of the Invisible Empire of the KKK. Exploiting its usual race hatred of African Americans, the revived Klan also attacked Roman Catholics and Jews. Now the Empire was not simply in the South but had great appeal in the northern states and in northern and southern cities. At its height, in 1925, the Klan boasted that it had five million members and effectively controlled states like Indiana (Chalmers, 1965; Jackson, 1992).

The Depression and New Deal

Many white Americans experienced the poverty known by millions of African Americans during the Depression years of the 1930s. White southerners, faced with the Dust Bowl, followed black southerners into the cities of the North or tracked further west to the golden state of California. The state of Mississippi by 1932 was literally bankrupt, with barely $1000 in its treasury and with debts of $14 million. As an historian of the South has pointed out, Mississippi was not untypical: 'The shrinking tax base throughout the South resulted in cutbacks in state services, and schools closed, road construction ended, and government offices closed, more workers were laid off. Low commodity prices and farm failures made a shambles of the South's economy' (Daniel, 1986). Despite many benefits from Franklin D. Roosevelt's New Deal, such as the social security scheme, many African Americans either faced discrimination in hiring and pay on the employment schemes or were forced from the land because of the workings of the Agricultural Adjustment Administration. Commodity prices could only be raised by restricting the supply and farmers were paid to plough cotton crops under. The result was the forced dismissal of sharecroppers on a massive scale. The drop in production required less labour and tenants and croppers were now encouraged to go North. As Daniel has pointed out, the structure of the Agricultural Adjustment Administration 'made it well-nigh impossible for a sharecropper to appeal eviction' (Daniel, 1986). But white and black tenants and sharecroppers did form the Southern Tenant Farmers Union in an effort to protect their rights and land, and even conducted a successful strike (Grubbs, 1971).

Although the limited reforms of the New Deal did not restore the economy, they were sufficient to persuade African American voters to give up their traditional allegiance to the Republican party. As early as 1936 eligible black voters overwhelmingly supported the re-election of Franklin Delano Roosevelt (FDR) and they have remained loyal to the party, which had earlier defended slavery, ever since. And by 1940, before its entry into the war, America was booming. As in World War I, African Americans benefited from the hostilities and their loyalty to the Democratic party was strengthened. A. Philip Randolph, who was head of the Brotherhood of Sleeping Car Porters, threatened a march on Washington in 1941 unless the President acted to abolish job discrimination. Following intense pressure from Randolph and the NAACP, FDR issued Executive Order 8802 on 25 June, which established the Committee on Fair Employment Practices. This was designed to ensure 'full and equitable participation of all workers in defense industries, without discrimination because of race, creed, color, or national origin'. This was the first time the federal government had introduced affirmative action, with any company seeking defence contracts being required to include this clause in their contracts and federal agencies responsible for vocational and training programmes to ensure they did not discriminate. A Roosevelt biographer claims: 'The order – which someday would be called a landmark step in the nation's greatest internal struggle – was greeted with mixed feelings by Negro leaders and with subdued interest on the part of the big-city press. The President granted the committee limited funds, and it was slow to get under way. But it was a beginning' (Burns, 1970; see also Wynn, 1976). In response to criticisms, FDR issued another executive order in May 1943, 9346, which gave the committee independent status, field offices and staff and $500 000 budget (Reed, 1991). Despite these shortcomings there was significant improvement for African Americans, such as the integration of the San Francisco shipyard, and the order would provide the basis for legislation after the war.

World War II

The attack on Pearl Harbor ensured the mobilisation of the whole nation regardless of race, religion or gender. The need for labour in northern factories required massive recruitment of black workers and, despite resistance from some trade unions, the first large-scale organisation of black workers in predominantly white unions. The willingness of African Americans to join trade unions, especially those organised by the Congress of Industrial Organization, would help win them an ally in the future struggle for civil rights. This was particularly true in the case of the United Auto Workers Union, which would later do a great deal in providing funds for organisations such as the Southern Christian Leadership Conference (SCLC), the Student Nonviolent Coordinating Committee (SNCC) and the Students for a Democratic Society (SDS).

Although the rhetoric of war was similar to that in World War I – making the world safe for democracy – the war against Nazi Germany added a new element. The National Socialist state was built on the premise of racism and sought to justify the extermination of so-called inferior races such as Jews. Every assault on the racism of Germany by administration officials was an attack on racism in the United States as far as African Americans were concerned. Ironically, fearing the power of southern Democrats, FDR was reluctant to act and the United States fought to destroy a racist regime and its military with a segregated army. Five hundred thousand African Americans fought in Europe and the Pacific in these segregated units with white commanding officers. Angry with their treatment, African Americans used their patriotism as a means of protest with the 'Double Victory' campaign, which sought victory over the enemies of democracy overseas and in the United States (Weisbrot, 1990).

However, protests against segregation and racial violence did not start in World War II and it would be wrong to portray African Americans as passive victims of southern violence. There were blacks, North and South, who protested against Jim Crow. Much earlier, a group of these black intellectuals attacked Booker T. Washington's policy of accommodation. They included the great academic and activist W. E. B. Du Bois, who established the Niagara Movement in 1909 which would later give birth to the NAACP. Du Bois, who had praised Washington for his 1895 speech in Atlanta, roundly criticised the pre-eminent black leader, arguing that his education policy would leave most Negroes with an inferior education. As a graduate of Harvard University, Du Bois stressed academic excellence, which would create a 'talented tenth'. Edwin Redkey points out: 'Different as these tactics were, bitter as were the struggles between the advocates of accommodation and protest, they shared the same basic strategy. Each ideology expected a black elite to win the dignity sought by all Afro-Americans' (Redkey, 1969).

Black Nationalism and Changing Attitudes

Just as there were blacks in the nineteenth century, like Frederick Douglass, who fought for civil rights in the United States there were also strong advocates within the African American community who argued in favour of black nationalism or supported going back to Africa. Black delegates to a convention in 1854 called on the 'colored inhabitants of the United States to leave the country and settle in the West Indies, Central and South America, or western Canada if that country should remain under British control' (Bracey et al., 1972). Edwin P. McCabe, a black man from Kansas, urged African Americans to move into the Oklahoma territory and create an all-black state. Although McCabe failed, several black towns were established and those who were disillusioned by their experience turned to Bishop Henry McNeal Turner and his plans to establish a nation in Africa. This black nationalism, as Redkey points out, 'shares many attributes of other nationalisms.... Afro-Americans had a political past of slavery, oppression, and isolation by whites who took special pains to exclude them from American life. As a result, blacks had overflowing recollections of collective humiliation and regret.' But, as he makes clear, this nationalism was not merely based on the negative experience of African Americans in the

United States but also 'stressed the glories of their African ancestors and the American rhetoric which claimed that all men are equal' (Redkey, 1969). This black nationalism had widespread appeal in the 1920s when its main exponent was Marcus Garvey and it would gain many supporters in the late 1960s, especially among the followers of the Nation of Islam (Essien-Udom, 1964).

However, the majority of African Americans in the nineteenth and twentieth century overwhelmingly sought to be full American citizens. The leaders in this struggle were members of the NAACP and one of their first successes came in 1915, against the state of Oklahoma. This new southern state, like several other southern states, sought to disenfranchise black Americans by declaring in its constitution that residents of the state whose grandfathers had not been eligible to vote should not be allowed to exercise the franchise. The Supreme Court declared the 'Grandfather Clause' unconstitutional because it violated the Fourteenth Amendment (Meier and Rudwick, 1970). The willingness to turn to the courts was encouraged during the reform environment of the 1930s which sought to exploit New Deal support for equal opportunity without demanding integration. The NAACP in the 1930s 'launched a concerted attack on school segregation that slowly stripped the judicial fences around Jim Crow'. The aim was to prove that, as a result of the *Plessy* decision in 1896, facilities were not separate and equal but rather unequal. The Supreme Court upheld their view and ordered that graduate and law schools in states such as Maryland and Missouri be integrated, or equal facilities be provided. It was cheaper for the states to integrate than to pursue segregation with equal facilities.

Combined with these efforts of white and black professionals in the NAACP and labour leaders in the unions, the war saw an increasing number of Americans speaking out against racism, building on the work of scholars such as Franz Boaz, who demolished the 'scientific' claims of racists that African Americans were inherently inferior. The Swedish sociologist Gunnar Myrdal, in collaboration with black and white American scholars, produced a massive (1483-page) report called *An American Dilemma*. His study stressed the gulf between the American Creed – that all men are created equal with the inalienable rights of life, liberty and the pursuit of happiness – and the American 'Deed', which was of segregation, racism and inequality. In 1944 Myrdal wrote:

> From the point of view of the American Creed the status
> accorded the Negro in America represents nothing more and
> nothing less than a century-long lag of public morals. In
> principle the Negro problem was settled long ago; in practice
> the solution is not effectuated. (Myrdal, 1964)

Myrdal and his American associates doubted that African Americans
would eventually share all the benefits of the American Creed.

But it was not only the changing attitudes of many Americans,
brought about by sociologists or the war against the Nazi regime in
Germany, which would give grounds for hope that African Americans would be included in the American Creed. Ironically it was the
very denial of this creed with the segregation laws of the South that
encouraged the development of black institutions such as the
church, the colleges and the fraternal organisations, some of whose
leaders would eventually cast their lot with the civil rights movement. The preachers had always played a crucial role in the African
American community, as had the college leaders such as Booker T.
Washington. Frequently the religion of the African American
community led to a conservatism, a desire to stress forgiveness
rather than struggle (Branch, 1989). However, after the war,
increasing pressure on preachers from their congregations and by
black students on the college campuses transformed these bastions
of a segregated society into battering rams which would do much to
destroy the southern way of life. But in 1945 most southerners were
sure that segregation was safe, and most northerners had no idea of
the disturbances that were to come.

1

TRANSFORMATION OF POLITICS:
CIVIL RIGHTS 1945–58

After World War II there were an increasing number of Americans willing to accept the views of sociologists and academics which openly challenged the assumptions of racism. The continued Great Migration of African Americans from the South into the industrial cities of the North also forced politicians to question their own assumptions. Of the African Americans living outside the South in 1940, 17 per cent were residents of New York City, and the cities of Detroit, Cleveland, Chicago, Philadelphia and Pittsburgh were home to 30 per cent of African Americans living in the North and the West (Issel, 1985). It was now necessary for the Democratic party, the party which had its strength among the working class in the North, to face up to the challenge of the 'New Negro', as the black sociologist E. Franklin Frazier had described them. They resided in the growing urban ghettos, increasingly were members of a trade union and had since 1936 transferred their allegiance to the Democratic party. Ironically, in 1944 Franklin Delano Roosevelt had won his unprecedented fourth term as President largely owing to the combined votes of African Americans and the segregated, Jim Crow, Democratic South. In the same year the black vote ensured the election of Adam Clayton Powell of New York, who became the second black congressman to be elected in the North, and 20 years later there would be six, all from the major industrial cities (two from Detroit and the others from New York, Philadelphia, Chicago and Los Angeles) (Meier and Rudwick, 1970). The political manoeuvring that would radically change the Democratic party after World War II would be in response to these demographic changes.

According to a biographer, Harry S. Truman, the Vice President and former shopkeeper from Missouri who took over the presidency after the death of Roosevelt, 'moved to establish himself as a friend of the Negro' (Hamby, 1973). Although he favoured some legislative help for blacks, Truman's support for African Americans never matched his support for Jewish Americans and his unwillingness to act decisively was characteristic of white liberals, both Republicans and Democrats, after the war (Fraser, 1994). Growing up in Missouri, he never escaped the prejudices of his region. 'Privately, he could still speak of "niggers," as if that were the way one naturally referred to blacks' (McCullough, 1992). In the 1920s as a young politician he had paid the $10 membership to the KKK, an act of 'amazing naiveté', demonstrating that principle could be sacrificed for ambition. His sister Mary Jane was confident, but mistaken, in her belief that 'Harry is no more for nigger equality than any of us' (McCullough, 1992).

Fair Employment

The victory in Europe and over Japan in 1945 was a mixed blessing for African Americans. Since 1944 there had been discussions in the administration about the conversion of military to civilian working. Members of the Fair Employment Practices Commission (FEPC) were only too aware that this would mean severe disruption for many African Americans and they even feared the outbreak of race riots in the cities. Although the rioting did not materialise, as it had after World War I, the disproportionate dismissal of black workers started as early as the spring of 1945. One company in Buffalo, for example, laid off 9000 female workers. 'Black women were affected in a five-to-one ratio because discrimination forced them to be the last hired and trained' (Reed, 1991). These workers, who had been earning from 80 cents to $1.42 an hour, were pressurised to apply for jobs that paid less and many were denied unemployment benefits. A similar pattern of discrimination existed across the country. 'By November, 1945, the exodus of minority workers from wartime jobs had turned into a virtual rout, and discrimination was "rapidly approaching pre-war levels," columnist Ted Poston reported in the New York *Post*' (Reed, 1991).

The first test of Truman's liberalism came in 1945 when the FEPC sought to end the discriminatory hiring policies of the Capitol Transit Company of Washington, DC. The FEPC had been successful in changing the policies of transport companies in 16 cities in the North and West but had been defied in the District of Columbia for three years. Senior members of the Committee sought the support of the President. Three months passed. Finally, the presidential assistant, John Steelman, told the Committee they could not act; a request to meet the President was refused and the chairman resigned. According to Truman, ordering the company to desist in its discriminatory practices was a violation of congressional law. Truman's support for a permanent FEPC has been described as 'routine' (Hamby, 1973). However, it has been suggested that many 'failed to understand ... that as President he could no longer sit idly by and do nothing in the face of glaring injustice' (McCullough, 1992). Although he issued an executive order, he knew it gave the Committee the ability only to collect data, and he also knew that Congress had stripped the FEPC of its funding. Despite all these limitations: 'In the new agencies created by federal legislation in the 1960s, some of these FEPC veterans would help revive the struggle for fair employment practice.' For example, John Hope Franklin II, a distinguished black historian, worked in the 1960s and 1970s in the Office of Civil Rights and on the presidential Commission for Equal Employment Opportunity (CEEO), and Marjorie Lawson served as a federal judge and on the Task Force on Urban Renewal. Former FEPC workers were active at the state and city level, such as Theodore Jones, the former budget officer, who set up an accounting business in Illinois where he was regional director of the Office of Economic Opportunity, a trustee of the state university, and also worked for the Chicago Commission on Human Rights (Reed, 1991).

A cynic might argue that Truman's civil rights policy was more a matter of mirrors than anything of substance. In a message to Congress he briefly advocated the setting up of a permanent FEPC. He did nothing to stop southern conservatives from filibustering the proposal. He did speak to an NAACP rally on 30 June 1946 and he did appoint a special committee on civil rights, chaired by the president of General Electric, Charles Wilson, which submitted a report on 29 October 1947 entitled *To Secure These Rights*, with recommendations for an anti-lynching law, abolition of poll taxes, protection of people during voter registration, integration of the armed services, denial of federal funds going to recipients that discriminated, and an end to segregation in interstate transport (McCullough, 1992). These recommendations, combined with action by the Justice Department, meant that it 'was not certain by the end of 1947 just how far the administration was willing to go, but no one could doubt that it was moving in a more liberal direction on Negro rights' (Hamby, 1973).

The reception given to returning African American servicemen shocked Truman. The vicious assault and blinding of a black soldier in South Carolina was one of 56 attacks on African Americans between June 1945 and September 1946, and the bloody white police riot in Columbia, Tennessee, led to demands for a federal anti-lynching bill. Truman reassured a southern friend that he was opposed to social equality but he was in favour of equality of opportunity (McCullough, 1992). Truman, like FDR, did not support such a measure but he was persuaded of the need for action; in addition, there was the pressure coming from the African American community (Duberman, 1989). Concerned about the revival of KKK terrorism, Truman told the Committee on Civil Rights in January 1947 that he wanted the Bill of Rights 'implemented in fact. We have been trying to do this for 150 years.' On 29 June 1947 he told the annual meeting of the NAACP that, 'If ... freedom is to be more than a dream, each man must be guaranteed equality of opportunity. The only limit to an American's achievement should be his ability, his industry and his character' (Truman, 1956). This was the first speech by a President to the NAACP and 'it was the strongest statement on civil rights heard in Washington since the time of Lincoln' (McCullough, 1992). One of the groups putting pressure on the White House was the Congress of Racial Equality (CORE), set up in 1942 by James Farmer of Louisiana and a group of Quakers who were members of the Fellowship of Reconciliation (FOR). The aim of CORE was 'to eliminate racial discrimination' and it was prepared to use 'inter-racial, non-violent direct action' to achieve this end. Members of the organisation were involved in sit-ins in Chicago restaurants, and demanded the end of segregation on interstate transport (White, 1985).

Democrats Transformed

Despite the limited actions of the President in support of African Americans, black voters overwhelmingly supported the Democratic candidate in 1948 and ensured Truman's election. As Don McCoy argues, the limited action of the Democrats had had one effect: 'If Truman was not yet considered a significant champion of America's minorities, the ostensible interest of congressional Republicans in civil rights had been discredited' (McCoy, 1984). The transformation of the Democratic party into a predominantly northern liberal party was speeded up in the 1948 convention. Exhorted by the young Hubert Humphrey and the liberals of the Americans for Democratic Action (ADA), the Democrats adopted 'the most sweeping civil rights plank ever written into a Democratic platform' (Hamby, 1973).

Angry southerners, led by Strom Thurmond, Governor of South Carolina, walked out of the convention and set up their own Dixiecrat party, with Thurmond running as its presidential candidate. According to one scholar (Garson, 1974), 'The Democratic party, then, no longer represented the South's interests. It had become dominated by intellectuals, self-seeking labor leaders, and most poignant of all for white southerners, insensitive Negroes.' Mississippi senator James Eastland was convinced that Walter White, of the NAACP, was 'a negro, who, I am afraid to say, has more power in your government than all of the southern states combined' (Garson, 1974). Another enthusiastic supporter of the Dixiecrat party who would play a prominent role in later civil rights disturbances in his city was the police commissioner of Birmingham, Alabama, Eugene 'Bull' Connor.

Truman complained bitterly that his stand on civil rights was 'deliberately misconstrued to include or imply racial miscegenation and intermarriage. My only goal was equal opportunity and security under the law for all classes of Americans' (Truman, 1956). Truman's position was made even more precarious by Democrats who disagreed with his anti-Soviet stance, giving their support to former Vice President Henry Wallace, who was running as a Progressive. With the Democrats putting up three candidates, it was considered certain that the Republican, Thomas Dewey of New York, would be the next President of the United States. Without the support of the African American vote Truman would have been defeated (Garson, 1974; White, 1985).

The 1948 Election

Historians are agreed that the 1948 election established civil rights as the major issue, endorsed by three out of the four parties. During the election, Henry Wallace, the Progressive candidate, went into the South and campaigned for civil rights. All the meetings were integrated and in Virginia they were orderly but in North Carolina there was serious violence. It was not only the willingness of Wallace to defy segregation that was significant but also the determination of African Americans and some whites to support the Progressive campaign. Boss Crump in Memphis tried to stop Paul Robeson, the great singer and actor, who was awarded the Springarn Medal by the NAACP in 1945, from addressing a Progressive rally. The black community was not intimidated, however, and the meeting was held because an alternative meeting space was offered by a black minister. Several thousand white and black people attended. In Columbus, Georgia, the KKK surrounded but failed to attack a Progressive rally because, as the politicians later discovered, there were 100 armed blacks protecting them. Robeson's biographer comments: 'It gave him hope for the future, regardless of how the '48 election itself came out – even as the outright murder of other blacks (including several who merely tried to vote) continued to feed his anger.' In Alabama white mobs attacked the Progressive presidential candidate but Wallace 'managed to hold a dozen unsegregated meetings, and he set an example of courage and moral determination which even his bitterest liberal opponents found hard to denounce' (Duberman, 1989). Academics teaching in the South who supported Wallace were often dismissed.

Some Republicans were so alarmed at the loss of the African American vote, which was crucial in many northern and western states, that they formed the National Council of Negro Republicans. Cynical observers were to note that even the limited civil rights programme proposed by Truman did not have popular white support (Lawson, 1991). There were Republican strategists who noted that advocating civil rights for African Americans would not benefit the party and the seed of the later Republican southern strategy was planted.

Although it is easy to criticise Truman for not acting on the recommendations in his civil rights committee report, *To Secure These Rights*, he was prepared to take executive action. He did desegregate

Washington National Airport, his inauguration guests in 1949 were integrated and he did appoint a black judge, William H. Hastie, to the federal courts (McCoy, 1984). The Justice Department supported cases against restrictive covenants and was prepared by 1950 to challenge the doctrine of 'separate but equal' as laid down in the *Plessy* case (Diggins, 1989; Miller, 1967). The man from Missouri 'helped – often in spite of himself – to educate a nation to its obligations and its failures. In another sense, he unleashed expectations he could not foresee, desires he could not understand, and forces which future governments would not be able to restrain' (Bernstein, 1970).

Integrating the Military

Perhaps Truman's most important action was to issue executive orders. In Order 9980 he established the Fair Employment Board to ensure equal treatment of minorities in federal hiring. However, lack of funding, civil service rules and the conservative nature of those who ran the Board all limited its achievements. Executive Order 9981 stipulated that there should be 'equality of opportunity for all persons in the armed forces, without regard to race, color, or national origin' (White, 1985). Truman's action was partly a result of pressure from A. Philip Randolph, who threatened to organise a boycott of compulsory conscription into the armed services (the draft). Most historians regard Truman's integration of the armed services, despite the opposition from some of the leading generals, as having long-term benefits for African Americans. There are those who dissent strongly from this majority view (Pinkney, 1976). By 1952 the army, navy and air force were largely integrated. There were still too few minority officers and the executive order had not been enforced in the National Guard or reserve forces. 'The greatest battles had been won, however, thanks to the persistence of Truman and civil-rights groups' (McCoy, 1984). (And one consequence was the integration of the 1950s *Sergeant Bilko* television comedy about army camp life, in which the one black actor is never a figure of fun.)

Presidents and congressmen were reluctant to act; the same cannot be said of African Americans. The NAACP Legal Defense

Fund continued to challenge the accepted notion of 'separate but equal' in the courts and members of CORE resorted to sit-ins and Freedom Rides, tactics of non-violent direct action which were to become common in the 1960s. For example, in 1947 CORE members took a 'Journey of Reconciliation' through the border states in which they sought to ensure the enforcement of a Supreme Court ruling which had challenged segregation on buses in inter-state travel (White, 1985). These latter tactics were adopted because many avenues of agitation were closed to black Americans.

African Americans and Labour

This is particularly true of the labour movement which, during the anti-communist witch-hunt following the war, purged communists and radicals from organised unions. The American Federation of Labor and the Congress of Industrial Organizations (AFL–CIO) were reunited in 1955 under the leadership of the conservative George Meany. Only two black labour leaders were on the executive council of the AFL–CIO, James Carney, who had been secretary-treasurer of the CIO, and A. Philip Randolph of the Brotherhood of Sleeping Car Porters. Although participating unions were 'en-couraged' to recruit members without regard to race, liberals failed in their efforts to exclude racist unions in the same way that the AFL had expelled communists (Marable, 1984). Even a recent study which stresses the benefits of unions organising in the southern black community admits that the moral force of the civil rights movement came from the black church and not the unions. 'By abandoning the effort to organize the unorganized the CIO ceased being a labor movement; and this, in turn, deprived civil rights activists of political and social space in which to operate' (Stokes and Halpern, 1994). One example of an African American who learnt his activism from the trade union movement was E. D. Nixon, one of the leaders of the Montgomery Improvement Association and the bus boycott, and a member of both the Brotherhood of Sleeping Car Porters and the NAACP (Branch, 1989).

With limited access to the labour movement and virtually no power in politics, African Americans turned to the legal system and direct action. The limits of political action can be seen when the

NAACP sought to amend federal aid to education. The Association argued that such aid should not be given to segregated schools. But the man who had championed the civil rights platform at the 1948 convention, Hubert Humphrey, now a senator, opposed the suggested amendment. 'As much as I detest segregation, I love education more' (McCoy, 1984). Rejected by such politicians, the Legal Defense Fund of the NAACP had with increasing success turned to the Supreme Court. For example, southern states had passed legislation between 1890 and 1915 allowing the Democratic party to limit voting in the primary elections to whites only and in 1944 the Supreme Court ruled white primaries unconstitutional. However, as late as 1958 it upheld the literacy tests for the franchise in North Carolina (Miller, 1967).

Eisenhower

It was Truman's successor, the Republican Dwight David Eisenhower, who inadvertently strengthened the Supreme Court, which would become a major factor as Americans struggled to resolve the conflict between the American Creed and the American Deed. Certainly the new President was not prepared to act vigorously to defend the rights of African Americans. Even a sympathetic biographer admits: 'Essentially, Eisenhower passed on to his successors the problem of guaranteeing constitutional rights to Negro citizens' (Ambrose, 1984). After all, Eisenhower and the Republicans were aware that many southern Democrats had bolted the party because of the race issue. General Eisenhower, as candidate of the hated Republican party – a party which had been feared and loathed by most southerners since the Civil War, won four southern States – Virginia, Tennessee, Florida and Texas. He did well in other states such as Arkansas and North Carolina.

This does not mean that significant changes were not made before the 1960s but they came because of outside pressure and the impact of world events. Having won the election of 1952, the former general had to satisfy all the powerful elements in the Republican party, and one of these was the Governor of California, Earl Warren, and his supporters, who had delivered the California delegation at the 1952 convention in favour of Eisenhower as the Republican candidate (Blum, 1991). Bypassed for the post of Attorney General, Warren was promised the first vacancy on the Supreme Court. It was an appointment that Eisenhower deeply regretted (Ambrose, 1984). Chief Justice Warren, unlike President Eisenhower, was willing to meet the challenge of civil rights.

The *Brown* Decision

One of the most famous cases in US history was decided by the Warren court. The NAACP had successfully chipped away at the 'separate but equal' doctrine of *Plessy* and now it was decided to challenge segregation in schools in four states – Kansas, South Carolina, Virginia, and Delaware – as well as in the District of Columbia. Twice, in 1951 and 1952, the Supreme Court referred the South Carolina case to a three-man panel, who simply enjoined the authorities to ensure that the schools, if separate, were equal. Meanwhile, Oliver Brown decided to challenge segregation in the schools of Topeka, Kansas. Under state law any city with a population of over 15 000 could impose segregation in its grade schools. Under this legislation Oliver Brown was prevented from sending his daughter to the nearest school, a mere five blocks away, because it was white and instead she had to travel 20 blocks to attend an all-black school. Brown lost his case in 1951, when three federal judges ruled that Topeka schools complied with *Plessy*. He was given leave to appeal to the Supreme Court. The choice of this case, *Brown v The Board of Education, Topeka, Kansas*, to represent the findings of the Court was not accidental because it was ruling on a northern state with a flexible segregation law. The attack on *Plessy* was led by Thurgood Marshall, the leading black lawyer for the NAACP and director of the Legal Defense Fund. He relied not only on expert lawyers but also called on leading sociologists and psychologists to argue that segregation by race was inherently unequal and a denial of equal protection under the law as guaranteed by the Fourteenth Amendment. (Marshall would be the first African American to be appointed a Supreme Court justice.) Partly because of the Association's role in this case, it has been suggested that the NAACP was conservative and reluctant to support direct action. However, it was members of the Association who frequently organised and led direct

action campaigns and it was the Legal Defense Fund that represented people caught up in the mass arrests that were to come.

Earl Warren was insistent that the Court should be unanimous
and on 17 May 1954 the Court, in its decision written by Warren,
posed the question: 'Does segregation of children in public schools
solely on the basis of race, even though the facilities are equal,
deprive children of the minority of equal educational opportunity?'
And answered that it did. Warren and the Court also ruled
segregation in the District of Columbia was unconstitutional and a
violation of due process (Miller, 1967). These rulings were made
despite pressure from Eisenhower on Warren. The President had
invited the Chief Justice to the White House and insisted that
Warren sat next to John W. Davis, the lawyer representing the
segregationists before the Supreme Court. Eisenhower told Warren
that the southerners 'are not bad people. All they are concerned
about is to see that their sweet little girls are not required to sit in
school alongside some big overgrown Negroes' (Ambrose, 1984).
Eisenhower was not the first white man, nor the last, to seek to
exploit sexual fears in combination with racial prejudice. Eisenhower's efforts failed.

The ruling in *Brown* was a major achievement for the NAACP and
a vindication of its policy to seek redress through the courts and it
has been called 'the single most important moment in the decade,
the moment that separated the old order from the new and helped
to create the tumultuous era just arriving' (Halberstam, 1993). But
it was not a complete victory by any means. The Court had overturned *Plessy* but there was no attempt to set acceptable standards
for schools and especially there was no indication of when desegregation was to be achieved. On this latter point Marshall and the
NAACP lawyers were invited to return to the Court and argue their
case. In *Brown II* the Court was unanimous in ruling that integration
should be done 'with all deliberate speed'. There was no date for
compliance (Blum, 1991; Miller, 1967). In this decision the Court
made a serious error but it was based on Warren's belief that schools
were being desegregated and that school administrators needed
time to adjust to the new ruling (Ely, 1976). Previously the courts
had always ruled that a constitutional right was always personal and
present and, as Loren Miller points out, 'in the 1955 case [*Brown II*],
the Court held that a personal and present constitutional right
could be deferred and extended gradually to those who were

entitled to exercise it by virtue of a constitutional amendment. There was no constitutional warrant for such a ruling' (Miller, 1967).

Warren hoped for gradual compliance with the Court. In this he and his fellow justices underestimated the resistance of white southerners to change. After the first *Brown* case, White Citizens Councils were formed, starting in Indianola, Mississippi, to ensure segregation would remain. Within a year they had spread throughout the South and have been called 'the bourgeois Klan'. In Virginia there was a 'massive resistance' campaign against integration and some public schools were even closed. The Harry Byrd state political machine concerned itself with registering and caring only for the white voters of the state and frequently exploited the race issue. One former Governor recalled that during his term as Governor, 'Negro influence was nil'. There was little support for integration from academics at the University of Virginia and the weak AFL–CIO unions were actively opposed. For example, in Warren County from 1958 until 1960 the local textile workers' union paid to keep open a segregated school when the county schools were closed. In 1958 union members overwhelmingly voted for the Byrd machine despite its anti-union measures. James Kilpatrick, editor of the *Richmond News Leader* recalled: 'There was talk then of blood flowing ankle deep in the gutters. Men were saying "never" then; and then they meant it' (Ely, 1976). It was the Virginians and White Citizens Councils which used the Old South arguments that it was the duty of the leaders of the 'sovereign' states to interpose their authority between the federal government and the people of the state and nullify unconstitutional rulings of the Supreme Court or acts of the federal government. In virtually every southern state integration plans submitted by school boards were challenged in the courts, even by the NAACP, on the grounds that the plans were inadequate. Most of the congressmen and senators from the South signed the Southern Manifesto, in which they committed themselves to fight the *Brown* decision. There were three notable exceptions – Albert Gore Sr and Estes Kefauver of Tennessee and Lyndon Johnson of Texas (Ambrose, 1984; Dallek, 1991).

As for President Eisenhower, he insisted that the problem of integration of schools was a local matter. Despite rioting at Clinton, Tennessee, and Mansfield, Texas, he maintained that the federal government had no power to intervene. He angered members of the NAACP when he compared them to the white segregationists. At a press conference he said that the South was 'full of people of good will' but he condemned 'the people ... so filled with prejudice that they can even resort to violence; and the same way on the other side of the thing, the people who want to have the whole matter settled today'. His biographer admits 'he had gone to great lengths to divorce himself from the problem of race relations, and especially integration of schools' (Ambrose, 1984). He set the example for other Presidents who hoped that desegregation would be achieved by the courts. Eisenhower was later attacked by Truman, who argued that the General as President had failed to give leadership. 'He didn't use the powers of the office of the President to uphold a ruling of the Supreme Court of the United States, and I never did understand that' (Miller, 1973).

Little Rock

As politicians of both parties were soon to realise, attacks on the *Brown* decision and the Supreme Court were an easy way to gain votes. The chief executive officer of Arkansas, Democrat Governor Orville Faubus, was just one of many southern Democrats who used this tactic. Faubus was running for re-election in Arkansas and he faced stiff competition. His opponents had also discovered that Faubus' father had been a dedicated socialist and that his school-teacher son had been a student at the radical Commonwealth College before the war and had helped his father set up a socialist local (group) (Green, 1978). Seeking to divert the electorate from his radical past, Faubus played the race card and challenged the ruling of the Supreme Court. The city of Little Rock had drawn up plans for very gradual compliance with the *Brown* decision which would not see the integration of the schools until 1963 (Miller, 1967). Nine African American students reported to Central High School in September 1957 but found it surrounded by units of the Arkansas National Guard. Faubus issued orders that no black students were to enter.

The Arkansas Governor claimed that he was seeking to protect the lives and property of citizens of the state. But already one of the students, Melba Pattillo, who had volunteered and had been selected to go to Central High, had been the victim of violent assault and an attempted rape by a white man who yelled at her: 'I'll show you niggers the Supreme Court can't run my life' (Beals, 1994). Although the children had the support of the NAACP and most church leaders, the battle to integrate Little Rock Central also brought about divisions. Pattillo's father opposed her, arguing that it only endangered her life and his job (Beals, 1994). Writing under her married name, Melba Pattillo Beals graphically depicts the appalling treatment of the students who integrated the school. While the Governor sought to keep the students out by surrounding the school with troops, the administration in Washington was forced to act. After obtaining an injunction against Faubus preventing him from interfering with integration, Eisenhower was forced to send in the 101st Airborne because the Governor had withdrawn the National Guard and the children were being attacked by hysterical racist mobs (Beals, 1994; Miller, 1967). Pattillo drew strength from meeting Thurgood Marshall:

> I looked at this man who seemed to have none of the fears and hesitation of my parents or the other adults around us. Instead he had a self-assured air about him as though he had seen the promised land and knew for certain we could get there. We had only heard rumors of freedom, but he had lived it, and it showed in his every word, his every movement, in the way he sat tall in his seat. (Beals, 1994)

She survived the ordeal at Central High because she had strong support from her mother, grandmother and many members of the black community as well as encouragement from a small group of whites. In her own account she admits, 'I wonder what possessed my parents and the adults of the NAACP to allow us to go to school in the face of such violence' (Beals, 1994). And Arkansas put the Association under increasing pressure with the state Attorney General, Bruce Bennett, demanding all its records, including names of members, their addresses, telephone numbers as well as contributors to the organisation. As the young Melba Pattillo wrote in her diary: 'What will become of us if the NAACP is not strong? It feels as though segregationists are attacking from all sides' (Beals, 1994).

Despite the sacrifices she and the other eight made in 1957 it was not until 1960 that Central was integrated and by 1964 only 2.3 per cent of all African American children were attending desegregated schools (Blum, 1991). Beals observes: 'Once President Eisenhower made that kind of commitment to uphold the law, there was no turning back. And even though later on he would waver and not whole-heartedly back up his powerful decision, he had stepped over a line that no other President had ever dared cross' (Beals, 1994).

Ironically, the deeply conservative President, as a result of pressure from the African American community (to be discussed in detail in the next chapter) and the claim that the United States was a leader of the free world in a global struggle against atheistic communism, would be forced to act on behalf of the African American community. However reluctant he may have been to enforce the *Brown* ruling, the Supreme Court was not so reluctant to act. In 1958 in *Cooper v Aaron* it made a sweeping ruling which made unconstitutional any law, 'ingenious or ingenuous', which sought to keep public schools segregated. Three new justices appointed by Eisenhower after 1954 reaffirmed the *Brown* ruling, which had been made before their appointment (Ely, 1976).

Republicans felt that their work on civil rights had not been appreciated by African Americans. They pointed out that despite desegregation of military bases and the city of Washington, and the appointment of Frederick Morrow, a former NAACP field secretary to the White House, in 1956 blacks continued to vote for the Democrats. What Republicans did not stress was the failure of the President to condemn the killing of Emmett Till in Mississippi or his failure to comment on the expulsion of the first black student from the University of Alabama, Autherine Lucy. Miss Lucy successfully sued for admission to the university. However, it was a Pyrrhic victory because the university authorities expelled her, accusing her of lying as she claimed that she had not been admitted initially because of her race. In addition, Eisenhower refused to give any federal support for the Montgomery, Alabama, bus boycott. He believed that the South was law abiding and that it was impossible for decisions of the Court to be completely enforced (Ambrose, 1984).

The FBI and Black America

According to his biographer, Eisenhower's reluctance was partly based on the reports of the director of the Federal Bureau of

Investigation (FBI), J. Edgar Hoover, that the Bureau was concerned that communists had infiltrated the civil rights movement. If this was the case, it was a very different assessment from the one given to the House Committee on Un-American Activities two years earlier. The Committee, better known as HUAC, had published a report on 22 December 1954 entitled *The American Negro in the Communist Party*, which cited Hoover's assessment of the previous year. Of the 5395 communists who were considered leading members of the party by the FBI, 'only 411 were Negroes.... The fact that only 411 Negroes were found in this select group is strong evidence that the American Negro is not hoodwinked by these false messiahs'. Hoover's opinion underwent a dramatic change. In 1956 Hoover warned Eisenhower that the NAACP, along with members of the Communist party, were exploiting the murder of Emmett Till and a 1957 report, based on information obtained through illegal burglaries and telephone taps, was given to 'various opinion molders within the government, with portions leaked to "reliable and cooperative" newspaper reporters' (O'Reilly, 1994). Publicly, Hoover denied that communists were influential in the NAACP. In subsequent years he and his Bureau members would not just search for communists but would seek to destroy the civil rights movement and its leadership (O'Reilly, 1994).

The 1957 Civil Rights Act

It is undeniable that Hoover held great power in Washington, but the best assessment of Eisenhower's attitudes towards civil rights is that made by a survivor of Little Rock. Beals' suspicions that the President was not 'wholehearted' in his support for civil rights can be seen when his behaviour over the passage of the Civil Rights Bill is examined. The Attorney General, eager to court the black vote, submitted a broad civil rights bill which proposed a bipartisan civil rights commission, a new division in the Justice Department to investigate civil rights abuses and one which especially sought to ensure all citizens the right to vote. But the Republicans faced opposition from the powerful leader of the Senate, Lyndon Baines Johnson. His biographer has summed up Johnson's political shrewdness well: 'Johnson saw a Senate fight over civil rights legislation in

1956 as a losing proposition for the country, the Democrats, and himself'. As a result, he sent the Bill to the judiciary committee headed by Mississippi Senator James Eastland, where it was buried (Dallek, 1991).

The revival of civil rights legislation was due to black pressure and an acute awareness on behalf of the presidential aspirants that something had to be done. As Lyndon Johnson's biographer states:

> It was clear to Lyndon that pressure from southern blacks made change in the region inevitable.... If he could lead a major civil rights bill through the Senate, it would be the first Federal legislative advance in this field in eighty-two years. Such an achievement ... would be a boon to his presidential ambitions. A civil rights bill credited to Johnson would help to transform him from a southern or regional leader into a national spokesman. (Dallek, 1991)

Moreover his supporters, even Senator Russell, knew the need for such legislation if the Texan was to go to the White House. For the Republicans, Vice President Richard Nixon, who had never championed civil rights legislation before, was also a convert and eager to make a gesture to satisfy the demands of the African American community.

The Bill went before the House of Representatives in the winter of 1955 and Eisenhower gave public and private support. But things changed when the Bill ran into opposition when it was sent to the Senate in 1956. There the senator from Georgia, Richard Russell, denounced the Bill as not only seeking to ensure the right to vote but rather to give power to the Justice Department and 'the whole might of the federal government, including the armed forces if necessary, to force a comingling of white and Negro children'. Hubert Humphrey, who had so strongly advocated the civil rights platform in the 1948 Democratic convention, said that Russell's 'tremendous ability was weakened and corroded by his unalterable opposition to the passage of any legislation that would alleviate the plight of the black man throughout the nation. He was the victim of his region, the victim of a heritage of the past, unable to break out of the bonds of his own slavery' (Dallek, 1991). Russell was not completely opposed to the Bill but rather sought to weaken the powers of the Justice Department and he was particularly keen to retain jury trials for breaches of civil rights because he knew that only white voters were eligible to sit on juries. Like Russell, Eisenhower was prepared to allow a weakened Civil Rights Bill to pass and he even claimed that he did not understand what was in it, even though he had been supporting it for two years (Ambrose, 1984). Faced with southern opposition to it, the President refused to fight for the Bill. Although most historians agree that the Bill was more symbol than substance, they also agree that it was a radical break with tradition and that more effective legislation would be inevitable.

Strom Thurmond, who led the walk-out from the Democratic convention in 1948, bitterly opposed any legislation and filibustered for over 24 hours in an attempt to kill the Bill. Eventually a much weakened Civil Rights Bill was passed, the first since Reconstruction. For many African Americans struggling to survive and tear down the walls of segregation, the Bill was seen as a sham. Ralph Bunche, a Howard University professor, critic of the NAACP and active in the National Negro Congress, and A. Philip Randolph believed that it would have been better to have had no bill at all. Bayard Rustin, the black pacifist and CORE member, acknowledged that the legislation was inadequate, but he also believed that it was 'very important because it was evidence that Congress was prepared to act' (Dallek, 1991).

Truman, the Cold War and Civil Rights

Apart from the pressure from the African American community for change, it was America's role in world affairs after World War II that had a significant impact on the struggle for civil rights in the United States. The Democratic party and the Republicans and their presidential leaders Truman and Eisenhower were engaged in the Cold War with the Soviet Union. The stark contrast between America's claims that it was the leader of the free world and its treatment of the black minority was all too obvious. Truman's urgency to support democracy in Western Europe with billions of dollars in the Marshall Plan contrasted with his approach to democracy in the United States. No American President would ever show the same concern about the freedom or economic progress of

African Americans in Mississippi or Alabama as they expressed concern for the peoples of Europe and Southeast Asia.

Immediately after the war, Truman had capitulated to pressure from his European allies by supporting the French in their attacks on nationalists in Indochina. The Truman Doctrine according to the President was essential to stop totalitarianism. 'The free people of the world look to us for support in maintaining their freedoms. If we falter in our leadership, we may endanger the peace of the world – and we shall surely endanger the welfare of the nation' (Hamby, 1973). And it was this lack of 'national welfare' that concerned many in the South. One white southern historian argues that the South as a whole was a colony and its political leaders evaded the issue, preferring to preach racism and segregation. However, he notes:

> Like other colonial people, Southerners were restless, impatient with the oppression of the past, and uneasy about the direction of the future. National political leaders realized that the racial system of the South presented a diplomatic problem, for to attract countries emerging from colonialism, the U.S. could not afford the embarrassment of segregation and disenfranchisement. (Daniel, 1986)

Critics in the African American community were concerned about Truman's policies. Paul Robeson warned that the United States was supporting Britain in denying freedom to the colonial peoples of Asia and India. In addition, he argued that black Americans would have to fight to achieve democracy in the United States. Leaders of the NAACP, such as Walter White and Roy Wilkins, were concerned not to alienate potential allies and refused to support Robeson's crusade against lynching. But 3000 black and white delegates met in Washington, DC, to demand a federal anti-lynching law and Truman did agree to meet a delegation led by Robeson. Truman told them the time was not right for such legislation and when he was reminded of the Nuremberg trials then in progress he retorted that Britain and the United States represented 'the last refuge of freedom in the world'. Robeson rebutted this, accusing the British of being 'one of the greatest enslavers of human beings'. He also warned the President that the mood in the African American community was changing and if the federal government did not act to protect its black citizens then they would protect themselves (Duberman, 1989).

In an address to the World Freedom Rally at Madison Square Garden, New York, on 14 November 1945, Paul Robeson warned his audience that the American government was 'helping British, French and Chiang Kai-Shek governments to crush the people's struggles toward democracy, freedom and independence.' He pointed out that while the American administration relied on vast arsenals of weapons, world peace could not be secure so long as millions of Africans suffered from starvation, or the Jews were denied a homeland. As his biographer has pointed out: 'In Robeson's mind, the domestic civil-liberties issue was inescapably linked to the international question of peace' (Duberman, 1989).

It was not only Paul Robeson who made the link between America's support for European colonialism and its failure to defend the democratic rights of African Americans. W. E. B. Du Bois, the eminent black historian and for many years editor of *Crisis*, the magazine of the NAACP, published in 1945 a volume entitled *Color and Democracy*. In this study Du Bois linked civil rights, African nationalism and socialism. In 1947 he authored an appeal to the United Nations and, like Robeson, he attacked American intervention in the Korean War (White, 1985). Paul Robeson, addressing delegates of the National Labor Conference on Negro Rights in 1951, told his audience that they were not to be diverted by warnings of the threat of communism, but rather blacks, Jews and aliens should unite with the working class to attack 'White Supremacy and all its vile works'. The enemies of African Americans 'are the lynchers, the profiteers, the men who give FEPC the run-around in the Senate, the atom-bomb maniacs and the war-makers'. Despite Robeson's defence of the Vietnamese in their struggle against the French, the invasion of South Korea by North Korea saw the passage of a new and infamous Internal Security Act, the McCarran Act, which equated dissent with treason and set up detention centres for so-called subversives in times of emergency. The Act was passed over Truman's veto (Duberman, 1989).

Both Robeson and Du Bois were subject to persecution in the United States. Efforts were made by HUAC to have Robeson cited for contempt of Congress and the State Department refused to give him a passport (Duberman, 1989). Du Bois became increasingly disillusioned by the failure of white liberals to support civil rights in the United States. Liberal intellectuals such as Arthur Schlesinger Jr, David Reisman, Daniel Bell and Reinhold Neibuhr were, however, eager to join the anti-communist Congress for Cultural Freedom. Although the Congress attacked the excesses of HUAC and of Joseph McCarthy they also policed 'the intellectual community for signs of weakening will in the anti-communist struggle. Most of the Americans affiliated with the Congress presumably did not know that its activities were partly subsidized by CIA funds laundered through dummy foundations' (Matusow, 1986).

Eisenhower and the Cold War

While white liberals may have been policing the subversive activities of their fellows, they did not share that sense of urgency that African Americans felt about their treatment in the United States. With the election of Eisenhower, the crusade for a free world, especially Eastern Europe, still did not include the southern states. The Secretary of State, John Foster Dulles, made continual promises to free the captive nations of Eastern Europe from the oppression of Soviet domination. Although the United States had no intention of undertaking such a task, Hungarian students and workers were not aware of this. In 1956 they sought to overthrow the communist government and were crushed by an invasion of Soviet and Warsaw Pact countries. Those who could manage it fled into Austria and Vice President Richard Nixon was sent on a fact-finding mission and wrote a report for the US government. In his report on the Hungarian refugee crisis, Nixon wrote that 'it is essential that in our necessary and understandable concern over the immediate problem of providing for the needs of refugees we not lose sight of the historical significance of this mass migration of people from an area of slavery to an area of freedom' (Lasky, 1957).

Nixon's professed concern for the Hungarians was not shared by many black leaders. Paul Robeson attended the Soviet Embassy reception in Washington, DC, to celebrate the thirty-ninth anniversary of the Soviet revolution and later, despite the efforts of an angry crowd, attended an American–Soviet Friendship peace rally. And the singer's contempt for the majority Cold War views were shared by the wider black community. Black newspapers from

Pennsylvania to California shared his doubts about the attention given to Hungarian freedom fighters. The San Francisco *Sun Reporter* asked rhetorically: 'How can America in good faith blow such loud horns about the freedom of Hungarians, when such a large proportion of her own population is deprived of freedom guaranteed by the Constitution of the United States?' (Duberman, 1989).

African Americans were concerned about Eisenhower's policy with regard to European colonial ambitions. The administration was implacably opposed in 1956 to the British, French and Israeli invasion of Egypt and attempted overthrow of Nasser on the pretext of defending the Suez Canal. According to Stephen Ambrose: 'American policy, in general, was to support colonial peoples attempting to win national independence' (Ambrose, 1984). Certainly the United States imposed a financial and oil embargo on Britain and Eisenhower was able to follow his policy of trying to keep the support of the newer nations – many of which were attracted by the Soviet model or preferred to remain non-aligned. Whatever success Eisenhower can claim for his willingness to defy his three leading allies, it seems that African American doubts about Eisenhower's anti-colonialism were justified because of the administration's willingness to support French colonial rule in Indochina. And in any case, his eagerness to make a stand over Egypt was in marked contrast to his unwillingness to challenge southern governors who openly defied the rulings of the Supreme Court.

Indochina

Both Truman and Eisenhower were reluctant to confront the issue of civil rights in America, while they supported the French efforts to regain control over its former colony of Indochina. Both gave lavish monetary support to the doomed French effort and Eisenhower even contemplated intervention. Some have suggested that the French were offered the atomic bomb, but all are agreed that Eisenhower was determined to keep Vietnam divided, and he was confident that he could achieve another Korean solution. In his efforts to persuade the American people that action in Asia, unlike action in Alabama, was vital, he outlined why it was essential for the

United States to act. He stressed the advantages in raw materials essential to the economies of the industrialised nations; but more important was 'the possibility that many human beings pass under a dictatorship that is inimical to the free world'. And Vietnam would not be the last to fall. According to Eisenhower, 'You have the broader considerations that might follow what you would call the "falling domino" principle. You have got a row of dominoes set up, you knock over the first one and what will happen to the last one is the certainty that it will go over very quickly' (Ambrose, 1984). It was this domino theory which would drag the United States into the Vietnam War resulting in the killing of millions of Vietnamese and over 50 000 Americans, a disproportionate number of whom were African American. The war would also destroy Johnson's dream of a 'Great Society', and lead to the radicalisation of American politics.

Perhaps it was merely coincidence that in the same year as the Russians invaded Hungary and the British invaded Egypt, a civil rights bill was introduced in Congress and became law a year later after the British gave independence to Ghana, a former British colony in Africa known as the Gold Coast (Wiedner, 1962). There is no doubt that the rapid decolonisation of Africa by Britain and France had a marked impact on African Americans. Ironically, these new African presidents would not suffer the humiliations of Jim Crow legislation when they travelled in the United States.

Black Nationalism

To American black nationalists the link between their status and colonialism is explicit because 'Afro-Americans have always been responded to as a colonized people, not unlike the overseas victims of European colonialism, and relegated to a system of birth-ascribed stratification, similar to that of India's untouchable caste' (Pinkney, 1976). Whatever the status of African Americans in the United States, it was not only black nationalists who were influenced by the growing and successful independence movements in black Africa. Even groups such as the NAACP, which had traditionally avoided involvement in African politics, saw the need for cooperation. 'The contradiction of a "free" Africa and their "unfree" descendants in the US was an immediate and important parallel which was reiterated by many civil rights advocates' (Marable, 1984). It was not a black nationalist who acted as legal adviser to Kenyan nationalists in their talks with the British government in 1960, but rather Thurgood Marshall of the NAACP who, as director of the Legal Defense Fund, had argued before the Supreme Court in the *Brown* case (Wiedner, 1962).

And it was not only black leaders who were influenced by the demise of the British Empire. Gandhi, who did so much to influence African independence movements, also was a hero to those who formed the front line in the battle against the southern way of life. At the height of the harassment from white students at Central High, Melba Pattillo Beals' grandmother told her to read and understand what Gandhi had accomplished without resorting to violence. As she recalls: 'I knew about Gandhi, about his courage even in the face of people beating up on him and calling him ugly names. I didn't think I was that strong and pure' (Beals, 1994). But the young girl had heroes closer to home than the nationalist leaders in India or Africa. On 1 December 1955 she read in the local newspaper about the arrest of Rosa Parks in Montgomery, Alabama, who had refused to give up her seat on a bus to a white man. 'Our people were stretching out to knock down the fences of segregation.... I felt such a surge of pride when I thought about how my people had banded together to force a change. It gave me hope that maybe things in Little Rock could change' (Beals, 1994). It was that sense of hope that motivated hundreds of thousands of African Americans to take up the challenge and tear down the walls of segregation.

2

GRASS-ROOTS RESISTANCE
IN THE SOUTH

It was Thursday 1 December 1955. Mrs Rosa Parks, who did so much to inspire the young Melba Pattillo, was 42 years old when she was arrested. Returning home after her day's work as a tailor's assistant in a department store in Montgomery, Alabama, she took her seat on the bus and soon it was full and a white man was left standing. The bus driver ordered her and three other African American passengers to move because under the city ordinance no black was allowed to sit parallel with a white passenger. The others reluctantly moved but Mrs Parks did not. Three times the bus driver, J. F. Blake, told her to move and then she simply said: 'No.' Warned that she would be arrested, Mrs Parks told him to go right ahead. Blake left the bus, called the police, and Mrs Parks was arrested. The events that sparked off the Montgomery bus boycott were completed with her being charged with violation of the city bus segregation ordinance (Garrow, 1988).

All too often Mrs Parks has been portrayed as an old woman whose failure to obey the driver was due to her tiredness, or because her feet hurt. As Angela Davis has observed: 'Now of course, this particular way in which history is remembered represents the central woman as a passive participant – as someone without agency' (Davis, 1994). In her recent autobiography Rosa Parks has pointed out that at 42 she did not think of herself as old and although she was tired after a day at work her refusal to give up her seat was because she was tired of giving in.

African Americans throughout the South were tired of giving in. It was this emergence of a mass movement of African American women and men, young and old, middle class and poor that would destroy Jim Crow. The national parties were forced to act because of pressure from people, most of whom were denied the vote and all of whom were denied political office. By segregating their fellow black citizens, white southerners forced black southerners to teach in their own schools and to study in their separate colleges, to worship in their own churches. Out of these institutions African Americans forged an army and weapons to war against their daily humiliations. And although Marxists regard religion as an opiate of the masses, it was this Christian faith taught in the black churches which inspired the civil rights movement. The Bible, with its stories of slavery to the Egyptians and the flight of the chosen people to the promised land, had inspired African Americans when they were slaves. It was this deep and passionate Christian longing for justice and belief in redemption that inspired the struggle for freedom.

Many of these black church leaders and their congregations, educators and their students would find themselves in the front line in the assault on segregation because southern racists in their resistance to change in their way of life, following the *Brown* decision, attacked the major campaigning organisation, the NAACP. Many states either abolished it or restricted its activities and often forced state employees to resign from the Association. African Americans responded by turning to their community leaders, especially in the churches and educational institutions, and they formed groups which operated at city, state and regional level such as the Montgomery Improvement Association (MIA), the Alabama Christian Movement for Human Rights (ACMHR), the United Christian Movement Inc. (UCMI) of Louisiana, the SCLC and the SNCC. These were just a few of the many groups formed throughout the South. Many of the leaders had been members of the NAACP. Ella Baker served as national field secretary for the NAACP in 1941 and 1942 and in 1943 was director of branches. During these years she toured the South extensively, covering nearly 27,000 miles and attending 519 meetings. She was president of the New York branch of the NAACP after the war and became the first associate director of the SCLC (Morris, 1984). But these links between the NAACP and SCLC did not always ensure good relations with the Association's national leadership under Roy Wilkins.

Most white southerners in 1954 were surprised that African Americans wanted to go to integrated schools, and they were blissfully unaware of the growing dissatisfaction of their fellow citizens who were treated as second-class citizens. Ignorant of African American history, white southerners in the 1950s were unaware of the boycotts of streetcars by blacks that had occurred across the region between 1900 and 1906 (Meier and Rudwick, 1970) or of the 'wave of rebellion that engulfed most of the leading black colleges of the 1920s [which] was one of the most significant aspects the New Negro movement' (Wolters, 1975). Ignorance was not merely a southern problem. Most northern politicians, when not ignorant, were indifferent about the status of the African American community. Neither Truman nor Eisenhower was prepared to confront the Jim Crow system.

Louisiana Protest

Ignoring the views of politicians North and South, blacks in the South were prepared to act and the first major protest did not happen in Alabama but in Louisiana. In March 1953, more than a year before the Supreme Court's ruling in *Brown*, African Americans in Baton Rouge had successfully petitioned the city council to allow seating on local buses on a first-come first-served basis. Although the passengers on the city bus service were mostly black, all the drivers were white and they refused to obey the ordinance. After a four-day strike, the Attorney General supported the drivers and declared the ordinance was a violation of the segregation laws.

In June the black community began a mass boycott of the transport system. The leader of the boycott was the Reverend J. T. Jemison of the Mount Zion Baptist Church, who was a relative newcomer to the city, moving there in 1949. As pastor, community leader, and past president of the local branch of the NAACP, he was held in high regard in the community and his radio appeal on behalf of the boycott resulted in virtually total support. The church was used as a centre for meetings and when the audience of enthusiastic supporters proved too numerous for the church hall they moved to the segregated school. During the boycott the community leaders closed down the bars in the evening, organised a community police force, and provided thousands of cars which ensured a free ride to all the participants. The movement leaders knew that if they charged for the rides they would be prosecuted for operating an unlicensed taxi service.

Jemison was not the only black preacher who was prepared to challenge the Jim Crow system. All the black preachers took an active part in the Baton Rouge community action group, the United Defense League, and urged their congregations to stay off the buses. Sunday morning sermons were not only used to exhort the faithful but were also a time when money was raised to keep the boycott going. Although the Baton Rouge action ended with Jemison accepting a compromise solution, it was the first mass, direct action campaign led by church leaders. Other preachers were soon informed of the success of the Baton Rouge community. The Reverend C. K. Steele of Tallahassee, Florida, and the Reverend A. L. Davis of New Orleans both knew Jemison and about the action in Baton Rouge. They were leaders of similar action in their cities. Martin Luther King Jr and Ralph Abernathy in Montgomery, Alabama, continued the battle started by Jemison (Morris, 1984).

Mrs Rosa Parks

Although the first boycott took place in Baton Rouge, the action in Montgomery included all the elements that were characteristic of the civil rights movement. Activists in the NAACP joined forces with college lecturers and students, who in turn combined with the leading black preachers and their congregations. Mrs Parks was not just a tired seamstress on her way home from work but rather a member of the NAACP since 1943 who had served as secretary of the Montgomery branch of the Association for most of the previous decade. She had worked closely with the young members of the Association's youth council, which included Claudette Colvin, who had been arrested in March 1955 because she had refused to give her seat to a white passenger. Mrs Parks had taken part in the discussions with E. D. Nixon, a fellow member of the NAACP and Alabama branch president of Randolph's Brotherhood of Sleeping Car Porters, about the possibility of using Colvin's arrest as a way of challenging the Montgomery segregation law. No action was taken because Colvin was charged with assault as well as breaking the segregation ordinance. In addition, it was felt that Colvin would not win the support needed for a successful boycott because she was a pregnant, unmarried teenager.

Mrs Parks not only knew Nixon, who had been an activist in the black community since the 1920s, but she had worked with him on voter registration drives undertaken by the NAACP. And it was Nixon who had introduced her to Clifford and Virginia Durr, both of whom were white southern liberals. A friend of Lyndon Johnson and Hugo Black, the Supreme Court justice from Alabama, Clifford Durr had resigned from the Federal Communications Commission in protest over Harry Truman's loyalty programme. It was Clifford and Virginia Durr and E. D. Nixon who went to the jail on hearing of Mrs Parks' arrest. Nixon, who posted the bail bond, had agreed with the Durrs that Rosa Parks would be the ideal test case and it was his certainty that a boycott would succeed that persuaded her to agree, despite the reservations of her husband, to the test case (Branch, 1989; Garrow, 1988).

Not that she needed much persuasion. Mrs Parks was well aware of the implications of her action. She had attended the Highlander Folk School in Tennessee run by Myles Horton, a friend of Clifford and Virginia Durr – both of whom acted as sponsors to the school. In a letter to Highlander nearly six months before her arrest, Mrs Parks wrote that she was 'hoping to make a contribution to the fulfillment of complete freedom for all people' (Garrow, 1988). Highlander has been described as a 'modern American movement halfway house'. According to Aldon Morris these houses are distinctive because of 'their relative isolation from the larger society and the absence of a mass base'. Although not equipped to lead a mass movement, the organisers at Highlander, such as Myles Horton and Ella Baker, trained activists, held workshops, developed media contacts and imbued those who attended their meetings with a knowledge of past struggles and a vision of a multiracial democracy (Morris, 1984). Certainly, Mrs Parks' faith in such a democracy was reinforced by her stay in Tennessee. When she refused to obey the bus driver's order she was acting – not merely reacting.

Following her arrest she not only gained help from fellow activist E. D. Nixon but also from faculty at Alabama State College, an institution for black students only. Mrs Jo Ann Robinson had joined the English faculty in 1949 and was a keen community activist in the city. At the time of Rosa Parks' arrest she was president of the Women's Political Council (WPC). As soon as she was informed of the incident Mrs Robinson called E. D. Nixon, with whom she and the WPC had worked throughout the early 1950s in attacking the poor treatment of African Americans on the Montgomery buses. Robinson, Nixon, and Rufus Lewis, former football coach at the college, businessman and head of the Citizens Steering Committee, had applied pressure on city commissioners to modify the segregation ordinance. As early as 21 May 1954, Jo Ann Robinson had written to the Mayor, W. A. Gayle, warning him that the WPC were considering a bus boycott. With the arrest of Mrs Parks, Robinson and Nixon agreed that the WPC should write a leaflet which would call on the black community to stay off the buses on the day of the trial. With the aid of student volunteers thousands of copies of the leaflet were run off using the college's mimeograph machine and distributed throughout the community. In the leaflet she appealed to all, including children, to stay off the buses. About Mrs Parks' arrest she wrote:

> This has to be stopped. Negroes have rights, too, for if Negroes did not ride the buses, they could not operate. Three-fourths of the riders are Negroes, yet we are arrested, or have to stand over empty seats. If we do not do something to stop these arrests, they will continue. The next time it may be you, or your daughter, or mother. (Garrow, 1988)

Now that the decision had been made to boycott the buses it was important to win the support of the wider African American community who were not members of the NAACP or the WPC. The people who could mobilise the necessary mass support were the ministers of the segregated churches. Nixon realised that he needed the support of black preachers such as Ralph D. Abernathy, secretary of the Baptist Ministers' Alliance. And it was Abernathy who told Nixon to call the young minister at the Dexter Avenue Baptist Church, Martin Luther King Jr.

Martin Luther King Jr and the Boycott

The boycott was already in advanced planning when King was called and even then he hesitated. He had already declined a request to lead the local NAACP branch because of other commitments but, following a call from Abernathy, he eventually agreed to hold a meeting at his church which was attended by 70 black leaders. It did not augur well for the success of the boycott because the meeting was disorganised and confused but Abernathy, supported by Jo Ann Robinson, took over the meeting and those who were still present voted to support the boycott. It was also agreed that a mass meeting should be called for the Monday night, and after this meeting King and Abernathy issued new leaflets urging people to attend the Monday meeting as well as boycott the buses. Over 200 volunteers distributed the new leaflet and black taxi drivers agreed to carry passengers on the day of the boycott at a standard charge of 10 cents.

E. D. Nixon told Montgomery *Advertiser* reporter Joe Azbell about the planned protest and urged him to get a leaflet and interview people in the community because it would be a good story for the Sunday paper. And as Nixon hoped, the newspaper duly featured the story, which in turn led to local television interviewing the racist City Police Commissioner Clyde Sellers, who charged that the boycott was going to be enforced by black 'goon squads'. He was confident that the black community would not be intimidated and that the boycott would fail. The white-owned newspapers and television had ensured that any African American who had not read the leaflet or listened to the sermons that Sunday morning, appealing to everyone to stay off the buses, would either have seen the headline in the paper or heard Sellers on television. It was not the first time, and certainly not the last, when white folks would give unwitting support to the movement (Branch, 1989; Garrow, 1988).

On the Monday morning, 5 December 1955, the boycott was more successful than the leaders had dared to hope and later, in an unprecedented display of solidarity, several hundred blacks went to the court house to witness the case against Rosa Parks. The hearing took only five minutes and she was fined $10. Following the trial it was agreed that the bus company should allow for seating on a first-come first-served basis with blacks filling the bus from the back and whites from the front. Under this system no one would have to give up their seat or be forced to stand over an empty seat. The second demand was simply that drivers should be polite to African American riders at all times and that any driver who was rude or assaulted a black passenger should be disciplined or fired. The last demand, put by Ralph Abernathy, was about the hiring of black drivers, because it was the black community which made up 75 per cent of the passengers. And if these modest demands had been met nothing more would have been heard about the boycott. However, the white council's determination to resist any change ensured that the boycott would continue. The city commissioners chose to resist rather than accept modification of the segregation ordinance and the one-day boycott was transformed into a year-long struggle in which the black community would only accept total desegregation.

Leaders of the boycott were aware that existing groups could not coordinate the campaign and that a new organisation was needed. The NAACP did not have the mass membership, the WPC leaders could not openly organise the movement because they were employees at Alabama State College and would be dismissed, and the Interdenominational Ministerial Alliance was not appropriate because the Reverend L. Roy Bennett was unsuitable as a leader. As in any mass community action movement, there were divisions about who would best be suited to lead the new organisation, which they called the MIA. All the factions did agree that the ideal leader would be Martin Luther King Jr, who had only recently arrived in the city, who was minister at one of the most prestigious black churches in the town and who had been educated at Union College Seminary in the North (Garrow, 1988). The pattern that was established in 'the walking city' would be recreated throughout the history of the civil rights movement. As J. Mills Thornton has pointed out, there is a danger that King's role 'may be very easily overstated. In Tallahassee, Tuskegee and Greensboro, it is only his example with which we are dealing.... In Albany, Birmingham, St. Augustine and Selma, he and his organization came into the city in response to the invitation of local black leaders to assist them in effecting goals of local importance, whatever may have been the national implications of their decision to do so.' Thornton stresses, 'In Montgomery ... King's role was even more completely than elsewhere a function of local circumstance. He played no significant part in creating the Boycott' (Thornton, 1989).

The black community leaders in Montgomery joined forces with the Alabama Council on Human Relations (ACHR), which was holding a meeting in Montgomery. A member of the ACHR board, Thomas Thrasher, a Montgomery minister, set up talks between the MIA and the city commissioners. The talks failed. The Chicago company National City Lines which controlled the Montgomery bus service refused to send an arbitrator as requested by MIA. And the resistance of the white community grew, with threats against the alternative transportation service the African American community had established. King called his friend Jemison in Baton Rouge, who told him about the free-ride service they had organised in their boycott and King followed his friend's advice, making the necessary arrangements at a second mass meeting.

White Resistance

The refusal of city commissioners to compromise encouraged more extreme elements in the city. Obscene and threatening telephone calls were received by MIA leaders. City police commissioner Clyde Sellers was the first to join the White Citizens Council and was later followed by Mayor W. Gayle and commissioner Frank Parks. It was estimated by local newspapers that membership of the Council had grown from 6000 at the beginning of February 1956 to 12 000 by the end of the month (Thornton, 1989). This growing white resistance resulted in the harassment of the black community and led to the first arrest of King, on 26 January 1956 for speeding at 30 miles per hour in a 25 mile per hour zone. Four days later his house was bombed and his father and father-in-law pleaded with King and his wife to leave the city. Martin Luther King Jr later recalled the vehemence with which southern whites sought to defend segregation and how he was so fearful of the hatred that surrounded him that he almost quit leadership of the boycott. He had not done so because he had prayed.

And it seemed at that moment that I could hear an inner voice saying to me. 'Martin Luther, stand up for righteousness. Stand up for justice. Stand up for the truth. And lo I will be with you, even until the end of the world.' ... I heard the voice of Jesus saying still to fight on. He promised never to leave me alone. No never alone. No never alone. (Garrow, 1988)

The bombing of his home made him more determined to fight on and not merely make segregation more pleasant for the African

American community but rather to challenge the Jim Crow system itself. He agreed with the proposal of Cifford Durr and E. D. Nixon to challenge segregation on the Montgomery bus system and the segregationists' response was to attempt to bomb Nixon's home.

The city commissioners resorted to law, not the bomb, in their efforts to break the boycott. Alabama had an anti-boycott law and in February 1956 the city fathers were determined to use it and 100 members of MIA were charged by the grand jury, whose members asserted that: 'We are committed to segregation by custom and law and we intend to maintain it' (Garrow, 1988). But their determination to resist the demands for justice from the African American community only strengthened the resolve of the black community, and all those indicted reported en masse to the court determined to demonstrate that they would not be intimidated. As King would tell a mass rally:

> There are those who would try to make this a hate campaign. This is not a war between the white and the Negro but a conflict between justice and injustice. This is bigger than the Negro race revolting against the white. We are not just trying to improve the Negro of Montgomery but the whole of Montgomery. (Garrow, 1988)

The genius of King was his ability to articulate the African American struggle in terms that were immediately understood by millions of Americans, white and black. Later his determination to follow the example of Gandhi, who had also inspired young Melba Pattillo and her grandmother in Little Rock, would transform municipal struggles over segregated buses or later student protests against segregated lunch counters into a great crusade for democracy in America. He would force black and white Americans, northerners and southerners, to challenge the system they had never questioned. The white resisters of Montgomery, and other southerners who simply said 'Segregation now and segregation forever,' only made King and other black leaders more determined to triumph.

The resistance from the white South in the form of the mass indictments for the first time stirred the indifferent northern public and press. As a direct result of the mass indictment, the MIA received $12 000 collected in the North. Both the leading New York papers, the *Times* and the *Herald Tribune*, carried front-page stories of the events in Montgomery and King's address to the mass rally was his first to get national coverage. On network television, which limited news coverage to 15 minutes, ABC compared the Alabama protesters to Gandhi and the Montgomery city officials to the British trying to shore up their empire. Such a comparison would have delighted Martin Luther King and it was a theme he took up in his first of many speeches about the boycott in a northern city. Addressing an audience of 2500 at Brooklyn's Concord Baptist Church, he reminded them that Gandhi had brought down the British rule in India with passive resistance. The major source of inspiration for the movement was Christian. As he told a reporter, 'I have been a keen student of Gandhi for many years. However, this business of passive resistance and nonviolence is the gospel of Jesus. I went to Gandhi through Jesus' (Garrow, 1988).

'Not a One Man Show'

This was not just a protest led by a charismatic leader but rather, as Jo Ann Robinson correctly described to a black reporter at the time, it was a mass movement.

> The amazing thing about our movement is that it is a protest of the people. It is not a one man show. It is not the preachers' show. It's the people. The masses of this town, who are tired of being trampled on, are responsible. The leaders couldn't stop it if they wanted to. (Garrow, 1988)

Although Robinson's assessment was correct, the leadership of King was increasingly emphasised, especially by sympathetic outsiders such as the African Methodist Episcopal (AME) Church, the National Council of Churches and the FOR. Bayard Rustin, the African American pacifist, and the Reverend Glenn Smiley, a white officer of the FOR, came to Montgomery from New York to speak with King and other black community leaders. Smiley, a Texan and fellow southerner, was profoundly influenced by the nonviolent direct action teachings of Gandhi but found that although King admired the Indian leader he admitted that he did not know very much about him. After the interview Smiley wrote that, 'King can be a Negro Gandhi, or he can be made into an unfortunate demagogue destined to swing from a lynch mob's tree' (Garrow, 1988). King would choose to follow Gandhi and not the role of demagogue chosen by his white political opponents.

King had to face the court and not the lynch mob. He was the first indicted boycott leader to be tried, found guilty and fined $500 with another $500 in court costs or 368 days in jail. His conviction was appealed and all other cases were held over until the appeal court had ruled. Meanwhile the suit challenging the constitutionality of the city bus segregation ordinance had been filed on 1 February 1956 and on 5 June the federal district court ruled in *Browder v Gayle* that segregation on the buses was unconstitutional. The city commissioners were not willing to accept the ruling and they decided on two further steps: first they appealed to the Supreme Court, and second, on 13 November, they filed for an injunction to end the car pool. But it was too late. The Supreme Court on the same day upheld the lower court ruling. It was agreed at a mass meeting on 14 November that the boycott should be called off as soon as the desegregated buses started to move. After over a year, on 21 December, the first African American to climb aboard the Montgomery buses was Martin Luther King Jr.

The victory at Montgomery was based on a mass movement of the black community that practised nonviolent direct action combined with the NAACP strategy of using the courts to overthrow the Jim Crow system. As the first tentative steps to challenge segregation met resistance from the white community so the goals were changed from amelioration of the system to its overthrow and just when blacks were determined to fight for justice the white resisters would turn to violence and threats of violence. On 10 January 1957 two homes, including the home of Ralph Abernathy, and four black Baptist churches were bombed. Later that month a bomb made of 12 sticks of dynamite was found on the porch of Martin Luther King's home and defused (Garrow, 1988).

White Sympathisers

One of the houses bombed that 10 January was the home of the Reverend Robert Graetz, the white minister at the black Lutheran church in Montgomery. Graetz had been the only white person openly to provide support for the boycott movement. The deeds and words of a few white people played a part in the success of the movement. It was all very well for King and Abernathy to talk of a multiracial democracy but in the segregated world of Montgomery very few blacks had any reason to believe that there were whites who shared their dream. Robert Graetz and his wife by their daily actions were living proof that such white people did exist. And they were not alone. The Texan Glenn Smiley of FOR did much to persuade King that Gandhi provided the role model that he was searching for. Clifford and Virginia Durr gave advice and help throughout the boycott and they were two southerners who contributed to its success. It was not only people who had long been associated with the struggle for civil rights who gave encouragement to black protest leaders. In Montgomery several white citizens wrote to the *Advertiser* supporting black complaints against the bus system. In such a rigidly segregated society letters from citizens such as Mrs I. Rutledge, who said that she did not know one white person who thought it was 'right that a Negro may be made to stand that a person may sit', must have reassured those who participated in the boycott. Miss Juliette Morgan compared the boycott to Gandhi's salt march. She was convinced that: 'Passive resistance combined with freedom from hate is a power to be reckoned with' (Garrow, 1988).

Even in the darkest moments there were other whites who supported the black struggle for justice. Two years later in Little Rock, Arkansas, the 15-year-old schoolgirl Melba Pattillo along with eight other African American teenagers had to face the bayonets of the National Guard and the fury of the white racists as they attempted to integrate Central High School. She drew strength from brave women like Rosa Parks and the calm self-assurance of Thurgood Marshall. The extent of her and other young black people's ignorance of whites can be seen in the beliefs of her friend Marsha. 'She said white people didn't perspire, so I had to be certain I didn't let them see me perspire. I was petrified on that first morning I was to go to school.' Her fear was increased with the actions of the mob and their threatening attack on her friend Elizabeth Eckford. The next Sunday the newspaper carried an advertisement showing the white mob with 'the twisted, scowling faces with open mouths jeering.' The advertisement had been paid for by a white man from a small Arkansas town and it read: 'If you live in Arkansas study this picture and know shame. When hate is unleashed and bigotry finds a voice, God help us all.' As she recalled, 'I felt a kind of joy and hope that one white man was willing to use his own money to call attention to the injustice we were facing. Maybe the picture would help others realize that what they were doing was hurting everybody.' And during her time at Central High she was helped by a white student named Link, who took great risks but managed to prevent her from being attacked on many occasions. Her grandmother and mother were worried. 'Although I, too, was undecided about trusting Link, I continued to defend Link as both of them came up with dozens of reasons why I shouldn't trust this white boy. Still, there was something inside me that said he had taken a big risk giving me his car that day' (Beals, 1994).

It was not only individual acts of courage and statements of support that made African Americans aware that there were white Americans who shared their dream. White southerners played a leading role in the Southern Conference Education Fund (SCEF), an organisation which had fought for civil rights and equality during the 1940s and 1950s when the white majority sought to retain segregation. Aubrey Williams, president of the SCEF, came from an old southern family in Birmingham, Alabama, and had graduated from Maryville College in Tennessee. After a short time as a minister he went into social work, worked with FDR and his New Deal programmes and while at the Works Progress Administration was made aware of racist practices. He fought hard to combat them and became a good friend of A. Philip Randolph and Mrs Roosevelt. Forced out of his job in 1943 he returned to the South to work with the National Farmers Union in Alabama, where he edited a farming journal and built homes for black families. Throughout the postwar period Williams warned that the poor whites of the South, who had been so badly mistreated, were 'the likeliest material in the country for the lumpen proletariat, the mass base for a racist, fascist movement'. Because of the Depression they had been forced in their millions across the land and they took their virus with them. The poor white 'is a very dangerous man, and he must be cured, and during the process of cure he must be guarded from destroying others' (Klibaner, 1989).

Williams, despite his isolation from the majority of white southerners, did influence people like James Dombrowski, a Tampa Florida native and graduate from Emory University in 1923. In graduate school in the North he became interested in labour history and Christian socialism and published his dissertation in 1936, *The Early Days of Christian Socialism in America*. A founder member of the Highlander Folk School in 1932, he served as its staff director until 1942 when he joined the Southern Conference of Human Welfare. An historian of the SCEF has assessed his career: 'For thirty years he devoted himself to the gradual, peaceful change of Southern society, and under his influence a number of white and black clergymen of repute joined the Southern Conference Educational Fund' (Klibaner, 1989).

Williams also persuaded Carl and Anne Braden to stay in the South and offered them positions as field secretaries for the SCEF. Carl Braden was a Kentucky native whose father, a railroad worker, was a socialist. Carl's socialism was profoundly influenced by his mother's Catholicism. Although he had gone to seminary, he turned to newspaper reporting and while at the Louisville *Courier-Journal* he met and married Anne. Unlike Carl, Anne Braden had never experienced grinding poverty but rather came from a middle-class family and was brought up in Mississippi and Alabama. She had attended a series of private schools and after graduating from an exclusive college she worked as a journalist in Birmingham and Louisville. 'For Anne, Carl's world was a shattering, albeit liberating experience. The emotional and intellectual walls that segregation and years of indoctrination in white superiority had built around her crumbled under the impact of sharing social, political, and simple human experiences on an equal basis with black people.' In 1954 they agreed to help a black friend, Andrew Wade, who wanted a better home and so they bought a house in an all-white neighbourhood and sold it to him. The racial tension was inflamed by the belief that Braden was a communist. Found guilty of conspiracy, he served eight months of a 15-year sentence until the Supreme Court ruled that the state law was unconstitutional (Klibaner, 1989).

All these people active in the SCEF realised that people of goodwill, both black and white, needed encouragement. They organised meetings and the Fund became 'a nerve center of inter and intra-racial communication in the South'. As part of that effort to improve communication Carl and Anne edited the *Southern Patriot* and later they would help students in SNCC establish their own paper, *The Student Voice*. Their activities they believed would also bring pressure on the federal government. The Fund members turned their semi-annual meetings into workshops which involved the wider community and in 1958, for example, a workshop was held at the black Fisk University in Nashville, Tennessee, which was addressed by Aubrey Williams. Fisk students would play a major role in the campaign of the 1960s.

Frequent trips to the North led to friendships with other whites who sympathised with the aims of the boycott leaders in Montgomery. Rustin introduced King to Harris Wofford, the first white man to graduate from Howard University Law School, the premier black university in the United States. Wofford was also a friend of E. D. Nixon of the MIA. Rustin also introduced King to Stanley Levison, a New York lawyer who, working with Ella Baker, had raised funds in that city for the MIA. All were agreed that now was the time to organise a regional group that would bring an end to segregation in the South. As the bombs were being planted in Montgomery on 10 January Rustin drew up the plans to challenge bus segregation throughout the South but he knew also that they meant to challenge 'the entire social, political and economic order that has kept us second class citizens.... Those who oppose us understand this.' The two weapons chosen to win the war were voting power and mass direct action. The new organisation, the Southern Leadership Conference, later called the Southern Christian Leadership Conference by Martin Luther King, was set up in 1957. Although the Conference had had Medgar Evers of the NAACP on its committee as it became SCLC, Evers agreed with Roy Wilkins of the NAACP that he, Evers, would resign from the committee. NAACP officials worked with King but this did not overcome the deep distrust between the two organisations.

Although often distrustful of one another, the leaders of these groups presented a united front when in negotiations with any administration. Wilkins, King, Randolph and Lester B. Granger of the National Urban League met with President Eisenhower. The four men agreed that Randolph would make the opening statement and the other three would address three points each. In the meeting, Eisenhower defended his administration and refused to give any promises about further action. And the pressure at a local level seemed even less successful with the City of Montgomery refusing to respond to demands for desegregation of schools or even parks. The city commissioners did not feel any urgency and the

MIA was divided by factional disputes over issues such as which organisation spoke for black America.

Following a short visit to India, King took part in the second march on Washington to demand school desegregation. The march on 18 April 1959 was reasonably successful, with an estimated 26 000 participating. King, Tom Mboya of Kenya and Roy Wilkins were the three main speakers. The consequence of this rally was a meeting for King with the Vice President, Richard Nixon. King was very impressed with the Vice President's support for the civil rights movement and added: 'If Richard Nixon is not sincere, he is the most dangerous man in America' (Garrow, 1988).

Despite their efforts, Rustin, King, and Levison had not created an effective national lobbying organisation. With the increasingly acrimonious feelings between King and E. D. Nixon the MIA had become moribund and King decided to leave Montgomery and go to Atlanta. Despite the success of the mass boycott in integrating the bus service and the contribution such grass-roots activism had had on drafting the Civil Rights Acts of 1957 and 1960, white southerners had shown they were just as determined to resist the burgeoning movement as African Americans were prepared to struggle for justice. Perhaps in King's gloomiest moments he recalled a visit he had made with Ralph Abernathy to the Highlander Folk School in Tennessee in 1957 where they heard Pete Seeger sing 'We Shall Overcome'. As King had said to Anne Braden, 'There's something about that song that haunts you' (Garrow, 1988).

3

A New Frontier? JFK, Civil Rights and Mass Protest

Despite the sit-ins and boycotts of the late 1950s which sought to capitalise on the success of the Montgomery boycott it was not at all clear as the new decade began whether the African American community would still be singing 'We Shall Overcome' at the end of the decade. Martin Luther King had moved with his family to Atlanta where he had the advantages and many disadvantages of being close to his strong-willed father. As he started a new career in the unofficial capital of Dixie, southern Democrats were pleased that a young senator whom they had promoted for the vice presidency in 1956 was preparing his assault on the executive office. Although King met with John Fitzgerald Kennedy on 23 June 1960 privately he was not impressed with the young senator from Massachusetts. The black preacher was convinced that the senator's voting on the 1957 Civil Rights Act was decided by his desire to win southern support for his presidential campaign rather than any set of principles.

The Greensboro Sit-In

However, while Kennedy was campaigning for power in the Democratic party, and Martin Luther King dreamed of winning control over the National Baptist Convention, four black students in Greensboro, North Carolina, entered the Woolworths store and went to the whites-only luncheon counter. They sat at the counter on the afternoon of 1 February 1960 and promised to return at ten o'clock the next day. This was not the first of the sit-in protests. As Branch has pointed out, 'In the previous three years similar demonstrations had occurred in at least sixteen other cities. Few of them made the news, all faded quickly from public notice and none had the slightest catalytic effect anywhere else. By contrast, Greensboro helped define the new decade' (Branch, 1989).

In assessing what was happening, the Southern Regional Council, an inter-racial group of moderates, issued a report a few months after the Greensboro sit-in entitled *Reflections on the Latest Reform of the South*, authored by Leslie Dunbar. He wrote: 'Almost from the beginning the sit-ins have been referred to as a "movement." ... No one ever speaks of the "school desegregation movement." One accomplishment, then, of the sit-in was to achieve, almost from the start, this recognition' (Laue, 1989). During the summer of 1960, 79 sit-in demonstrations were led by students, 78 of which were in the South and border states, with North Carolina (18 sit-ins), Florida (12) and Virginia (10) being the most involved. Among the reasons given by students for their involvement in the movement was not only their sense of personal frustration but also their sense of commitment and belief in justice. 'Your relationship with the movement is just like a love affair,' said one. 'You can't explain it. All you know is it's something you *have* to do' (Laue, 1989).

Perhaps the 1960s sit-ins came to be called 'the movement' because the four students from North Carolina Agricultural and Technical College captured the spirit of the moment. The ageing General Eisenhower sadly was better known among the younger generation for his golf and his heart attacks than he was for his opposition to the military industrial complex. It is difficult to explain the heady sense of optimism that the young generation felt – that anything was possible and no problem need go unresolved. It was time for the older generation, who had made so many mistakes, to move over and let the newcomers solve the world's problems. Surely they would not repeat the mistakes of the older generation with their wars and crusades against the 'red menace'. It was this intense idealism that motivated the black students in the South and their white supporters. Regardless of what they actually achieved, the young black Baptist minister Martin Luther King Jr and the young Catholic politician John F. Kennedy from Massachusetts expressed the hopes and dreams of this baby-boom generation.

It was this young generation that had loyally pledged allegiance to the flag each morning in school and it was in the schools across the nation that they were told of the unique promise of America. For the older generation the latest Chevrolet or Ford with its new layers of chrome came to represent the ideal which could be achieved by hire purchase. Conspicuous consumption and leisure were the concern of adults, but for many of the younger generation who had been constantly reminded in high school of their fortunate status as citizens of the wealthiest democratic society on earth, the determination was to make the American dream a reality. The older generation's warnings about the dangers of communism had lost their impact. This was especially true for the South, where the schools and churches preached white supremacy as a bulwark against communism. As Paul Goodman observed in *Growing up Absurd* in 1960, 'Now that Law and religion side against them, the Southerners are maniac with wounded conceit and sexual fear; their behavior on integration should be referred not to the Attorney General but to the Public Health Service'. He added, 'All this has come banging down on the children as the battleground. Yet, paradoxically, among all young people it is perhaps just the young people in the South, whites and Negroes both, who most find life worth living these days, because something real is happening' (in Howard, 1982).

News of the Greensboro sit-in swept not only through the local community but also across the South. Floyd McKissick, NAACP youth council leader, was told about the sit-in by one of the protesters. The following day the vice president of the predominantly white National Student Association had heard about the demonstration and had gone to Greensboro. And this was before news of the sit-in had been reported in the media. By the third day of the protest the number of students involved was over 80 and the word had spread to James Lawson in Nashville. On that day sympathy demonstrations were held in Durham, Raleigh and other cities in the state. By the weekend over 400 students had taken part in the sit-in, which was extended to other stores in Greensboro. On the following Thursday, the Reverend Fred Shuttlesworth had arrived from Birmingham, Alabama, to preach a midweek service. He was immediately aware of the historic significance of the events and telephoned Ella Baker in the SCLC office in Atlanta and told her: 'You must tell Martin that we must get with this'. He was certain that the sit-ins would 'shake up the world'. King was the first black leader to give his full support to the students when black newspapers were dismissing the demonstrations as merely student pranks. Three weeks after the sit-ins started in Greensboro King spoke to a rally in Durham and he reiterated that: 'Men are tired of being trampled over by the iron feet of oppression'. He continued with praise for the students: 'What is fresh, what is new in your fight is the fact that it was initiated, led, and sustained by students. What is new is that American students have come of age. You now take your honored places in the world-wide struggle for freedom' (Branch, 1989).

The Nashville Sit-In

Meanwhile in Nashville, James Lawson found himself overwhelmed by volunteers to take part in similar demonstrations. Approximately 500 students, mainly from the city's four black colleges – Fisk, Tennessee State, Meharry Medical and the Baptist Seminary – were insistent that they should hold their own demonstration. Lawson tried to dissuade them, pointing out that only 75 of them had completed training at Highlander in nonviolence. In addition, he said they did not have bail money and many would be arrested by the Nashville city police. Despite his reservations, the students were determined to act and he gave them a crash course on nonviolence. As one historian has written: 'The Nashville students – destined to establish themselves as the largest, most disciplined, and most persistent of the nonviolent action groups in the South – extended the sit-in movement into its third state. Their success helped form the model of the student group – recruited from the campuses, quartered in the churches, and advised by preachers' (Branch, 1989). It was a Fisk student – Marion Barry Jr – who was elected chairman of the SNCC, which was set up at a meeting sponsored by the SCLC at Shaw University, Raleigh, North Carolina, on 17 April 1960 (*The Student Voice,* June 1960).

Only 12 days after the students had made their protest in North Carolina, the students in Nashville, whose leaders included Chicago native Diane Nash, sat in at lunch counters in the dime stores in the city. The protesters were attacked and in the weeks that followed almost 150 were arrested. Nash told the judge that she and 15 others would prefer to go to jail than pay the fines because if they did they 'would be contributing to and supporting the injustice and immoral practices that have been performed in the arrest and conviction of the defendants' (Branch, 1989). On hearing her remarks 60 others joined and chose to go to jail. By 10 May the downtown stores capitulated, lunch counters were integrated and African Americans were hired in nonmenial positions for the first time. On 7 March in Knoxville, Tennessee, the black students from Knoxville College and white students from the University of Tennessee at Knoxville held a series of sit-ins and eventually the counters were integrated. In Chattanooga white shoppers rioted rather than integrate (*The Student Voice*, August 1960).

At a SNCC meeting held at Atlanta University 13–14 May 1960, the students adopted a statement of purpose drawn up by the Reverend James Lawson. They would be motivated by nonviolence because they declared:

> Through nonviolence, courage displaces fear; love transforms hate. Acceptance dissipates prejudice; hope ends despair. Peace dominates war; faith reconciles doubt. Mutual regards cancel enmity. Justice for all overthrows injustice. The redemptive community supercedes [*sic*] systems of gross social immorality. (*The Student Voice*, June 1960)

Also present were Ella Baker and the Reverend Wyatt Walker of SCLC, the Reverend Edward Brown of Atlanta Congregational Churches, Max Heirich of the Friends Service Committee (Quakers) and Len Holt of CORE. The committee of SNCC was divided into three subcommittees for coordination, communication and finance. It was agreed to have an office in Atlanta and to have regular monthly meetings. They agreed to raise funds for their work but sought close cooperation with the NAACP and its Legal Defense Fund. The importance of good communications was clear, and they agreed to publish a newsletter which would be distributed to every group and cover action throughout the South. They also stressed the need for a 'system of flash news to alert the nation to emergencies and serious developments' (*The Student Voice*, June 1960). They also provided for press releases on the movement, public relations pamphlets and interpretative statements for the outside press. Carl and Anne Braden, of SCEF, used their skills as professional journalists to help the students.

The sit-in movement was a mass protest organised by African American students from black campuses but it did have support from a few white southern students. Those whites who did participate were mentioned in the SNCC newsletters. In October a story was headlined 'PARKER STILL JAILED'. Richard Parker of Florida State University was in the Duval County Jail, Jacksonville, with a broken jaw. He was sentenced to 90 days in jail having been charged with inciting a riot in Jacksonville. He took part in the sit-in in Jacksonville on 25–26 August and was arrested three days later. According to the report he had lost 25 pounds since his imprisonment (*The Student Voice*, October 1960).

From the very beginning sit-ins were more than just asserting the right to be served at previously all-white lunch counters. For the students 1 February 1960 was Freedom Day. In an editorial in *The Student Voice* in August 1960 entitled 'Politics and the Student Movement' the editors complained: 'The political ramifications of the student protest movement are often underestimated and glossed over'. But as the movement gained strength they should widen the battle and 'it is imperative that we look into the possibility of engaging in political activity on all levels, local, state, and federal'. They had to inform politicians of their views 'forcefully'. 'Elections are coming in November, and we have done our part in seeing that both parties have included in their platforms the strongest civil rights planks ever written'. However, this was not good enough and students were urged to dramatise 'the most blatant denial of civil rights that exists in this country today – the denial of the right to vote to millions of citizens of the South'. The editorial called on students North and South to hold protest rallies and pickets on election day. 'As citizens working for the betterment not only of our communities, but of the country and the world, again we are called to witness that we are willing to do that which is often unpopular to see that neither we nor our fellow-citizens are forced to endure second-class citizenship'.

King Meets Kennedy

The members of SNCC were following a policy that had been set out by the union leader A. Philip Randolph and by Martin Luther King

Jr of SCLC. On 9 June, Randolph and King jointly called on voters to picket the Democratic and Republican national conventions. They both attacked the Civil Rights Act of 1960 as inadequate and pointed out that millions of Americans were still second-class citizens. They argued that marching on the conventions would force the political parties to act. One man who stridently opposed their efforts was Harlem congressman Adam Clayton Powell, who denounced King as the 'captive of socialist interests'. Although the row with Powell eventually forced Rustin to resign as coordinator of the New York office of SCLC, King's visit to New York resulted in him having a breakfast meeting with presidential candidate John F. Kennedy. The two men agreed that firm executive leadership was needed and that urgent action was required to ensure the right to vote and to end discrimination in housing. Before this meeting, King did not consider the young man as a politician of principle but after the meeting he admitted, 'I was very impressed by the forthright and honest manner in which he discussed the civil rights question. I have no doubt that he would do the right thing on this issue if he were elected President' (Garrow, 1988).

A second meeting with Kennedy in mid-September revealed the young senator to be better briefed on civil rights issues. Again Kennedy reassured the Atlanta preacher that he supported strong measures to ensure the right to vote. King refused to endorse Kennedy but the presence of the first white graduate of Howard Law School, Harris Wofford, in the Kennedy campaign must have influenced King. Although King's campaign with Roy Wilkins was called a 'Nonpartisan Crusade to Register One Million New Negro Voters', most involved knew it was an attempt to register more Democratic voters.

King had more pressing things on his mind such as the determination of African American students at the five black colleges in Atlanta to be part of the crusade for freedom. The students were impatient with the store owners, especially Richard H. Rich, owner of the biggest downtown store. Despite meetings with the students, Rich refused to integrate his facilities and three student leaders – Lonnie King, Herschelle Sullivan and Julian Bond – persuaded Martin Luther King Jr that he had to join their sit-in. On 19 October, starting at 11 o'clock, 75 students from the five colleges moved on to the stores and the first arrest was made at the Magnolia Room of Rich's store 30 minutes later. King was arrested and like the students he refused to post bond and spent his first night in jail (*The Student Voice*, October 1960). He was unaware that he had broken the conditions of a probation order and when the students were released King was transferred to DeKalb County handcuffed and guarded by a large police dog. Despite appeals from many people, King was sentenced to four months for violating his probation. Having avoided prison in Alabama on trumped up charges of tax evasion, King now found himself in prison for the first time (Garrow, 1988).

News of King's imprisonment was sent to Vice President Richard Nixon on the campaign trail but he refused to send telegrams because he and his advisers were aware that Eisenhower had broken into the previously solid Democratic South and Nixon wanted to retain the recent white converts to the Republican party. Nixon's press officer Herb Klein pocketed the drafts of telegrams drawn up by campaign staffer E. Frederick Morrow. While Nixon ignored the advice of black Atlanta Republican John C. Calhoun, King's wife Coretta called her friend Harris Wofford, who was working for the Kennedy campaign. John Kennedy called Mrs King. Robert Kennedy was furious and he accused Wofford, 'You bomb throwers probably lost the election. You've probably lost three states ... the civil rights section isn't going to do another damn thing in this campaign'. But he was also angry about the behaviour of the judge whom he telephoned, arguing that it was a constitutional right for defendants to post a bond. The next day King was released. Although John Kennedy denied any deliberate attempt to win the African American vote (Schlesinger Jr, 1979), the Democrats issued a small flyer in black precincts which read '"No Comment": Nixon versus a Candidate with a Heart, Senator Kennedy: The Case of Martin Luther King' (Garrow, 1988). Martin Luther King Jr spoke of Kennedy's 'moral courage' and Daddy King, a Republican voter, was more enthusiastic: 'I'll take a Catholic or the Devil himself if he'll wipe the tears from my daughter-in-law's eyes. I've got a suitcase full of votes – my whole church for ... Senator Kennedy' (Schlesinger Jr, 1979).

Executive Action

Although the election of JFK was largely due to the African American vote, his appointment of his brother Robert as Attorney

General did not augur well for those involved in the civil rights movement. Although Robert knew that action was necessary he was not the most distinguished graduate of Harvard or of Virginia Law School. As one historian has noted: 'he had not known many black people, knew little about segregation, and had not considered the federal role in promoting desegregation' (Bernstein, 1991). However, he did make an excellent choice of Assistant Attorney General by appointing the Tennessean Harris Wofford, who did know a lot about the civil rights movement. And it was Wofford who urged the Justice Department to support the policy of voter registration that had been adopted by the students in SNCC, as well as SCLC and the NAACP. In addition, he advised Kennedy to use executive orders rather than rely on the conservative Congress to advance civil rights. The Civil Rights Commission, renewed in the Civil Rights Act of 1960, was to be continued, the President appointed more African Americans to senior posts and avoided segregated meetings. A sympathetic historian, Irving Bernstein, claims: 'The Kennedy policy on civil rights in 1961 called for a minimum of legislation and a maximum of executive action' (Bernstein, 1991). However, civil rights activists such as Roy Wilkins of the NAACP became increasingly frustrated at Kennedy's lack of action, especially his failure to desegregate federally funded housing, something he had promised to do during the campaign with 'one stroke of the pen'. As the days passed the White House received thousands of pens all emblazoned with the famous phrase. Kennedy refused to act because he was aware that segregation in housing was a national issue with the potential for great violence and that 'Any governmental intrusion of race into housing was certain to arouse deep emotions' (Bernstein, 1991). Eventually, in November 1962, after the congressional elections, Kennedy did sign the executive order but it was merely a symbolic act with no effective enforcement powers.

In federal employment the President ensured the integration of the Coast Guard Academy and set up the Commission on Equal Employment Opportunity (CEEO) with the Vice President, Lyndon Baines Johnson, as its chairman. Although based on the FEPC principle as operated by FDR and Truman, Executive Order 10952 drawn up by Johnson and signed by Kennedy for the first time combined federal employment and government contractor agencies under such a commission. And Johnson pointed out that it was not good enough simply to forbid discrimination. 'It is necessary that affirmative action be taken to make equal opportunity available to all who, directly or indirectly, are employed by the nation' (Bernstein, 1991). Although CEEO had the power to refuse contracts to companies that had discriminatory policies, this sanction was rarely used, although there were notable successes such as the integration and promotion of African Americans at the Lockheed plant in Marietta, Georgia. Following the Lockheed agreement, Johnson announced 'Plans for Progress'. But, despite the great publicity, these produced very poor results and a Southern Regional Council study demonstrated that in the Atlanta area only three out of 24 companies were in compliance. Only rarely did the federal government threaten to bar companies from competing for federal contracts but it is possible that the publicity surrounding two firms, one in Arkansas and the other in Illinois, may have persuaded others to end discrimination.

Employers frequently, and with justification, complained that they were simply complying with demands from their workers for segregated facilities. Randolph had been campaigning for years against the racist practices of American labour unions. In November 1962, Johnson, President George Meany of the AFL–CIO, and the officials of 116 unions signed an agreement to end discrimination on the basis of race, creed, colour or national origin in hiring, apprenticeship training and promotion. It was useful in that it educated people, but practically it made little difference to the unions and there is no evidence that the construction unions did anything after they signed the agreement (Bernstein, 1991).

Although John and Robert Kennedy sought to bring about gradual change largely through executive action, they were under constant pressure from activists in SNCC and CORE, in addition to the traditional lobbying of groups such as the NAACP and the Urban League. As one commentator on the 1960s has observed:

> The Kennedy emphasis on the young, the bright, the chic and the tough was enormously appealing: it dampened criticism by its very style, and so begged for a while the questions of substance which must inevitably come. A program like the Peace Corps seemed to say that one could change the world a little for the better and have an exciting time doing it. It could also shake up establishment liberalism, which had become shop-worn. (Knight, 1989)

Whatever the intentions of the Kennedy administration, the students in SNCC and in CORE were certainly not prepared to accept merely gesture and style. Throughout 1960–1, students participated in voter registration drives. Lane College students registered the black voters in Fayette and Haywood Counties in Tennessee and 861 African Americans voted in Haywood County for the first time in 1960. The response of the wealthy white landowners was to evict their black tenants who were organised into a 'Freedom City' by SNCC workers (*The Student Voice*, November 1960). In addition to voter registration, students were involved in church kneel-ins and theatre stand-ins.

The Freedom Rides

The events which gained international news coverage were the Freedom Rides organised by James Farmer of CORE, who explained later:

> We planned the Freedom Ride with the specific intention of creating a crisis. We were counting on the bigots of the South to do our work for us. We figured that the government would have to respond if we created a situation that was headline news all over the world, and affecting the nation's image abroad. An international crisis that was our strategy. (Bernstein, 1991)

Certainly at the time CORE made it clear to the President that they were seeking an international crisis. Following the bombing of the Freedom buses and the violent assault on Freedom Riders in Birmingham, Alabama, Edward B. King, administrative secretary of SNCC, sent a telegram to Kennedy in which he stated: 'At a time in the history of our great nation when we are telling the people of Asia, Africa, Latin America and the free world in general that we desire to be their friends Negro Americans continue to be assaulted by the Southern reactionaries' (Bernstein, 1991).

The aim of the Freedom Riders was also to test Kennedy's willingness to support civil rights through executive action. As early as 1946 the Supreme Court had ruled in *Morgan v Virginia* that enforcement of state segregation laws on interstate transport was a burden on interstate commerce and therefore was unconstitutional.

In 1958 in the case of *Boynton v Virginia* the Court had also ruled that segregated bus depots were illegal. The Riders, six black and six white, left Washington, DC, on 4 May 1961 to test these rulings. On 14 May, after several minor incidents, the Greyhound bus pulled into Anniston, Alabama, 60 miles from Birmingham and was met by the Ku Klux Klan. After their first attack on the bus they followed it out of town and when it was forced to stop because of a puncture the mob set the bus on fire. The students continued in another bus to Birmingham where the racist chief of police, Eugene 'Bull' Connor, told his men to take the day off and visit their families because it was Mother's Day. A howling mob armed with baseball bats, lead pipes and bicycle chains assaulted the students. Although an FBI informer, Gary Thomas Rowe was one of the gang and had told Hoover about the planned attack on the Freedom Riders; nothing was done. A group of students from Fisk University, led by Diane Nash, insisted on completing the journey. Governor John Patterson of Alabama, a friend of Kennedy, refused to give the now 21 riders, only three white, protection and they were badly beaten by a mob in Montgomery. They were attacked again in Jackson, Mississippi. All this was carried on the national and international news just as Kennedy was preparing to meet Krushchev shortly after his humiliation in Cuba. But as Farmer knew, the lawyers in the Justice Department could no longer ignore the failure of southern states to uphold the law and by September 1961 the Interstate Commerce Commission had issued regulations ordering the end of segregation on interstate transport. However, as African Americans were only too well aware, it was one thing to issue orders and another for them to be obeyed. Years later, when the author arrived at the bus station in Selma, Alabama, in 1966 at three in the morning, there were no 'whites only' signs anywhere but the bus station was rigidly segregated. Therefore it is not correct to suggest as Bernstein does that, 'By the end of 1962 James Farmer's Freedom Riders and Robert Kennedy's lawyers had abolished Jim Crow in interstate transportation' (Bernstein, 1991).

The Integration of 'Ole Miss'

The very confrontation that Kennedy wanted to avoid was now brewing in Mississippi. It would make the events at Little Rock seem quiet by comparison. The son of a Mississippi sharecropper and an air-force veteran James Howard Meredith applied to attend the University of Mississippi ('Ole Miss'), at Oxford. The Democrats who ran the state were divided between moderate racists such as John Coleman and rabid racists such as Ross Barnett. They were supported by equally racist judges who upheld the right of the University to refuse Meredith entrance. Judge Sidney Mize argued that Mississippi was not racially segregated, even though no African Americans either studied or taught at the University.

After a series of appeals Supreme Court Justice Hugo Black, a native of Alabama, ordered that Meredith be enrolled. Ross Barnett went on television and threw down the gauntlet. The people of Mississippi had a choice: either they submitted to tyranny from the federal government or they acted like men and resisted. In his determination to defend white supremacy, the Governor called on the arguments of his ancestors who had fought to keep slavery. 'Mississippi, as a Sovereign State, has the right under the federal Constitution to determine for itself what the federal Constitution has reserved to it'. He would interpose the authority of the state between the people of Mississippi and federal government tyranny.

Attempts to enrol Meredith peacefully were futile. The Board of Trustees of the University voted to surrender their authority to Barnett. On several occasions the Governor and his deputy played out the act of interposition on the University steps. As the days dragged by the students became more agitated and Kennedy realised that he would have to use force. The cabinet agreed that the army should be kept in reserve and that federal marshals and prison staff should be used to minimise the risk of violence. The extreme right-wing General Edwin Walker called for volunteers to protect the University. As Barnett postured in front of the students at a football game, he failed to realise the changing situation in Washington. Initially reluctant to have a repeat of Little Rock, Robert Kennedy cynically sought political advantage from the crisis. He told his assistant Nicholas Katzenbach: 'If things get rough, don't worry about yourself; the President needs a moral issue'.

On Sunday 30 September Meredith was flown into Oxford with 170 federal marshals. A mob of students, joined by outsiders, started to riot, throwing bricks and setting fires. The highway patrol was withdrawn, not strengthened, and this seemed to be the green light for major violence. The use of tear gas only made matters worse.

The students were too busy rioting to listen to the appeal of John Kennedy in which he vainly flattered the state for its prowess on the battlefield and gridiron. By nine o'clock that evening the first fatality occurred when Paul Guilhard, a reporter for Agence France-Presse was shot in the back. An Oxford resident was killed and many others were wounded by either rocks or gunshots. The rioting lasted through the night and order was not restored until nearly seven that morning. Ross Barnett and 'Ole Miss' gave the President the moral issue he had been looking for and also gave him and his brother Robert the tactics they would need later to beat George Wallace of Alabama.

Internal Divisions and External Pressures

The Kennedy brothers had not made any commitments on civil rights. The students had won the support of King and direct action had proved successful despite the deep reservations of the NAACP. Roy Wilkins and the older leaders resented young leaders like Martin Luther King Jr. The latter had to stop Wyatt Walker at SCLC from introducing individual membership because it would mean direct competition with the NAACP. However, the New York lawyer Stanley Levison and Jack O'Dell raised hundreds of thousands of dollars by direct mailing and King raised an equal amount with his speeches.

However, because of Levison's former connection with the Communist party, Robert Kennedy gave the FBI the authority to wiretap telephone calls and even burgle the lawyer's office. The Bureau, under J. Edgar Hoover's leadership, was increasingly concerned about the communist influence in the civil rights movement. Levison warned King that O'Dell had been a member of the Communist party and a report of this conversation was sent to the Attorney General. In a further effort to weaken King the FBI informed newspapers, such as the *New York Times*, that O'Dell was a communist. King was embarrassed by this revelation, and publicly claimed O'Dell had resigned when he, and the FBI, knew that O'Dell was still working for the SCLC (Garrow, 1988).

Not only the FBI was causing problems for King. The students in SNCC were increasingly restive about their lack of funds. They

believed that it was their direct action that had brought in money
from sympathisers from around the world but was now being used
by Wyatt Walker to promote SCLC. While SNCC, under the
formidable and inspirational leadership of men such as Robert
Moses, faced great danger as they struggled to register voters in
Mississippi, it was King and SCLC who got the celebrity status in
New York. The fact that Ella Baker was now working for SNCC
following her replacement at SCLC by the Reverend Wyatt Walker
did not make for easy relationships between SNCC members and
the older leaders of SCLC (Garrow, 1988). Ironically it was King and
his supporters who were viewed as the young upstarts by the even
older leadership of the black Baptist Convention. Whereas King as
vice president of the Convention had supported the sit-ins, the
autocratic president, the Reverend Joseph Jackson, had openly
criticised them. King was too young to challenge Jackson but a
friend of his did. The election saw the triumph of the autocrat and
King lost his position as vice president. From then on the black
Baptist church would remain deeply divided and the Convention
not only refused formal support for the SCLC but actively opposed
King (Branch, 1989).

The Albany Movement

These divisions within the civil rights movement help to explain its
failure in Albany, Georgia. Charles Sherrod, who worked with
Robert Moses in Mississippi, decided to tackle the repressive regime
in southwest Georgia. He chose to organise the young African
Americans in Albany, especially the students at Albany State College,
bypassing the older black leadership, all of whom were active in the
NAACP. Administrators at the College were alarmed at the activities
of the students and tried unsuccessfully to remove SNCC organisers
from the campus. The efforts of the students are generally assumed
to be a failure, despite the support of Martin Luther King Jr and
Ralph Abernathy, who were both arrested. Certainly the police chief
Laurie Pritchett made many claims about his understanding of
Gandhi and newspapers reported that he defeated nonviolent direct
action with nonviolence, such as ensuring that all protesters were
treated courteously when arrested. In turn the establishment press

provided Pritchett with details of the students' demonstrations and intended targets, something which was to lead to deep distrust of journalists by students in the movement. They knew they needed publicity but the distrust planted in Albany would result in the banning of journalists from mass meetings. It would lead to an alternative newspaper system. Pritchett, when he did not have the press giving him information, relied on either older members of the black community to report to him or even used paid informers. His much vaunted nonviolence relied on journalists who were too lazy to investigate jails outside Albany where student demonstrators were taken and subjected to Georgia's old-fashioned brutality. The city fathers knew that the student protests had been effective; business was seriously affected and their concern was evident when they insisted that King should be released from jail. But the most shocking revelation for many in the movement has been described by King's biographer:

> It was a painful irony to movement activists, who concluded accurately that the national public had taken little offense at Albany's establishment of what one observer termed 'an efficient police state'. So long as the Laurie Pritchetts of the South succeeded in maintaining segregation in a fashion that eschewed public violence and brutality, it seemed that the Kennedy brothers would be content to leave civil rights on the back burner. (Garrow, 1988)

Fortunately for Martin Luther King, the movement and the United States, there were very few Pritchetts enforcing white supremacy in the South. Much more typical, and well known to members of the movement, was the violent racist police chief in Birmingham, Alabama, Eugene 'Bull' Connor. So when white racists bombed the Bethel Baptist Church, King was able to use the incident to demand action from the President. African American leaders on a visit to the White House demanded improved relations with the newly independent African countries and called on Kennedy to take a stronger stand on the civil rights issue at home. The President refused to give any promises and argued that legislation on civil rights was bound to fail in Congress. It would take one more action in the struggle for justice, which would be met with violent white resistance, to force the Kennedy brothers to act.

King and Birmingham, Alabama

King went to New York and informed the singer Harry Belafonte of their plans and he agreed to raise money for those who would be jailed and gave substantial sums himself. Meanwhile in Birmingham things did not go well at first, with few taking part in the marches and the newspapers eager to print attacks on King. While King explained the need for action with black preachers and businessmen, Eugene 'Bull' Connor proved how he intended to deal with the protesters. On Monday 8 April 1963 a small group of demonstrators led by A. D. King were stopped by snarling German shepherd dogs. The dogs' assault on a demonstrator was captured by a news photographer and the picture appeared throughout the world.

As a result of the police brutality, King decided to march on Good Friday despite a court injunction against him. His arrest, with Abernathy, meant that the administration could no longer duck the challenge of the movement. With King in solitary confinement the President called Coretta King to reassure her that everything would be done to protect her husband. While in prison King was able to write his famous 'Letter from Birmingham City Jail'. His absence while in jail also gave control of the movement to James Bevel, who had married Diane Nash and both of whom worked for SCLC. It was Bevel who realised that the movement had never fulfilled its commitment to fill the jails and he was also aware that the students at the black Miles College were not willing to be jail bait. He did know that high-school students were eager to join the protests and had been held back by adults. Bevel had no such doubts. Ignoring the protests of their teachers and parents, thousands of high-school students took to the streets. The police were fooled by diversionary marches and Bevel, Andrew Young and other volunteers armed with walkie-talkies organised march after march. On 3 May the police used dogs and fire hoses on the teenagers and 250 students were arrested. Three days later this had increased to 1000. By 7 May the jails were full, with 2500 arrests. Birmingham was a mass movement and one that the administration could not ignore. Despite the criticisms of the Birmingham settlement by David Garrow, Adam Fairclough is correct when he writes: 'The success of Birmingham should not ... be judged according to its impact on Congress: the initiative for the civil rights bill came from the administration, not the legislature. And the evidence strongly suggests that SCLC's demonstrations played a decisive role in persuading the Kennedy administration to introduce legislation' (Fairclough, 1987).

The Attorney General had for two years sought to defuse black protest and the Kennedy brothers were seriously alarmed about the possibility of all-out race war. This fear was heightened following Robert Kennedy's meeting with black intellectuals, novelist James Baldwin, sociologist Kenneth Clarke, playwright Lorraine Hansbury and with singers Lena Horne and Harry Belafonte, plus CORE activist Jerome Smith, who was in New York for medical treatment following one of his many beatings. Smith and Baldwin were furious with Kennedy's apparent indifference. Smith told Kennedy about the abuse he had received in the South and warned him: 'When I pull the trigger, kiss it good-bye'. When asked by Baldwin if he would fight for the United States, Smith shouted, 'Never! Never! Never!' Robert Kennedy was shocked and angered by the meeting but as his friend and biographer writes: 'He began, I believe, to grasp as from the inside the nature of black anguish. He resented the experience, but it pierced him all the same. His tormentors made no sense; but in a way they made all sense. It was another stage in his education' (Schlesinger Jr, 1979).

The March on Washington

Another part of his education were the efforts of SNCC, CORE and SCLC throughout the summer of 1963 to register voters and the failures to do so in any number in Gadsden, Alabama, Danville, Virginia and Plaquemine, Louisiana, underlined the ease with which southerners could maintain their white supremacy. For the Attorney General it became obvious that the courage alone of civil rights workers would never bring democracy to America. For Martin Luther King Jr these individual failures could not be allowed to destroy the faith that had made the challenge possible in the first place. Taking up an idea first proposed by A. Philip Randolph, King decided that a march on Washington, if they could get a hundred thousand, would be sufficient pressure to demonstrate a mass demand for justice. Fairclough argues that the march on Washington had minimal impact on the legislative process. It is difficult to be certain. This underestimates the amazing scene of at least 250 000 demonstrators in front of the great American icon, the Lincoln Memorial. For the first time leading representatives of the major religions and denominations were united behind the civil rights cause. Tens of millions of North Americans watching on television heard a young Baptist minister articulate African American demands for justice in terms of the American Dream. It was a familiar theme to many who had heard King before but it came as a revelation to millions who had not.

Despite the success of the march, the FBI still spent most of its time trying to undermine the SCLC, which Hoover saw as merely a communist front organisation. Robert Kennedy, despite his education, outraged young people in the movement with the federal indictment of the 'Albany Nine' – students who were accused of obstructing justice during the Albany protest. However, this concession to the segregationists did not stop the racists and their violence. Just three weeks after the march on Washington four young black girls were killed by a bomb at Birmingham's Sixteenth Street Baptist Church. This was the seventh bomb in six months, and since 1956 there had been 17 bombings in that city alone. Leading southern politicians were content to remind southerners of the Civil War with their appeals to interposition and nullification. George Wallace stood in the doorway of the University of Alabama vowing to keep segregation forever and these actions were fuelling the violence of the resurgent Klan. Wallace's racist appeal to southern white nationalism was met by John Kennedy's televised address to the nation in which he committed himself to a civil rights bill providing a federal remedy to integration of public accommodation. Only seconds after the President had stopped speaking a shot rang out in the humid Mississippi night in Jackson. Mrs Medgar Evers ran out to find her husband, the head of the state NAACP, dead on the front porch (Garrow, 1988).

The very violence that southern politicians had encouraged and which the FBI had done nothing to stop was further aided by the indifference of the northern newspapers and network television. It was in such a climate of fear, hate and violence that the President went to Dallas, Texas. The murder of the young President plunged the nation into mourning and into a period of great uncertainty. Blacks and liberals were worried about the obvious popularity of politicians such as Goldwater and Wallace. There were dire predictions that if the supporters of these two men joined forces then the United States was on the brink of becoming a fascist state.

4

THE GREAT SOCIETY AND THE LIMITS OF LIBERALISM

As Lyndon Baines Johnson took the oath of office aboard Air Force One, Jacqueline Kennedy stood next to the Texan, the dried blood of her husband still clinging to her pink suit. It was the sort of tragic scene that many in the civil rights movement knew all too well. The terrible events in Dallas, Texas, would not be the last time that the Kennedys would be the victims of political assassination, just as the death of Medgar Evers would not be the last death among those who fought for justice in America.

For some writing about the civil rights movement in later years, the extraordinary union of black massive resistance with white liberal forces in the United States in 1963 also had its dangers. According to one African American, 'The central dilemma of the first stage of the black freedom movement emerged: the existence and sustenance of the civil rights movement neither needed nor required white aid or allies, yet its success required white liberal support in the Democratic Party, Congress and the White House' (West, 1993). According to Allen Matusow, John Kennedy, a traditionally conservative politician, had 'inadvertently helped arouse among millions a dormant desire to perfect America' and as a consequence he became 'the reluctant champion of Martin Luther King'. 'Only later, during Lyndon Johnson's term as President, would the limits of liberal good will become apparent and the flaws of liberal reform be exposed' (Matusow, 1986). This view conforms to the majority opinion that the liberalism of the 1960s was limited, and there are those who argue that it not only failed to achieve its limited goals but also it did positive harm to the United States as well as to the people it sought to help.

The very existence of this liberal goodwill was in doubt when LBJ took office. Despite his insistence that he was a national leader from a western state, many in the North viewed him as a vulgar Texan from the region of the Deep South. There are parallels with 1945 after the death of FDR, when Truman was little known and deeply distrusted by northern voters, especially African Americans. Despite his limitations FDR had done a great deal for black Americans and he was the champion of the liberal cause. Although Truman's achievements for African Americans were limited, he was the first President of the United States openly to attack the evils of discrimination in American society. John Kennedy, despite the early distrust of liberals and his attempts to appease southerners in his judicial appointments (Navasky, 1971), came to be hailed as the liberal President with his championing of the 1963 Civil Rights Bill introduced into Congress which sought to enfranchise blacks by strengthening voting rights. It also proposed that the Justice Department could initiate desegregation suits and thus overcome massive resistance to the integration of schools, and discrimination in public places was to be illegal. The President wanted power to cut funds to state programmes that discriminated. Although the majority of Americans supported his civil rights stand, Harris poll findings showed that 6.5 million Americans who had voted for Kennedy in 1960 said they would not vote for him in 1964, and 4.5 million of these indicated that it was because of his stand on civil rights (Matusow, 1986). The question that worried African Americans and their liberal supporters was what would be the reaction of the new accidental President? Would he be true to his region, would he simply push through the Kennedy legislation or would he be an enthusiastic supporter of the civil rights movement? Many Americans remembered the day that FDR had died and the uncertainty felt about Truman. Now once more they had to cope not only with the sudden death of their President but with his assassination. It is not surprising that many worried about the future of their country and had doubts about the man from Texas who was about to take power.

The Civil Rights Act 1964

Initially, Johnson overcame these doubts and the Civil Rights Act of 1964 has rightly been 'heralded as one of the great achievements of

Lyndon B. Johnson and his presidential administration'. Segregation was banned in all public facilities in America. It also 'raised the issue of "public" versus "private". Contrary to conservatives, the administration supported the view that any privately owned enterprise that accepted tax-payers' funds or business was public' (Anderson, 1995). The federal government could withhold money from private companies that discriminated. The Equal Employment Commission was set up. Passage of the Act paved the way, in part, to the very important Voting Rights Act of 1965 and the Housing Rights Act of 1968 (Loevy, 1980). Johnson supported the Civil Rights Bill as Vice President, and therefore when he took office black leaders in the nation trusted him to get it passed. He did 'a masterful job of using the publicity powers of the presidency to press for the Civil Rights Bill'. He took the lead in opposing George Wallace's campaign for the Democratic nomination in 1964 and LBJ used Wallace's vehement opposition to the Bill to persuade Everett Dirksen, the leader of the Senate Republicans, to support the legislation.

Although Hugh Davis Graham accepts Robert Kennedy's opinion that he told Johnson that he needed Dirksen to get the votes, it is very unlikely that such a master manipulator of the Senate as LBJ would have even asked Kennedy for advice (Graham, 1994). In fact, the search for a bipartisan approach to ensure passage of the Bill was first outlined by Johnson to Assistant Attorney General Norbert Schlei on 3 June 1963. The Vice President took part in planning meetings and joined the President when he met civil rights leaders. After the death of Kennedy many liberals expressed their fears about the legislation. 'As a southerner, Lyndon Johnson was mainly concerned with winning political support in the north. He would have to run for reelection in 1964, and he had less than a year to convince sceptical northern and western liberals that a southerner was an acceptable leader of the national Democratic party'. To achieve this end and stop the worst racist abuses, Johnson actively worked with Congress, civil rights leaders and the media to ensure the passage of the legislation. In his State of the Union address in 1964 he declared: 'As far as the writ of Federal law will run, we must abolish not some but all racial discrimination. For this is not merely an economic question – or a social, political or international issue. It is a moral issue – and it must be met.' He linked his battle for civil rights to his battle against international communism. 'Today Americans of all races stand side by side in Berlin and Vietnam. They died side by side in Korea. Surely they can work and eat and travel side by side in their own country' (Loevy, 1980).

Johnson succeeded in getting stronger legislation than that conceived by Kennedy and in doing so achieved an historic first by stopping a filibuster of the Bill in the Senate with a two-thirds vote for a closure motion. This success was achieved because Johnson was a 'consummate legislator' who had 'great faith in the passage of laws to obliterate racial discrimination'. It has been observed that the Texan 'drew energy from the lawmaking process and never seemed to tire from participating in it' (Lawson, 1991). To draw energy required successful legislation achieved by consensus across party lines and this meant give and take if the legislation was to be passed.

Unfortunately for LBJ, his search for consensus would become increasingly difficult. His dream of a 'Great Society' to complete the unfinished business of the New Deal was defeated by the failure of this 'consummate legislator' to win the support of Martin Luther King Jr and the young leaders in SNCC as much as the increasing difficulties he would face in Vietnam. As a President worried about 'the burden of national unity', Johnson was concerned that only days after signing the Civil Rights Act riots broke out in Harlem and Brooklyn in New York City. In the following days Rochester, New York, and Jersey City, Paterson and Elizabeth, New Jersey, were also torn by rioting (Johnson, 1971). The predominantly white student body at the University of California at Berkeley rebelled against the paternalistic regime and demanded the civil liberty of free speech and assembly, a rebellion led by students who had been active in CORE and SNCC during the 'Freedom Summer' of 1964 (Blum, 1991).

The Mississippi Freedom Democratic Party

For Johnson and the civil rights leaders the main aim of 1964 was the victory of the Democratic party under the leadership of LBJ against the challenge of Alabama Governor George Wallace in the party and from Senator Barry Goldwater, the ultra-conservative Republican from Arizona. Meanwhile in Mississippi Robert Moses, a student from New York, had been working with SNCC to register voters. A black woman attended one of the meetings arranged by Moses. Fanny Lou Hamer, at 44 the youngest of 20 children of black sharecroppers who had grown up in Sunflower County not knowing that she had the right to vote, volunteered to go to the court house and register. As she said: 'The only thing they could do to me was kill me and it seemed like they'd been trying to do that a little bit at a time ever since I could remember'. Dismissed from the plantation because she refused to give up her efforts to register, there was an attempt to murder her and she was brutally beaten in Winona – a beating that left her permanently injured. This did not stop her and many more from fighting on and she joined SNCC in 1963 (Carson, 1981). Hamer, Moses and many African Americans struggled to bring democracy to Mississippi. In the process they formed the inter-racial Mississippi Freedom Democratic party (MFDP) and challenged LBJ.

Men and women, black and white, were part of the Voter Education Project supported by several civil rights groups. To avoid disputes over funding, the groups had united under an umbrella organisation entitled the Council of Federated Organizations (COFO). Moses was director of voter registration and Aaron Henry of NAACP was elected president. Voter registration was concentrated in the area of both the highest black population and largest number of White Citizens Councils. And the students, many from segregated institutions, used the all-black churches and black newspapers to make links with residents and their other organisations such as youth groups (Carson, 1981). As Julian Bond, a SNCC activist, recalled a few years later: 'The biggest change in SNCC came in '63–'64 when we decided to build political organizations as well as just try to get people to register to vote' (Stoper, 1989).

The Freedom Summer was designed to register voters to support the MFDP, which had been formed in April 1964. It was also used to expand the freedom school programme, an idea of Charles Cobb. It was Cobb who suggested recruiting northern college students to come to Mississippi (Carson, 1981). On 13 June the first white volunteers started training at Western College for Women. Although subject to tough scrutiny and psychological tests, Oxford, Ohio, was paradise compared with Oxford, Mississippi. As David Dennis, Robert Moses' assistant, told an interviewer 10 years later, 'We knew that if we had brought in a thousand blacks, the country would have watched them slaughtered without doing anything about it. Bring in a thousand whites and the country is going to react.' Young African Americans had already been beaten and murdered but there was no protection provided by federal forces and no publicity in the major newspapers. However, similar attacks on white students would force the FBI to protect civil rights workers and the newspapers and television would report every assault. As Dennis admits, it was SNCC's 'sorta cold' assessment that if it was going to take deaths to achieve justice in Mississippi 'the death of a white college student would bring on more attention to what was going on than for a black college student getting it' (Raines, 1977).

Eight days later two whites (and a black) did 'get it'. Three COFO workers left Meridian, Mississippi, to investigate the burning of a black church. They disappeared. Two CORE members, James Chaney, a black Mississipean, and Michael Schwerner, a white social worker and CORE member from New York, were reported missing, along with Alan Goodman, one of the first student volunteers in Ohio, to the Justice Department. As usual there was no immediate response on the part of the FBI. Not that this came as any surprise to SNCC workers. Bob Zellner, a white student from Alabama and SNCC staffer, recalled the FBI response when a mob in McComb, Mississippi, tried to murder him. After the assault, in which his assailants sought to gouge his eyes out, Zellner was imprisoned. Then three or four FBI men arrived to take pictures of him and reassured him that he had not been alone – they had taken notes throughout. This was his first experience of the FBI and 'I realized they were a bunch of gutless automatons.... This guy thought it would comfort me to let me know that he was out there recording my death' (Morrison and Morrison, 1987).

Prior to the disappearance of Chaney, Schwerner and Goodman there had been over 150 cases of violence and intimidation against black civil rights workers and local residents who supported the movement. In none of these cases was there any action from the federal authorities. In contrast, the news of the disappearance of the three men 'immediately focused national attention on the Summer Project' but it did not lead to a basic change in federal policy as far as providing protection for civil rights workers was concerned (Carson, 1981). This was despite appeals to Robert Kennedy by the parents of Goodman and Schwerner to provide more protection for civil rights workers. Twenty-four incidents were reported between 21 and 26 June despite the presence of FBI agents and the international press (*The Student Voice*, 30 June 1964). A further 39 incidents, including bombings and shootings, occurred between 26 June and 10 July (*The Student Voice*, 15 July 1964).

The federal government drafted in 200 naval personnel, Justice Department officials and 150 FBI men to search for the bodies of the three civil rights workers. After paying informers, the bodies of the three men were found on 4 August in an earth-fill dam near the town of Philadelphia (Carson, 1981). Leaders of CORE were aware that despite their anger and frustration with the Mississippi authorities, demonstrations against the President would only exacerbate the situation and help the conservative Goldwater. In early August James Farmer assured administration officials that they would not picket Johnson on a visit to Syracuse, New York. Farmer persuaded CORE members to petition the President's staff instead (Lawson, 1991). Relations between Farmer and federal officials became increasingly strained. None of the 20 men arrested by federal authorities, including the sheriff of Nashoba County, were charged with the state offence of murder. They were accused of the federal offence of depriving the men of their civil rights. LBJ had preserved his liberal consensus. Three years later only seven men were convicted and sent to prison (Carson, 1981).

As the bodies of the three COFO men were being dug out of the dam, SNCC leaders and their supporters were planning to unseat the delegates selected by the segregated Democratic party of Mississippi. They were confident that an inter-racial group who, unlike the regular party, were all dedicated to the election of Johnson would see the replacement of the old order with the new. Ella Baker would claim four years later that she had never been optimistic about the challenge to the regular delegation. She argued: 'The fact that liberals and most of the black civil rights leadership were committed first to elect Johnson was crucial' (Stoper, 1989). But certainly at the time SNCC and their supporters lobbied hard in the convention to win (*The Student Voice*, 5–19 August 1964). LBJ, the man they were struggling to support, does not even mention the MFDP in his memoirs but rather he recalls 'happy, surging crowds and thundering cheers. To a man as troubled as I was by party and national divisions, the display of unity was welcome indeed' (Johnson, 1971).

However, this unity was bought at a high price. Johnson used Hubert Humphrey, an acknowledged leader of liberal Democrats, in a failed effort to get the MFDP to accept two delegates. Southern Democrats did not walk out because Johnson preferred to listen to the threat from Governor John Connally of Texas that 'If those baboons walk onto the convention floor we walk out' (Burner, 1994). Robert Moses' biographer points out: 'The administration and the party in this critical juncture lay bare their inability to understand not only the moral premise on which the creation of the MFDP rested but also the very real and dangerous physical battle the delegates had fought to be there' (Burner, 1994). Humphrey and Walter Mondale were instrumental in appeasing the racists from Mississippi and it was an appeasement that would prove costly to both men in their later presidential ambitions (Burner, 1994; McAdam, 1988).

Significantly, LBJ had not lost the support of Martin Luther King Jr and the SCLC, Roy Wilkins of the NAACP or Whitney Young of the National Urban League, a group dedicated to helping African American business development. Although his relationship with LBJ has been correctly characterised as 'volatile', King supported the administration compromise and urged the MFDP to reach a consensus with the liberals. The Atlanta preacher argued that a coalition of unions, liberals and blacks would deliver progressive reform and that the influence of the coalition would grow as the southerners left and joined the Republican party (Lawson, 1991). King was correct only in his views that the southerners would shift their party allegiance. A white activist from Mississippi, Bill Higgs, was present at the meeting and recalled Moses' response: 'We're not here to bring politics into our morality but to bring morality into our politics'. And as he reflected later, one of the major reasons for their defeat was not solely race: '[the] Democratic Party has organized around the middle class. And we were challenging them not only on racial grounds ... but we were challenging them on the existence of a whole group of people who are the underclass of this country, white and black, who are not represented' (Burner, 1994).

The 1964 Campaign

The campaign by Johnson and Humphrey against a bitterly divided Republican party led by the conservative senator from Arizona,

Barry Goldwater, resulted in a landslide victory for the Democrats. Significantly the traditional base of the Democratic party in the South was beginning to crumble. Of the six former Confederate states that supported the party, four, Arkansas, Florida, Tennessee and Virginia, did so solely because of the African American vote. Only in Johnson's home state of Texas did the majority of white voters support the party. As the editors of *The Student Voice* of 25 November 1964 pointed out: 'The rejection of Negroes from the traditionally integrated Republican party, the lack of support the Democratic ticket received from local and state Democratic party figures in the deep South, and the clear delineation of Senator Barry Goldwater's position favoring states' rights and "local option" of segregation all contributed toward a Democratic victory.' Goldwater's southern strategy had failed, but the Republicans would not give up trying.

Following the election and despite his later protestations (Johnson, 1971), President Johnson was reluctant to push for further civil rights legislation, preferring to wait for the South to implement the Civil Rights Act. But the experience of SNCC, CORE and SCLC volunteers trying to register voters made them determined to force the issue. The mass movement of African Americans and their white supporters forced a showdown in Selma, Alabama. The nation was once more forced to witness the violence of the 'genteel South' fighting to preserve white supremacy. Out of a possible five million black voters in the South only two million were registered. In Mississippi only 6.4 per cent of the African American voters were registered despite the efforts of Robert Moses and others.

The Challenge at Selma

The situation was just as dire in Alabama. In the city of Selma, African Americans were a majority of the 29 000 population but only 3 per cent of the electorate. The sheriff of Dallas County, including Selma, was Jim Clark, a violent racist demagogue who had attacked blacks in 1963 when they tried to register to vote. With support from a racist judge and indifferent federal officials, Clark almost succeeded in destroying the voting rights drive. James Bevel of the SCLC knew that dramatic action was required and called on Martin

Luther King Jr to defy the ban on black marches and meetings. King and 15 black groups in Selma decided to challenge Clark and his paramilitary forces and in doing so force the federal government to act.

The division in the white community in Selma was between those who supported Clark, the 'stupid segregationists', and those who backed the Director of Safety, Wilson Baker, the 'smart' racists. According to one white resident: 'The trouble is, too many of our people fear the white man more than they do the Negro and won't speak up against Clark' (*The Student Voice*, 26 March 1965). Despite Baker's successful detention of American Nazi party leader Lincoln Rockwell, on 19 January Sheriff Clark arrested 67 blacks who were trying to register to vote. Six days later surprised whites saw one black woman retaliate against the sheriff, knocking him down twice after he had hit her. Immediately dragged to the ground by three of Clark's deputies, Annie Lee Cooper found the sheriff was willing to ignore the newsmen, sat on her stomach and clubbed her senseless. As one historian has put it, 'The sound of the clubbing could be heard through the crowd that had gathered in the street. By the next day the political echoes of the beating had resounded through the country' (Weisbrot, 1990).

Even as Johnson was instructing the new Attorney General, Nicholas Katzenbach, to draw up legislation giving federal protection to those registering to vote, Clark defied federal court rulings. With hundreds in jail, he moved quickly to imprison the two men he believed were communist agitators – Martin Luther King Jr and Ralph Abernathy. From his prison cell King wrote a letter to the American nation demanding federal protection for those who sought to use the vote.

'Bloody Sunday' and the March to Montgomery

Nearby towns held marches in support of the Selma campaign. On 18 February in Marion, state troopers shot and wounded Jimmy Lee Jackson. Refused treatment in the local hospital he was taken to Selma, where he died. His death was just one of many that were not prosecuted. William Moore, a postman, had been shot and killed and the man responsible was freed. Four girls were blown up in the Sixteenth Street Baptist Church and the three white men arrested were freed for lack of evidence. A 13-year-old boy, Virgil Ware, was shot and although his killers confessed, they were charged only with manslaughter and after a few days in jail were released on probation. In addition, police in Birmingham had shot and killed Johnny Brown Robinson, aged 16 (*The Student Voice*, 26 March 1965). None of these murders resulted in convictions and, despite pleas from the black community, J. Edgar Hoover spent most of his time trying to discredit King and the civil rights leaders.

The failure to act in any of these cases makes 'Bloody Sunday' of 7 March 1965 seem inevitable. King planned a march from Selma to Montgomery, to provide mass support for the Voting Rights Bill proposed by Lyndon Johnson and supported by Republican Everett Dirksen. Hosea Williams of SCLC and John Lewis of SNCC led 600 marchers from the AME Church towards the Edmund Pettus Bridge, where they were met by hundreds of state troopers wearing Confederate badges and armed with clubs and electric cattle prods. Although given two minutes in which to return to their church, the charge of the troopers came in less than a minute. John Lewis, who had bowed his head but refused to retreat, was the first to be struck, suffering a fractured skull. Five women were also among the first to be beaten, including Amelia Boynton, who was clubbed and tear gassed. With blacks fleeing for safety, Sheriff Clark unleashed his mounted paramilitary forces and they later took part in the riot, attacking innocent people in the city's black section.

Pictures of the beatings were broadcast around the world as well as across the nation. The majority of Americans were horrified by what they saw and liberal senators such as the Republican Jacob Javits of New York denounced the reign of terror. As Lyndon Johnson recalled, 'The Alabama state troopers took matters into their own hands. With nightsticks, bullwhips, and billy clubs, they scattered the ranks of the marchers.... The march was over. But the struggle had just begun' (Johnson, 1971). But while the vast majority of the whites in America were united in their horror at Selma, for those involved in the movement it was a crucial turning point. Many young members of SNCC were eager to retaliate. As Julian Bond recalled a few years later, the problem with nonviolence was that many African Americans in the Deep South 'carried guns for self-defense as a matter of custom' (Stoper, 1989).

Nonviolence may have been a way of life for John Lewis; it was not for most African Americans. King flew in from Atlanta and the divisions between him and the majority of SNCC members came into the open. King had agreed to lead a symbolic march to the bridge. State troopers and Sheriff Clark waited on the other side and then seemed to leave the road open, inviting King to lead a march past the troopers on the road to Montgomery. Cleveland Sellers and James Forman wanted King to march. Ralph Abernathy, King's associate in SCLC, recalled that SNCC workers 'felt betrayed' and that King lacked courage. 'It was the first time that such accusations would be made, though not the last. Soon, very soon, the advocates of violence would be saying that Martin was too timid to lead the movement, and then that he was too cowardly' (Abernathy, 1989). The minister refused either to defy a federal court injunction or to walk into the trap and led the marchers back to the church, where James Forman argued that the only reason they had not been attacked was because white folks were in the march. Sellers, Forman and Stokely Carmichael were increasingly restive with the tactic of nonviolence, and bitter that the suffering of African Americans was barely noticed whereas the slightest injury to whites was widely reported.

Despite the killing and maiming of many blacks it was the assault by a white mob on four white Unitarian ministers that galvanised the President into action. The Reverend James Reeb of Boston, a 38-year-old father of four, was savagely beaten and died two days later in hospital (*The Student Voice*, 26 March 1965). Johnson immediately telephoned Mrs Reeb to express his sympathy but refused to send in federal troops because he believed that it would jeopardise the Voting Rights Bill. Instead, he met Alabama Governor George Wallace at the White House. Johnson was angry with Wallace but also with the demonstrators who accused him of lack of action. And, typical of southern politicians, he bemoaned that: 'Once again my Southern heritage was thrown in my face. I was hurt, deeply hurt. But I was determined not to be shoved into hasty action' (Johnson, 1971). The President told Wallace to protect the rights of Negro citizens. Wallace claimed he lacked funds to protect the marchers, who had been given authority to march by federal judge Frank Johnson. LBJ federalised the state troopers and sent Ramsey Clark, the new Attorney General, to take control. When the marchers reached Montgomery, King assured them that 'segregation is on its deathbed in Alabama' and concluded, perhaps seeking to answer his young critics, as to how long it would take:

How long? Not long, because no lie can live forever.
How long? Not long, because you still reap what you sow.
How long? Not long, because the arm of the moral universe is
long but it bends toward justice.
How long? Not long cause mine eyes have seen the glory of
the coming of the Lord, trampling out the vintage where the
grapes of wrath are stored. He hath loosed the fateful
lightning of his terrible swift sword. His truth is marching on.
(Abernathy, 1989)

The fateful lightning struck the next day when Mrs Viola Liuzzo was
driving several marchers back to Selma. As a white woman driving
with a black man, Leroy Moton, Mrs Liuzzo was breaking one of the
southern codes of 'honour'. She had been subject to various attacks
during the day, and now a car sped past and three shots were fired.
Mrs Liuzzo was killed. Moton stopped the car and in trying to revive
Mrs Liuzzo was covered in blood. Her blood saved his life. When the
assassins came up to the car they assumed Moton was dead also
(Abernathy, 1989). Unlike the murders in Mississippi, this murder
did not take long to solve because an FBI agent, Gary Rowe, was one
of the attackers.

While the consensus among SNCC, SCLC and CORE was breaking down at Selma, LBJ struggled to maintain unity with liberal
Republicans and Democrats to meet the crisis. Initially reluctant to
take precipitate action, LBJ agreed with the leaders in Congress to
address a joint session on the evening of 15 March. In his address
Johnson linked the violence in Selma with the opening skirmishes
of the American Revolution and the end of the Civil War. Then he
contended: 'There is no issue of states' rights or national rights.
There is only the struggle for human rights,' and he ended with the
words of the movement: 'Their cause must be our cause too.
Because it is not just Negroes, but it is all of us who must overcome
the crippling legacy of bigotry and injustice. And ... we ... shall ...
overcome' (Johnson, 1971).

The Voting Rights Act 1965

Four months later, on 6 August 1965, Johnson signed the Voting
Rights Act. The strain between some of the civil rights leaders and

the man from Texas was evident even at this ceremony. James Farmer of CORE was invited to the signing ceremony but LBJ, who 'could be as petty as he was generous, tried to snub Farmer by refusing to give him one of the souvenir pens' (Lawson, 1994). Julian Bond of SNCC commented in 1968 that, 'The '64 and '65 Civil Rights Acts took the pressure off the country. People weren't as concerned about civil rights because they figured they'd done what they should do for it' (Stoper, 1989). This view is underlined by LBJ in his memoirs where he writes that: 'With the passage of the Civil Rights Act of 1964 and 1965 the barriers of freedom began tumbling down. At long last the legal rights of American citizens – the right to vote, to hold a job, to enter a public place, to go to school – were given concrete protection' (Johnson, 1971).

During the recent years of triumphant conservatism, politicians and scholars have tended to deride the liberal response to the challenge of the civil rights movement. The very stridency of these attacks against liberals, federal government power and the conservatives' attempts to repeal the Voting Rights Act, or to dismantle the Great Society programmes, suggests rather that liberals were successful. In the 11 southern states 430 000 blacks registered to vote in 1966. 'It was,' one South Carolinian observed, 'more than anything else that occurred during the movement years, an expression of the will to citizenship and responsibility of the mass of Negro Southerners – the underlying strength of the people that had given rise to the movement in the first place' (Watters, 1971). Gradually segregation and denial of the vote would become part of history. These liberal reforms brought about a quiet revolution in the South. In 1965 a white woman was murdered because she was driving a car with a black man as a passenger but 30 years later an African American would write a book to explain to his children that before the Civil Rights Acts they would not have been allowed to stay in the same hotel as their white mother (Gates, 1995). He did not tell them that in most southern states their parents' marriage would have been illegal, and that their daddy might have been lynched for marrying a white woman.

Civil Rights and the Anti-Vietnam War Movement

Despite these long-term gains, the tensions between LBJ and groups such as SCLC, CORE and SNCC were evident in 1965. Howard Zinn, the history professor and SNCC member, criticised NAACP leader Roy Wilkins and James Farmer, leader of CORE and spokesmen of the Urban League, for attacking SNCC's opposition to US intervention in Vietnam. Zinn argued: 'Movement people are perhaps in the best position to understand just how immoral are this nation's actions in Vietnam.... They understand just how much hypocrisy is wrapped up in our claim to stand for "the free world".' Just as civil rights workers were labelled 'outside agitators' in the South, so those who fought American imperialism were dubbed communist, a term which was the same as 'nigger', because both were labels which denied a person's individuality. 'SNCC always prided itself on a special honesty, on not playing it "safe", in saying exactly what it felt like saying. Shouldn't it now say, at this crucial moment, that FREEDOM NOW must be international?' (*The Student Voice*, 30 August 1965).

In the same month that Zinn posed the question, 'Should civil rights workers take a stand on Vietnam?', Martin Luther King urged the President to stop the bombing of North Vietnam and seek negotiations with the Viet Cong. King was increasingly concerned about the underfunding of Great Society programmes. He was determined to attack the problems of poverty in northern ghettos. Although King privately urged Johnson to change his policy in Vietnam, he did not become a leader in the anti-war movement until 1967 and it was King, not Johnson, who broke off relations. King refused invitations to the White House (Lawson, 1994).

While King left the leadership of the anti-war movement to the SDS he still found himself at odds with President Johnson over another issue – the problems of the inner cities. LBJ saw this as yet another unfair criticism of his efforts. But the Atlanta minister was determined to heighten awareness of the plight of those in the ghettos of the North. The first announcement that SCLC intended to 'close down' Chicago was made by James Bevel at Northwestern University, two weeks after the march on Selma. Five months later King and Andrew Young announced that SCLC would work with the Coordinating Council of Community Organizations and attack discrimination in housing and problems of urban poverty. Most historians have judged their efforts a failure and a defeat. Adam Fairclough shares the view of King's critics that 'white exclusiveness was an unshakeable reality, to confront it head-on, from a position of political isolation was self-defeating'. It also made white liberals question 'the viability of nonviolent tactics' (Fairclough, 1987).

King Goes to Chicago

Certainly, by challenging the Mayor of Chicago, Richard Daley, SCLC were taking on one of the most powerful men in the Democratic party and threatening the liberal desire for consensus. Johnson and the federal leadership needed the Irish American's support, as it was widely believed that Daley had rigged the election of John Kennedy. In addition, challenging housing discrimination in Chicago with nonviolent protests led to white mobs and a white backlash that many liberals feared. Racial violence by white and black in the city only intensified the distrust between the city officials and the leaders of SCLC. The white residents, angry at liberal efforts to integrate their neighbourhood, stoned Martin Luther King as he led a nonviolent march through Gage Park. The marchers were called 'cannibals', 'savages' and 'niggers' and one sign read, 'The only way to stop niggers is to exterminate them'. The veteran of so many struggles in the South, King told the press that he had 'never seen as much hatred and hostility on the part of so many people'. For those who knew the city's long history of racial violence, the scenes were reminiscent of the riot in 1919.

In the political fallout, a liberal congressman who had voted for the Civil Rights Act struggled for re-election and Senator Paul Douglas, who had supported fair housing legislation, was defeated by Republican Charles Percy. The beneficiary of the white backlash would be George Wallace in his 1968 campaign. The Catholic Church was divided, with a white supremacist priest defying his cardinal and eventually being elected as a city alderman.

Did the Chicago freedom movement make any gains? SCLC received $4 000 000 from the Housing and Urban Development, working with the Community Renewal Foundation, to rehabilitate housing in Chicago. The federal Office of Education provided a $100 000 grant for a scheme to improve the skills of Lawndale residents. There were several community groups which did effective work for several years, especially Operation Breadbasket, organised by Jesse Jackson. And the resistance of the Daley machine to the nonviolent strategy persuaded most African Americans in the city, and some whites, that the machine could not be reformed. In 1983, activists of 1966 supported the successful challenge by Harold Washington to bossism (Ralph, 1993).

The FBI and Martin Luther King

The SCLC in Chicago and in Cleveland in 1967 was increasingly faced with institutional racism of the northern cities. King realised that African Americans and the poor of the cities, just as much as in the rural South, fought each other for scraps from the table. His experiences in Chicago radicalised him and he stressed the need for dramatic change in the economic structure and advocated Christian socialism. Such views took him further from the liberals and only seemed to confirm the view of J. Edgar Hoover of the FBI that King and his followers were a communist menace. And Hoover needed no persuading. It was Hoover in 1964 who described King as a 'most notorious liar' shortly after it was announced that the Atlanta minister had been awarded the Nobel Prize, and William Sullivan of the FBI sent a letter to King which described the civil rights leader as 'a dissolute, abnormal moral imbecile' who was guilty of 'incredible evilness'. King was encouraged to commit suicide: 'You are done. There is but one way out for you. You better take it before your filthy, abnormal fraudulent self is bared to the nation' (Garrow, 1988).

It is hardly surprising that King and his supporters had little faith in the FBI and instead of being praised by the administration for his awareness of the problems posed by ghetto poverty, he was accused of fomenting trouble. If Johnson had trusted King and his supporters he would have been aware of the pending violence. As it was, in 1967 presidential assistants visited the major cities in the North and West and were oblivious to the dangers. Those who went 'to Detroit in May 1967 did not turn up a clue that a disastrous riot would break only two months later, nor did travelers to Oakland in March mention the Black Panther party' (Lawson, 1994).

The Black Panther Party, Malcolm X and Black Power

Dismissed by some as a 'gun-toting cadre of youths' (Lawson, 1994), the Black Panther party had its origins in Lowndes County, Alabama, following the 1965 registration of 2000 black residents. Because they believed they would never 'pierce the present white power structure' they decided to form a separate party and elect Negroes to office (*The Student Voice*, 20 December 1965). It is not surprising that young African Americans abandoned the Alabama Democratic party and although the rhetoric of Black Power distressed King and alarmed many white Americans, the demands of these young men and women were not that far removed from those of King. Both believed in the institutional nature of racism in America; both believed that only massive expenditure would eradicate the endemic poverty in many parts of America; both believed that socialism provided a constructive alternative to American capitalism. They disagreed about the role of the churches; they disagreed over the redemptive power of nonviolence. Black Power advocates learnt from the rural black communities of Mississippi and Alabama that weapons were needed in self-defence. Their arguments were the same as those put by the National Rifle Association. The difference, as King realised, was that white folks had more guns and would be prepared to use them. And King was right when he wrote: 'Beneath all the satisfaction of a gratifying slogan, Black Power is a nihilistic philosophy born out of the conviction that the Negro can't win' (King, 1967).

However, just as some African Americans questioned Martin Luther King's appeal to nonviolence, there were an increasing number who questioned the prevailing Christian world view of the black community. One of the most charismatic men who challenged the Christian, nonviolent view of the world was Malcolm Little, better known as Malcolm X. Both his parents, Earl and Louise Little, were involved with the black nationalist movement of the 1920s headed by Marcus Garvey. This involvement led to their being driven from their homes in Omaha, Nebraska, and in 1929 a white hate group torched their home in Lansing, Michigan. In later years Malcolm would claim that his father had been lynched by a white mob but there is no evidence for this. On the other hand, there is much evidence from Malcolm and others that he was subjected to harsh punishment by his father. Despite claims made about the profound influence of Garveyism on Malcolm Little, there is little evidence for this and Malcolm's youth was spent in petty crime, robbery, drug abuse and pimping. During a stay in prison he met a member of the Nation of Islam, or Black Muslims, and was converted. He dropped his 'slave name' Little and replaced it with X.

Although a small sect, founded in 1930, the Nation of Islam grew in the northern cities in the 1950s. The religious views of the Muslims were based on the arguments of its leader, Elijah

Muhammad. Unlike the teachings of the Koran, Elijah Muhammad argued that Allah had made all people black and that it was the evil acts of a black chemist that created the white race. Allah in his anger swore that his chosen black people would be enslaved by the white devils but at the time of judgement the whites would be destroyed. It has been suggested that the fact that Malcolm X 'used vituperative language against whites did not mean that he hated whites or that he was trying to make blacks hate them. Rather his purpose was to wake up blacks to the need to love each other' (Cone, 1993).

Whatever his intentions were when he was a disciple of Elijah Muhammad, his attacks on white devils and his demand for segregation not only frightened and angered white conservatives, they had the same effect on white liberals. In addition, the strong anti-Jewish attacks, which were a central theme of the Black Muslims, were accepted by the wider black nationalist movement. Cultural black nationalists such as Ron Karenga and LeRoy Jones (Imara Baraka) shared this anti-Semitic view and the alliance of Jewish Americans and African Americans was severely damaged as a result.

Just before he was assassinated in 1965, Malcolm X visited Mecca, where he discovered that Muslims came in every colour. It has been suggested that Malcolm was reluctant to leave Elijah Muhammad (Cone, 1993), but upon his return from Mecca he set up his own mosque based on Sunni Muslim belief. He argued that black and white Americans should struggle to overcome the oppression of racism. In comparing African Americans and Jews, Malcolm X maintained: 'The biggest difference between the parallel oppression of the Jew and the Negro is that the Jew never lost his pride. He knew he had made a significant contribution to the world, and his sense of his own value gave him the courage to fight back. It enabled him to act and think independently, unlike our people and our leaders' (Dyson, 1995). And eventually Malcolm even apologised for his bitter assaults on Martin Luther King Jr. His murder, probably by fellow Muslims, means that we will never know if he could have worked with King and the SCLC. Unfortunately in recent years it is the early Malcolm that is heard in the speeches of Louis Farrakan, the current head of the Nation of Islam, and not the Malcolm of reconciliation who returned from Mecca.

Johnson's response to the challenge of Black Power was to say that he was 'not interested in black power or white power'. As he reflected later, it was an easy remark for a white person to make and he acknowledged: 'Black power had a different meaning to the black man, who until recently had had to seek the white world's approval and for whom success had come largely on white people's terms. To such a man, black power meant a great deal more in areas that mattered the most – dignity, pride, and self-awareness' (Johnson, 1971). It is a pity he did not show such sensitivity when he was in the White House. But assailed by many for his policies in Vietnam, Johnson could not take criticism from people who did not share his liberal beliefs and values.

The President was even more aggrieved when his National Advisory Commission on Civil Disorders reported on the cause of the 1967 urban riots. Headed by Otto Kerner, the Democratic Governor of Illinois, the Commission was carefully selected to reflect Johnson's desire to maintain a consensus between the two main parties. The appointment of Roy Wilkins of the NAACP and black Republican Senator Edward Brooke also reflected his faith in moderate leaders. His anger was thus the greater when the report blamed the riots on white racism and recommended a massive federal spending programme. Johnson claimed that to meet the report's recommendation would have required an additional '$30 billion, in addition to the $30 billion plus already in the budget for the poor'. Such a figure he believed was unrealistic and he argued later: 'Setting such an unattainable goal could easily have produced a negative reaction that in turn might have endangered funds for the many invaluable programs we had fought so long to establish and were trying so hard to strengthen and expand' (Johnson, 1971).

Whatever the doubts and grievances felt by the President, King decided to fight the backlash by highlighting the fact that poverty was not just a problem for African Americans. The majority of the poor and illiterate in the United States were white, brown and red. King planned another march on Washington but this was to be a rainbow coalition of the disadvantaged. The Poor People's Campaign would involve Native Americans, Mexican Americans and poor whites as well as African Americans and they would live in Resurrection City in the capital until legislators acted.

Murder in Memphis

King never led the march. Flying to Memphis, Tennessee, at the request of his friend the Reverend James Lawson, King gave his support to striking garbage workers. On the second visit, on 3 April 1968, he recalled how he had almost died in 1959 after he had been stabbed while on a visit to New York. He referred to a letter he had had from a young white girl who wrote: 'I read in the paper of your misfortune and of your suffering. And I read that if you sneezed you would have died. And I'm simply writing you to say that I'm so happy that you didn't sneeze.' And King continually reiterated that he was pleased that he did not sneeze, because if he had he would not have seen the advances they had made. As for the future, they would triumph despite 'the difficult days ahead'. He only wanted to do God's will. 'And He's allowed me to go up to the mountain. And I've looked over. And I've seen the promised land. And I'm happy tonight. I'm not worried about anything. I'm not fearing any man. Mine eyes have seen the glory of the coming of the Lord' (Washington, 1991).

The next morning, standing on the balcony of the Lorraine Motel, Martin Luther King was assassinated. Despite appeals for calm, rioting swept across the United States. For a week 100 towns and cities saw major riots, with 46 killed, 3000 injured and 27 000 arrested. It took 21 000 federal troops and 34 000 National Guardsmen to restore order after $45 million worth of property had been damaged. Congress, which earlier had defeated a minor budget measure for rat control in the slums (sneeringly dubbed a 'civil-rats bill'), did pass a weak fair-housing bill following the assassination. Although discrimination in renting or buying houses was made illegal it was up to individuals to act. The legislation included a clause to appease whites because incitement to riot was now listed as a serious federal offence. It was a far cry from the early years of the administration when 60 education acts, including the Headstart programme, and the Medicare legislation did so much to help in the education and health of some of the poorest citizens in America.

One student of the Johnson presidency has written that 'the black freedom struggle converted him from a routine defender of African Americans into the most vigorous advocate of racial equality ever to occupy the Oval Office. This progression, however laudatory, did not prepare him for the bitterness and anger that accompanied the black revolution in its later stages' (Lawson, 1994). However, it was not just the bitterness and anger that alienated so many from a President who had sought to do so much. Many Americans who had benefited from the liberal reform programme now turned to Johnson's arch enemy, Robert Kennedy. As the New York senator's friend wrote later: 'He [Johnson] had always known that, as in the classic Hollywood western, there would be the inevitable walk down through the long silent street at high noon, and Robert Kennedy would be waiting for him'. Robert Kennedy was convinced that he could heal the division, stop the violence and end the disenchantment of white and black. He told a victory rally in Los Angeles after winning the California primary: 'We are a great country, an unselfish country and a compassionate country. I intend to make that my basis for running' (Schlesinger Jr, 1979). He left for a press conference and took a short cut through the kitchen. He was assassinated.

In 1968 America lost the last white politician that millions of the disadvantaged, especially African Americans, felt they could trust. However, Kennedy's last speech did not give enough credit to the achievements of his old rival and in many ways Johnson had led a quiet revolution which had dramatic effects, especially on his beloved South.

5

Nixon, Reagan and the New Right

For those caught up in the civil rights movement, 1968 seemed to be the year in which the rule of the old elites was coming to an end. In Northern Ireland, France, Germany and Japan students seemed to be in the vanguard of a major revolution that would sweep away the old liberal and conservative establishments. Johnson had refused to seek re-election, the Democratic candidate and liberal Vice President Hubert Humphrey campaigned on the 'politics of joy' and the voice of the new conservatism was the deeply distrusted former Vice President, Richard M. Nixon. Humphrey had to rely on LBJ and the boss of Chicago, Mayor Richard Daley, at the Democratic convention in Chicago. Despite the death of Robert Kennedy, the first senator to challenge LBJ, Eugene McCarthy of Minnesota, was still in the nomination race and after Robert Kennedy's murder in Los Angeles his popularity was rising. But he failed to win over the Kennedy supporters and behaved more as a spectator of events rather than trying to shape and mould them and as a result many delegates supported the anti-war senator from South Dakota, George McGovern.

Chicago, 1968

At the Democratic party convention, millions of American viewers saw the ruthless assault on anti-war protesters in the convention hall by Daley's lieutenants and in the streets by his police force. The most trusted man in America was CBS newsman Walter Cronkite, who watched helplessly while one of the CBS news team was beaten up in the convention. Cronkite deplored what he called 'fascist' tactics. Under pressure from his bosses, he gave Daley an easy time in an interview the next day in which Daley claimed that the police were upholding law and order in response to violent assault from hippies and others. For many Democrats, such as Senator Abraham Ribicoff, the tactics of Daley were reminiscent of the Gestapo. The majority of Americans, however, would have agreed with LBJ about the radicals. The President had wanted, in his own words, 'to get them by the balls'.

George Wallace of Alabama was determined to appeal to the growing numbers of voters who were alienated by the civil rights movement – not just southerners but blue-collar workers in the North. He ran for the presidency as an American party candidate. Eager to attract sufficient support to throw the election into the House of Representatives, Wallace combined his racism with a populist assault on banks, Wall Street and federal government bureaucrats. Unfortunately for Wallace, he chose as his running mate the outspoken retired air-force general Curtis LeMay. The general's desire 'to bomb the North Vietnamese into the Stone Age' scared some Wallace supporters, and the general's support for civil rights, pointing to the armed services as the ideal integrated society, angered others. Disillusioned Wallace supporters either drifted back to the Democratic party or turned instead to the man who had returned from the politically dead – Richard Nixon.

Nixon had been defeated in 1960 by the narrowest of margins by John Kennedy, and his hatred for the Kennedys was deep and lasting. In 1962 he lost again in his bid for the governorship of California. The disgruntled candidate told the press: 'You won't have Nixon to kick around any more'. But whatever pleasure the journalists may have gained from writing his political obituary, Nixon never gave up his quest for the presidency (Ambrose, 1989). He hoped the Republican party would turn to him in 1964, but instead they preferred Goldwater, and following the defeat of the conservative cause, those same journalists were writing the obituary of the party. Meanwhile Richard Nixon methodically travelled the 'rubber chicken and green pea' circuit, talking to American Legion groups and frightened suburbanites, building a powerful base in the party at grass-roots level. As the civil rights marches continued and young Americans protested against the war in Vietnam, Nixon spoke to the angry and scared white people and reassured them that they were the 'silent majority' and that civil rights workers, communists and radicals should not take the law into their own hands.

For Nixon the great achievement of Martin Luther King Jr was that 'he worked to resist extremists in the movement, those who wished to resort to violence to reach their goals'. Nixon was confident that it was pressure from these 'extremists' that 'sometimes caused him [King] to be more extreme in his public views than he otherwise would have been'. However, in his memoirs the disgraced former President did admit that King's 'death left black America without a nationally recognized leader who combined responsibility with charisma'. And while others might be 'reasonably effective' he was sure that 'none could match his mystique and his ability to inspire people – white as well as black – and to move them' (Nixon, 1978). Nixon ignored the failure of southern states to fulfil their constitutional duties and their reluctance to protect the lives and rights of African American citizens.

Nixon's Southern Strategy

Whatever qualified praise he had for King in later years, Nixon knew that opinion polls which excluded Wallace showed the vast majority of the Alabama Governor's supporters preferred Nixon for President. The aim of the southern strategy adopted by the Republicans was not to attack George Wallace, as Humphrey did, but to argue that a vote for Wallace was a wasted vote. While Nixon was prepared to concede the Deep South states to the Alabama Governor he was determined to win the border states of Tennessee, Kentucky and Virginia as well as the Carolinas and Florida (Nixon, 1978). To ensure the success of his southern strategy, Nixon chose the Governor of Maryland, Spiro Agnew, as his vice presidential candidate because the Governor, after the Baltimore riots in 1968, had denounced the black leadership as 'Hanoi-visiting ... caterwauling, riot-inciting, burn-America-down type of leaders'. When informed about this intemperate outburst Nixon's response was: 'That guy Agnew is really an impressive fellow. He's got guts. He's got a good attitude' (Ambrose, 1989).

Leaving running mate Spiro Agnew to attack Humphrey as 'soft on communism' and 'soft on crime', Nixon wrapped himself in the

American flag and appealed to the wounded nationalism of the American electorate. He told a cheering crowd in Springfield, Ohio: 'We must gain respect for America in the world. A burned American library, a desecrated flag, a ship captured by international outlaws on the high seas – these are the events which in effect squeeze the trigger which fires the rifle which kills young Americans.' As Humphrey gained in the polls Nixon attacked the Great Society programmes' attempts to deal with poverty, which Democrats saw as a major cause of crime. Johnson's 'war on poverty was not a war on crime' according to Nixon, 'and it was no substitute for a war on crime' (Nixon, 1978).

Central to Nixon's law-and-order strategy was an attack on the Supreme Court. The Republican candidate attacked the *Miranda v Arizona* decision in which the Court insisted that suspects must be notified about their rights upon arrest. For Nixon the mid-sixties was a time when a 'new liberalism was fashionable, in which there appeared to be more concern for the rights of the accused than for the protection of the innocent' (Nixon, 1978). In addition, in an appeal to southerners, Nixon argued that the Court should follow a strict construction of the constitution, an argument that southerners had used against the earlier rulings of the Court, such as *Brown*. He assured southerners and northerners opposed to integration of schools that he would not withhold federal funds from school districts that were slow in complying with the Court ruling (Blum, 1991).

Despite a remarkable fight by Humphrey, Nixon was elected. In the popular vote Nixon received 43.4 per cent and Humphrey 42.7. George Wallace got 13.5 per cent and all the polls indicated that if he had not been a candidate, most of his vote would have gone to Nixon. The result was not the close decision that it at first seems, but rather reflected a marked shift to the right in which blue-collar workers in the North deserted the Democratic party despite the efforts of union leaders in the AFL–CIO.

Nixon as President, although serious and intelligent, was an isolated figure who had passionate hatreds for intellectuals, dis-senters and critics, especially the press and television. A leading conservative Republican, Barry Goldwater, claimed Nixon was the most dishonest person he had ever known and that Nixon would readily lie to his wife, family, the Republican party, the American people and even the world. And his attitude towards African

Americans was not promising. During his campaign in 1960 he had complained that he would have to give a speech on 'all that welfare crap' and in 1967 he wrote in the *Reader's Digest* that America was 'far from being a great society, ours is becoming a lawless society'. According to Nixon the cause was the tolerance of lawlessness, not by Mississippi sheriffs, but rather civil rights groups which were aided by universities 'where civil disobedience may begin and where it must end'. And his first meeting with one of the leaders of civil disobedience was not auspicious (Ambrose, 1989).

Nixon and Abernathy

Ralph Abernathy, the new leader of SCLC following the murder of Martin Luther King Jr, had first sought a meeting with Nixon when the President was on a trip to South Carolina. Abernathy was helping Charleston hospital workers who were on strike in an attempt to increase wages from $1.30 an hour, and when Nixon declined the meeting Abernathy sent students to demonstrate and heighten awareness of the problems faced by the workers. The students were arrested. On 13 May 1970 Abernathy flew to Washington for a meeting with Nixon at the White House. It was disastrous.

In his memoirs Nixon describes the meeting with Abernathy and his associates as a 'shambles' because the black minister was 'either unprepared or unwilling, or both, to have a serious discussion. Instead he postured and made speeches. He began by reading a list of demands and spent the rest of the time restating them in more colorful ways. Nonetheless he seemed pleased that we had made the effort and at the end he thanked me profusely for taking the time to meet with them' (Nixon, 1978).

Nixon was not amused when Abernathy left the meeting and told the press that the meeting was one of the most 'fruitless' he had ever attended. According to Nixon he (Nixon) reassured his adviser Daniel Patrick Moynihan that it was actions not words that would demonstrate his sincerity. He does not refer to the note he sent to his advisers John Ehrlichman and H. R. Haldeman in which he wrote: 'This shows that my judgment about not seeing such people is right. No more of This!' (Ambrose, 1989). As for Abernathy, he writes that he was convinced that Moynihan and others were 'full of earnest resolve and high blown rhetoric'. However, he was not fooled. 'They had been so certain that their economic double-talk had mesmerized all of us' (Abernathy, 1989).

Following the meeting with Abernathy, Moynihan wrote to Nixon: 'The time may have come when the issue of race could benefit from a period of "benign neglect." The subject has been too much talked about.' According to Moynihan the debate was controlled 'by hysterics, paranoids, and boodlers on all sides. We need a period in which Negro progress continues and racial rhetoric fades.' According to Nixon the phrase 'benign neglect' was taken out of context by his critics in the media and Congress. In his own defence he points with pride to his 'affirmative action' programme. Although opposed to quotas in job hiring he was determined that all federal contractors would hire more minority workers. Each contractor had to set a goal for affirmative action and federally funded construction projects in Philadelphia were targeted with the intention of increasing minority workers from 4 per cent to 26 per cent. Conservatives argued that Title VI of the Civil Rights Act prohibited affirmative action. The proposals as laid out in the Philadelphia Plan violated the Act, which stipulated that no one could be denied the benefits of federal financial assistance based on race, colour or national origin. According to Nixon he was attacked by congressional conservatives and Everett Dirksen informed him bluntly: 'As your leader in the Senate of the United States, it is my bounden duty to tell you that this thing is about as popular as a crab in a whorehouse'. Dirksen warned him that the proposal would split the Republican party and as party leader in the Senate he could not support it (Nixon, 1978).

Nixon and Affirmative Action

Nixon ignored his advice. Affirmative action was introduced in October 1969 at a federally funded hospital project and was extended to building trade unions in New York, Pittsburgh, Seattle, Los Angeles, St Louis, San Francisco, Boston, Chicago, and Detroit. Nixon fought off opposition in Congress and from George Meany, the leader of the AFL–CIO. By 1972 affirmative action was extended beyond the construction industry to over 300 000 firms. Nixon recalled his disappointment with the 'luke warm support from most of the national black leaders who tended either to minimize the results we had achieved, or to complain that we had not gone far enough'. His response to this criticism was 'to wonder whether the black leadership was not more interested in dramatic tokenism than in the hard fight for actual progress' (Nixon, 1978; see also Graham, 1994).

Why would a conservative President dramatically expand a policy first outlined by the liberal LBJ in an executive order in 1965? According to one scholar it is not as paradoxical as it appears. 'Faced with growing urban violence, government leaders sought to fend off social chaos by launching benefit programs with quick and visible payoffs'. However, it was not just the pressure of civil rights groups or the courts which prompted Nixon to act. One of the main reasons was his desire to punish organised labour, which had led the opposition to his nomination to the Supreme Court of Judge C. F. Haynsworth of South Carolina. In addition, he wanted to break the coalition of the AFL–CIO and civil rights groups because unions would seek to maintain their seniority system and control over labour contracts, whereas African Americans would support his programme as a way of breaking down institutional racism. In the process Nixon would destroy the New Deal alliance which had maintained the Democrats as the majority party. By advocating black capitalism he was confident that he would build a black middle class who would return to the Republican party. But most important of all was the intent to ensure Republican control of the Congress, the White House and the federal judiciary (Graham, 1994).

Supreme Court Nominations

Nixon was determined to use the Supreme Court appointments as part of his southern strategy, and not merely to appoint more conservative justices. With the defeat of Haynsworth, Nixon defied the advice of many leading lawyers and law professors and submitted the name of Judge G. Harold Carswell for the vacancy on the Court. Without doubt it was the worst nomination to the Court in history. A lifelong segregationist, Carswell's rulings on the circuit court in Florida reflected his racist views and most of his decisions had been overruled by the Supreme Court. Even a sympathetic biographer of Nixon admits, 'his qualifications for the high court were simply nonexistent' (Ambrose, 1989). Nixon supporter Roman Hruska (Republican senator from Nebraska) declared in Carswell's defence that because many Americans were mediocre, they should have a representative on the Court!

Nixon continually denied that Carswell was a racist and despite warnings from his own party pushed ahead in April 1970 with the nomination, which he knew would be defeated. In response the President called a news conference in which he lashed senators for voting against good southerners and intelligent conservatives. 'When you strip away all the hypocrisy, the real reason for their rejection was their legal philosophy ... and also the accident of their birth, the fact that they were born in the South'. He was determined he would never nominate another southerner because it was not fair they should face such 'character assassination'. And he concluded: 'I understand the bitter feeling of millions of Americans who live in the South about the act of regional discrimination that took place in the Senate yesterday'. Nixon always defended his nominee, dismissing Carswell's support of segregation as 'youthful indiscretions' and maintaining that he still believed that 'Carswell would have passed muster by the standards of other times' (Nixon, 1978). As Nixon's biographer rightly points out, it was the South that was insulted by the nominations of Carswell, as if this fourth-rate judge was the best the South could offer. Senator Albert Gore Sr of Tennessee voted against Haynsworth and Carswell on the grounds that the two men were not fit to sit on the Court and he considered Carswell's nomination as 'an assault on the integrity of the Senate' (Ambrose, 1989). As a result, Gore would be one of the first casualties of the southern strategy. The nominations of strict constructionist and right-wing judges and his opposition to making Martin Luther King Jr's birthday a national holiday were all part of Nixon's gestures made in an effort to win over southern white voters. On reading about this proposal for the national holiday, Nixon wrote, 'No! Never!' Stephen Ambrose argues, 'the South wanted more than symbolic defiance' (Ambrose, 1989). Nixon was soon given the opportunity to advance his appeal to the South and at the same time continue his efforts to discredit the Supreme Court.

School Desegregation

His first attempt to deliver tangible benefits for most white southern politicians failed disastrously. The Secretary of Education, Health and Welfare, Robert Finch, had approved a plan for the desegregation of Mississippi schools which, if the state failed to comply with it, would result in loss of federal funding. Senator James Stennis of Mississippi demanded that the policy be reversed and Nixon forced Finch to go to the courts and request a delay of the plan. The Supreme Court in *Alexander v Holmes County Board of Education* ruled that *Brown II*, requiring compliance 'with all deliberate speed', no longer applied and ordered the immediate end of the dual school system. The solution to Nixon's dilemma came from the Attorney General of the United States, John Mitchell, who argued that desegregation should be left to the judicial process 'because seeking injunctions and bringing lawsuits was not only a slower, more careful procedure but would place the onus of enforcement on the courts instead of the White House'. The wrath of southerners would be deflected on to the hated federal courts (Greene, 1992).

This proved to be valuable advice. The federal courts were impatient with the tardy compliance with its rulings on desegregation, and they were determined to act and to speed up the process. Whites in the South had maintained virtual segregation of the school system by such devices as allowing families to choose their children's school and this 'freedom of choice' was ensured by bussing white children to white schools. In 1970 a North Carolina federal judge ordered bussing of children across Charlotte to ensure compliance with the *Brown* ruling. In 1971 the Supreme Court upheld the ruling in *Swann v Charlotte-Mecklenburg*.

Nixon opposed the bussing of school children between school districts in order to achieve desegregation. Millions of school children had been bussed in every American state for years, and it was viewed as a positive benefit because it allowed for consolidation of schools, especially in rural areas, which enabled the schools to offer a better education for their pupils. Now bussing was associated with race and the slogan was, 'No forced bussing'. In the Department of Health, Education and Welfare (HEW), which had responsibility to enforce the *Brown* rulings under the 1964 Civil Rights Act, there were many who were eager to support the courts but who felt that the administration and Nixon in particular were preventing them from achieving their goal of desegregation. One hundred and twenty-five HEW workers resigned and in response in March 1970 Nixon issued a statement supporting desegregation but opposing bussing (Ambrose, 1989). In his memoirs he reiterates statements he had made as President: 'I felt obliged to uphold the law; but I did not feel obliged to do any more than the minimum the law required, while hoping that the Court would eventually see how its well-intentioned ruling was both legally and socially counter-productive' (Nixon, 1978).

Throughout the next few years he reassured conservatives such as John Tower of Texas, Strom Thurmond of South Carolina and Richard Russell of Georgia that he would do everything possible to curtail the activities of HEW officials and in a memo to John Erlichman of 28 January 1972 he wrote, 'I believe there may be some doubt as to the validity of the Brown philosophy that integrating education will pull up the blacks and not pull down the whites'. But on another issue there was no doubt 'that education requiring excessive transportation of students is def-initely inferior.' He contended that his views on race were 'ultraliberal' and insisted he was correct in opposing 'forced integration of education and housing'. In the memorandum he maintained he was not motivated by politics and argued that he directed $2.5 billion toward improving schools (Nixon, 1978). He fails to point out that he proposed a 'moratorium' on court orders requiring bussing until 1973 and that many of his attempts to fund schools were efforts to support the various segregationist academies that had sprung up over the South as the wealthier whites withdrew from the public education system.

The immediate result, ironically, was the rapid integration of southern schools. When Nixon came into office 68 per cent of African American school children were attending segregated schools in the South. By the time he was forced to leave the White House in 1974 it was only 8 per cent (Greene, 1992). But it is the courts that should get the credit, because, as Nixon planned, it was they who took the blame. The courts came under assault in the North as well as the South. And efforts by the courts to break *de facto* segregation in northern cities would help Nixon's plan to destroy the New Deal coalition shaped by Roosevelt in the thirties.

Ironically, in June 1974, when Richard Nixon was fighting for his political life in the Watergate crisis, a federal judge attacked the public school system of Boston, Massachusetts, as segregated because blacks were confined to inferior schools, which were poorly equipped and staffed by inadequate teachers. Black students were to be bussed into South Boston. The consequences were similar to those of Little Rock in 1957. South Boston was an area of mainly Irish American working class who had always been staunch supporters of the Democratic party. Whatever the liberals, like Senator Edward Kennedy, may have preferred, they were not going to comply with the law. The students, parents and city officials were overwhelmingly opposed to bussing of black students from the Roxbury neighbourhood. The riots in Boston gladdened the hearts of southern segregationists.

While the courts sought to tackle segregation in Boston, a similar attempt was being made in Detroit; but in this case the court sought to overcome the white flight to the suburbs by linking the suburban schools with the inner-city schools. The Governor of Michigan, Henry Milliken, was opposed to the plan which linked segregation in housing to segregation of schools. Obviously, so long as African Americans and other minorities were prevented from moving into the suburbs because of restrictive covenant clauses, so the school systems could never achieve the objective as laid down in *Brown*. The judge's plan ensured the triumph of George Wallace in the 1972 Michigan primary.

In 1974 the Supreme Court in *Milliken v Bradley* overturned the Detroit bussing plan by a five-to-four majority, with the majority arguing that the suburbs were not responsible for the segregation and so should not be used to resolve the problem. All four of Nixon's appointees to the Court ruled with the majority. One of the four was William Rehnquist, who had been proposed because of his conservatism. His nomination had been approved by the Senate following the bitter battle over Carswell but Rehnquist's record was no better than that of the judge who had been defeated. In the 1950s Rehnquist had argued in favour of the *Plessy v Ferguson* ruling of 1896, which upheld segregation so long as facilities were separate but equal and he had maintained that 'it is about time that the Court faced the fact that the white people in the South don't like the colored people'. In addition, in 1964 he advocated the use of racial zoning covenants for private businesses (Greene, 1992).

The Politics of Euphemism

Bussing was all part of the politics of euphemism as practised by Nixon and the right. Opposition to 'forced bussing' was the code used to reassure conservatives in the North and the South that he would never support the goals of the civil rights movement. The persistent demand for 'law and order' was not meant as a rebuke to the southern states for failing to provide equal protection and rights for all their citizens, but rather an attack on any form of dissent whether expressed by civil rights groups, anti-war demonstrators, environmentalists or consumer groups. Nixon's 'New Federalism' was a way of attacking liberal social welfare reforms by transferring power to state programmes. By so doing he was simply supporting the contention of southern politicians who, in their resistance to the civil rights movement, had continually defended state sovereignty. His bitter personal attacks on federal civil servants were also an assault on the Great Society programmes. Although the vast majority who benefited from these schemes were white, it was the popular perception that they were designed only to benefit African Americans and other people of colour. And LBJ watched helplessly from his ranch in Texas as his 'beautiful woman', the Great Society, was taken apart by Nixon. 'It's a terrible thing for me to sit by and watch someone else starve my Great Society to death,' Johnson complained. 'Soon she'll be so ugly that the American people will refuse to look at her; they'll stick her in a closet to hide her away and there she'll die' (Kearns, 1976).

Black Capitalism

Nixon's dislike of the Great Society programmes and welfare was shared by many, including his Democrat adviser on minority affairs, Daniel Patrick Moynihan. Instead of getting government handouts, 'Nixon believed in government hand-ups, and he was convinced that the best way to help disadvantaged groups was with capitalism rather than welfare which he believed was "creeping socialism"'. Nixon notes in his memoirs, 'minority enterprises were getting only $8 million of business through government contracts. By 1972 they were getting $242 million. In the same period the total of all government grants, loans and guarantees directed toward helping minority business enterprises had jumped from $200 million to $472 million.' He points out that two-thirds of the top 100 black companies had been set up during his administration and that 'receipts of black-owned businesses jumped from $4.5 billion in 1968 to $7.2 billion in 1972' (Nixon, 1978).

Federal government assistance to black business was a method followed by subsequent Presidents and supported in Congress. An African American Democratic congressman from Baltimore, Maryland, proposed, in an amendment to the 1977 Public Works Employment Act, an appropriation of $4 billion to stimulate the economy and that 10 per cent of each grant should be for minority business. The set-aside programme was approved with virtually no discussion and no committee hearings. The programme of 1967 which had no racial basis designed to aid disadvantaged business enterprises now became set-asides for minority business enterprises. 'The set-aside model for federal grants and contracts proved attractive in the 1980s not just to liberal Democrats in Congress but also to Republican presidents Ronald Reagan and George Bush. Like President Nixon, they attacked racial quotas but supported affirmative-action programmes that encouraged entrepreneurship' (Graham, 1994). Ironically, affirmative action, which has come under severe criticism by the New Right in the 1990s, was developed and defended by Presidents who gave birth to and represented the New Right majority.

If Nixon's policy was to build a black middle class which would support the Republican party, it did not pay dividends in the short term. In his re-election in 1972 the African American vote stayed loyal to the Democratic party. Following the attempted assassination of George Wallace, which took the Alabama Governor out of the presidential race, Nixon saw the triumph of his southern strategy – all the former Confederate states voting overwhelmingly for the Republican party. But the Democrats still controlled Congress because 'Nixon completely wrote off local races, telling Erlichman that the Republicans had raised the "worst crop of candidates in history"' (Greene, 1992).

The failure to win African American support was not a surprise to Nixon. Although Stephen Ambrose stresses that in the fifties Nixon 'was the only one who would go into the South and tell southerners that segregation was morally wrong,' it is also true that since that time he was very quiet on the issue. It is evident that he had more sympathy for white southerners and their resistance to integration than he did for African Americans in their struggle for justice. He refused to give Robert Finch at HEW any support, preferring to follow the advice of John Mitchell, which was simply, 'Do only what the law requires, not one thing more'. Nixon was certain that they would never gain credit from the African American community and he wanted to keep 'as low a profile as possible' on desegregation. As Ambrose (1989) admits, 'he passed on his best opportunity for greatness'.

The opportunity was to complete the task in which Lyndon Baines Johnson had shown true presidential leadership – the task of solving the civil rights question. Nixon failed to give a forthright denunciation of segregation and he failed to provide 'an enthusiastic advocacy of integration, a wholehearted acceptance of the necessity for equality of opportunity in the marketplace, a compelling commitment to decency in race relations in all areas'. As Ambrose (1989) confesses, 'it was not to be, because in this area Richard Nixon did not want to be the nation's leader. He only wished the problem would go away.'

African Americans and liberals were only too aware of this lack of leadership. They were also aware that the legacy of Richard Nixon would last long after he left the White House in disgrace following the Watergate scandal because he had appointed four conservative justices to the Supreme Court. The Court, which had been the ally of the civil rights movement, could no longer be relied on for support and this in turn had long-term consequences for those, such as the NAACP, who struggled for justice through the legal system. Ralph Abernathy, of SCLC, recalled that in 1976, 'The civil rights movement was no longer as fashionable as it once had been'. He also believed that the future battles would be smaller and complicated and would not get the media attention. 'Watergate had been a better show than anything we had managed to stage' (Abernathy, 1989). He was not surprised when he was asked in 1976 to resign from the leadership of the SCLC.

Ironically, conservatives attacked Nixon because they thought he was too sympathetic to civil rights groups and had accepted a liberal agenda. Pat Buchanan, who had earlier supported Nixon, now complained that he had betrayed the conservative cause. In a seven-page memorandum to Nixon, Buchanan claimed that the President had surrounded himself with liberal advisers and that conservatives were 'the niggers of the Nixon Administration' (Ambrose, 1989). In order to rectify this situation Pat Buchanan and California Governor Ronald Reagan decided to take up the banner of the 'moral majority' and sweep the remaining liberals and communist dupes out of Washington.

Following the single term of the Georgia Democrat Jimmy Carter, whose major achievements were the appointment of minorities and women to prominent positions and the renewal of the Voting Rights Act, the former sports commentator, movie actor, FBI agent and Governor of California tried once again for the presidential nomination of the Republican party. Ronald Reagan, who had been a liberal Democrat as a young man, had embraced anti-communism and became in the 1950s an ardent supporter of McCarthy, the HUAC and the new conservatism.

Ronald Reagan and the New Right

An ardent supporter of Barry Goldwater in 1964, Reagan bitterly attacked the liberal Republicans, such as Nelson Rockefeller of New York, as traitors to the party. When Reagan first ran for the governorship of California in 1966 he was careful not to repudiate members of an extremist right-wing group, the John Birch Society, because he knew that Nixon had lost conservative support in 1962 when he had attacked the Birch group. Reagan compromised to keep extreme right-wing support; he campaigned for members of the Society but issued a statement criticising Robert Welch, the founder. When he was attacked in the Republican primary by a former Mayor of San Francisco for not supporting the Civil Rights Act of 1964 he lost his temper, shouting: 'I resent the implication that there is any bigotry in my nature. Don't anyone ever imply that' (Dallek, 1984). During the same campaign, he supported the American Medical Association in their battle against Medicare and argued that: 'Medical care for the aged is a foot in the door of a government takeover of all medicine'. He even alleged that income tax was a 'progressive system spawned by Karl Marx and declared by him to be the prime essential of a socialist state'. For Reagan the threat was not from liberalism but from the 'socialism' of the

Democratic party which would destroy individual initiative (Boyarsky, 1981).

Reagan courted the conservative vote when dealing with civil rights issues. A typical and frequently repeated story by Reagan concerned the black Chicago woman Linda Taylor. In this tale Reagan linked African Americans and welfare, reinforcing the popular perception that many black women exploited the welfare system paid for by hard-working white folk. In addition, his rendering underlined his typical cavalier use of statistics. Campaigning for the presidency in 1976 he claimed that a Chicago woman 'has eighty names, thirty addresses, twelve Social Security cards and is collecting veterans' benefits on four nonexisting husbands.... Her tax-free cash income alone is over $150,000.' In fact Taylor was convicted in 1977 of welfare fraud using two, not eighty, names which she used to collect 23 welfare cheques worth $8000, not $150 000. According to the *New York Times*, during this same campaign he used a typical racial epithet to a southern audience when he complained about a 'young buck' receiving food stamp benefits (Cannon, 1991).

Was Reagan a Racist?

It may be true that Reagan was not 'racially prejudiced in the normal meaning of the term', but it is also the case that his open support for African Americans was limited. In his early years at Eureka College he supported integration of the football team and when he was a sports broadcaster he spoke out in favour of integration of black baseball players into the major league teams. Since those early days he had attacked the 1964 Civil Rights Act and the 1965 Voting Rights Act, and opposed laws seeking to forbid discrimination in housing and the desegregation of schools by bussing. However, he did try to win over leaders of the 1960s civil rights movement with promises of job training for inner-city youth which would break the so-called 'dependency culture' that he and they believed the welfare state had fostered. Abernathy was concerned that the Republican southern strategy was winning over whites only and he blamed African Americans because of their blind loyalty to the Democrats. In the 1980 campaign civil rights activists, such as Ralph Abernathy, Charles Evers and Hosea Williams, endorsed Reagan rather than Jimmy Carter (Abernathy, 1989). Despite Abernathy's efforts, 'Ronald Reagan received the lowest percentage of the black vote of any Republican presidential candidate in history' (Shull, 1993).

Abernathy was rapidly disillusioned with the new President. Although 'honored guests' and despite being 'treated as important celebrities', Abernathy did not get a chance to speak with Reagan. All his efforts in the coming days and weeks to meet with Reagan or his senior staff failed and he 'didn't get past a third-echelon staff member.... No one, it seems, knew or cared about the president's promises' (Abernathy, 1989). What Abernathy failed to appreciate was that Reagan was a different type of civil rights activist. 'Instead of extending civil rights, he sought to reduce the government's role' (Shull, 1993). The former leader of SCLC was not the only one who was disillusioned with Reagan. Leaders of the NAACP were not pleased when he refused to give a speech at their annual convention in 1980 because he had a prior arrangement – a riding holiday (Cannon, 1991). When he made good the error and went to the NAACP meeting in July 1981 he angered delegates when he coolly informed them that the plight of many African Americans was due to government programmes passed by liberal Democrats. Reagan asserted:

> Many in Washington over the years have been more dedicated to making the needy people government dependent, rather than independent. They've created a new kind of bondage. Just as the Emancipation Proclamation freed black people 118 years go, today we need to declare an economic emancipation. (Dallek, 1984)

The New Right Budget

Reagan's first budget was to be the first step in the revolution that would sweep away years of accumulated state dependency. His budget director, David A. Stockman, proudly stated: 'The Reagan Revolution, as I had defined it, required a frontal assault on the American welfare state'. And he admitted that 'forty years' worth of promises, subventions, entitlements, and safety nets issued by the federal government ... would have to be scrapped or drastically modified'. This 'minimalist government' would offer 'even-handed public justice, but no more'. Instead of welfare dependency the nation would be liberated by free-market economics. He believed that removing regulations and restriction on private wealth would increase 'capitalist wealth and the expansion of private welfare that attends it'. According to Stockman, the failure of Reagan's budgets, with their huge tax cuts and massively increased expenditure on defence spending, was the failure to cut welfare programmes, which 'are family-destroyers. They subsidize a culture of poverty, dependency, and social irresponsibility' (Stockman, 1987). In an interview with William Greider of *Atlantic Monthly*, the 'high-sounding philosophy' of supply-side economics was, according to Stockman, nothing more than the old idea of giving tax breaks to the rich in the hope that eventually the good effects might benefit the poor. He admitted, 'It's kind of hard to sell "trickle down," so the supply side formula was the only way to get a tax policy that was really "trickle down." Supply side is "trickle down" theory' (Johnson, 1991). However, Stockman was not alone in his attacks on the welfare state. Ralph Abernathy attacked Democrats who saw welfare as a 'benign thing rather than as a millstone around the neck of the black population' (Abernathy 1989).

Despite Stockman's later complaints that the President failed to support his efforts, Reagan was a true believer and it was his passionate conviction which won over many doubters in the Republican and Democratic parties. Following the decision to cut taxes by 25 per cent over three years and increase military expenditure, one Republican moderate is quoted as saying, 'Pray God it works. If this economic plan doesn't jell, where are we going to get the money for anything?' They were forced to borrow and thus increase the budget deficit. Although the welfare state was not swept away by this budget or subsequent budgets, it was the poor who took the brunt of the cuts. The number of people eligible for food stamps, Medicaid, unemployment benefit, housing assistance, student loans, child nutrition programmes, public service jobs and legal aid were cut back. And the tax cuts did not benefit the people who had lost out. As Robert Dallek points out: 'The 31.7 million taxpayers making $15,000 or less a year were to receive only 8.5 percent of the reduction while 12.6 million people earning $50,000 or more a year were to get 35 percent of the money given up by the federal treasury'. In their determination to encourage the 'productive potential of free men in free markets' the contribution of corporations in federal taxes was reduced from 13 cents to 8 cents per tax dollar (Dallek, 1984).

Stockman attacks conservatives such as Irving Kristol for not going far enough and thus ensuring the persistence of the welfare state. Certainly, the much vaunted Reagan Revolution was merely a continuation of policies supported by Republican and Democratic administrations and congressional parties. According to congressional Budget Office statistics for 1977 to 1987 the family income after taxes in 1988 dollars, and adjusted for inflation, saw the richest 5 per cent increase their earnings by 37.3 per cent from $94 476 to $129 762. However, the poorest 10 per cent of the population with average earnings of $3673 in 1977 had had their earnings reduced by 10.5 per cent in 1987 to $3286. The after-tax income of the top 1 per cent increased by 87 per cent over 1980 to 1990 (Shull, 1993).

The anger of NAACP members over Reagan's priorities in his budget had been made clear by Benjamin Hooks, the head of the Association. Hooks denounced the budget plans as bringing 'hardship, havoc, despair, pain, and suffering on blacks and other minorities'. African Americans who supported his criticisms were Coretta Scott King, Martin Luther King Jr's widow, and the Mayor of Detroit, Coleman Young.

The Commission on Civil Rights and the IRS

Reagan was not only activist in his budget proposals which cut the welfare state – he was also determined to change the structure, personnel and mission of the US Commission on Civil Rights. In this he was also following the example set by Richard Nixon, who had demanded the resignation of Father Theodore Hesburgh because he refused to oppose bussing for integration. Nixon appointed a Republican, Arthur Fleming, in the hope that he would be more compliant to Nixon and the demands of the New Right. He was not and was outspoken in his criticism of Republican administrations, especially that of Ronald Reagan.

Fleming was fired by Reagan and the ousted Commission member complained at a news conference that his dismissal signalled a retreat on affirmative action. An NAACP spokeswoman commented: 'What the administration is trying to do is not just put civil rights on the back burner, but take it off the stove completely'. And the man Reagan chose to help him weaken the Commission was a conservative black Republican, Clarence Pendleton of the San Diego Urban League. He was an ideal choice for Reagan in that he was a strong believer in self-help, free markets, opposed to affirmative action and bussing to achieve integration. The President was not concerned that 'The increased politicization of the commission perpetuates [his] image as an opponent of civil rights'. Reagan won his battle with the liberals and transformed the Commission into a conservative body that accepted the New Right critique of affirmative action and bussing (Shull, 1993).

It has been argued in Reagan's defence that he 'was so cut off from the counsel of black Americans that he sometimes did not even realize when he was offending them' (Cannon, 1991), but if that is the case then as President he was responsible for that remoteness. One 'glaring example' of this remoteness, it is suggested, was his support in 1982 for Bob Jones University in South Carolina and the Goldsboro Christian Schools in North Carolina when they challenged the right of the Internal Revenue Service (IRS) to deny tax exemptions to segregated schools. This IRS policy was aimed at schools set up in the South to avoid integration and the policy had had the consistent support of three Presidents, Richard Nixon, Gerald Ford and Jimmy Carter. In the case of Bob Jones University, although it admitted a few minority students, interracial dating and marriage were prohibited by the school rules, which it claimed were based on the Bible. Later Reagan claimed: 'All I wanted was that these tax collectors stop threatening schools that were obeying the law' (Cannon, 1991).

In the resulting storm of protest, Reagan was told that African Americans viewed him as a traitor and he hastily sought a compromise in which he argued that his proposed legislation would not only end the role of bureaucrats in the IRS in making social policy but also prevent schools that were segregated benefiting from tax-exempt status. As Robert Dallek points out, this was 'the politics of symbolism' that would please everybody. 'Black Americans were supposed to accept the picture of a compassionate president opposed to discrimination, while conservatives were supposed to see his action as a victory over arbitrary bureaucrats and for the rule of law'. The Reagan administration had 'lined up with white sub-urbanites in opposition to government insistence on equal rights for minorities'. They backed away only when it seemed that the administration would lose moral authority but they still sought to keep conservatives reassured (Dallek, 1984). Perhaps this is a harsh judgement. There were many Republicans only too eager to court the racist vote, but Reagan's dislike of strong federal government had been a persistent theme of his campaigning since the 1960s. Arthur Aughey points out, 'The success of Reagan in the 1980s owes much to the forms of argument provided by conservative intellec-tuals in the previous two decades' (Aughey, 1992).

Renewal of the Voting Rights Act

The New Right conservatives, especially the growing numbers of southern Republicans, were not content with budgetary measures and symbolic gestures of opposition to school desegregation. They were particularly concerned about the Voting Rights Act of 1965, which had been renewed by Richard Nixon. They expected Ronald Reagan to fight the efforts of liberal Democrats and Republicans who were determined to renew the Act. The law, which enabled the federal government to register voters in districts where 50 per cent or more were not registered, transformed southern politics. In Mississippi, for example, the number of African American regis-tered as voters had increased from 6.7 per cent to 59.8 per cent in three years. Reagan made it clear that he was not in favour of renewal of the Act and very grudgingly accepted the revision of the Act which was designed to stop state and local officials from using registration and voting procedures that resulted in discrimination against minorities. This change ended the requirement to prove the intention to discriminate, a much harder thing to do in law (Dallek, 1984).

Reagan's opposition to the Voting Rights Act was based on a desire to ensure Republican strength in the South and among white working-class voters in the North and it was based on his reluctance 'to use federal authority in the cause of punishing discrimination of any sort'. Both were also factors in his opposition to the Civil Rights Restoration Act of 1988. The Act resulted from a Supreme Court ruling, *Grove City v Bell*, in 1984 that limited anti-discrimination laws to federally aided programmes and not to the institution where the discrimination occurred (Cannon, 1991). The result of this ruling meant that a department of a university that practised discrimination would lose federal funding, but not the university that had permitted the discrimination to take place. The Civil Rights Restoration Act has been considered by some as 'the most significant civil rights legislation in twenty years' (Shull, 1993). It was designed to reverse the *Grove City* ruling, which dramatically limited the scope of four major civil rights laws. Any organisation or institution had to be in compliance with the civil rights legislation if any part of the organisation was to get federal funding.

Even though he was a lame-duck President and had no need to court voters, he vetoed the Act in 1988. He had warned that he would do so because the legislation 'dramatically expands the scope of federal jurisdiction over state and local governments and the private sector, from churches and synagogues to farmers, grocery stores, and businesses of all sizes'. And according to Reagan it diminished individual citizens. His critics pointed out that the Act was merely restoring the situation to what it had been before the Supreme Court ruling. The vociferous support of the Moral Majority and its leader, the Reverend Jerry Falwell, harmed rather than aided Reagan's cause. The fundamentalist minister was convinced that churches would be forced under the Act to hire homosexuals or drug addicts with AIDS as teachers or youth workers. Even conservatives thought such attacks were nonsense and the law was passed, overriding the Reagan veto. The Republicans in Congress were deeply divided, with 21 Republican senators and 52 members of the House voting with the Democrats to override the presidential veto (Shull, 1993).

Just as Johnson had caught the liberal mood of the nation in 1964 to introduce sweeping reforms in his Great Society programme and civil rights activism, so Ronald Reagan personified, and exploited, the fears of a nation that had been transformed by the civil rights revolution. Although Jesse Jackson in 1980 and 1984 sought to rebuild a 'rainbow coalition' of the working class, minorities and women in his two bids for the presidency, it was Ronald Reagan who knew his audience the best. In his efforts he was aided by African Americans who had either benefited from the civil rights movement, such as Pendleton, or one-time leaders of the movement, such as Ralph Abernathy, who had been responsible for the transformation. In his memoirs Abernathy criticises young blacks for taking 'the past too much for granted', forgetting the sacrifices of an earlier generation.

> Had it not been for the character and courage of these simple people, we would not have raised a generation of leaders and nothing would have changed. We would still be looking from afar at the high walls of an impregnable city. So these are the first great heroes and heroines of our struggle. (Abernathy, 1989)

And he grieves for those who died for the cause and 'in the growing twilight my heart also aches for those anonymous generations who never saw the Promised Land, even from the mountain top' (Abernathy, 1989). It only makes it all the more sad that a sick and ageing fighter of the civil rights struggle should have campaigned for Ronald Reagan, who had for so long led the resistance to the movement to help those 'simple people'. When Reagan left office the city was more impregnable than at any time since the 1950s.

6

TRANSFORMATIONS: A NEW SOUTH?

Lyndon Baines Johnson had always wanted consensus politics but by 1968 he was facing mounting opposition over his foreign policy in Vietnam from the left, and vociferous attacks on his radical legislation on civil rights and economic policies from the right. He admitted: 'There were deep divisions in the country, perhaps deeper than any we had experienced since the Civil War. They were divisions that could destroy us if they were not attended to and ultimately healed.' On his return to the ranch in Texas he walked beside the Pedernales River and reflected that as President 'I had given it everything that was in me' (Johnson, 1971).

However, as President he had shattered the broad alliance which brought him so many legislative successes. Johnson sought to ensure continued support from a sympathetic Supreme Court after Chief Justice Earl Warren said he was to retire. LBJ persuaded his old friend and adviser, Abe Fortas, a liberal Tennessean, to be nominated as the new Chief Justice. Fortas would have been the first Jewish head of the Court. Republican senator Dirksen and James Eastland, the Democrat from Mississippi, were able to block the appointment of Fortas by two votes. Eastland was angered by a speech in which Fortas had urged Jews to support the civil rights movement. According to Johnson, Eastland interpreted that statement as a conspiratorial call for Jews and Negroes to take over America (Johnson, 1971). Eastland, with his paranoid fears of a Jewish–communist–black plot to destroy America, personified the old South.

The civil rights struggle and the anti-Vietnam War movement not only influenced African American lives: it transformed the lives of

121

many white southerners. The characterisation of the South as home only to those who are violent, racist, insular and forever reliving the battles of the Civil War is an oversimplification. Southerners have been accused of shackling themselves to a 'false image' but that image is as much an invention of northerners as of southerners. There has always been another South. Although many liberal southerners failed to meet the challenge posed by the civil rights movement, there were many who in the finest sense upheld the southern tradition of honour.

The civil rights movement transformed the South. Black southerners proved that with their courage when they challenged Eugene 'Bull' Connor and Sheriff Jim Clark. Their refusal to accept second-class citizenship and their determination to struggle for justice forced many southerners to question the received wisdom of their political, religious and educational leaders. Foremost in the struggle were the African Americans of the South – it was their battle and they were determined to make it their victory. However, it is important to remember that white politicians, such as Senator Albert Gore Sr, had the courage to face the challenge presented by the movement. Other moderates not only achieved state power but gained the ultimate prize that had alluded Gore – the presidency. Jimmy Carter was elected Governor of Georgia as an anti-segregationist candidate and eventually became President of the United States.

It is true that some southern judges such as E. Gordon West of Louisiana refused to enforce the *Brown* ruling. William Harold Cox of Mississippi called African Americans 'niggers' and accused some of them of behaving like 'a bunch of chimpanzees'. However, these Kennedy appointments to the federal court were not typical of all southern judges. Frank Johnson, appointed to the Alabama Middle District federal judgeship by Republican President Eisenhower and to the Fifth Circuit Court of Appeal by Democrat President Jimmy Carter, struggled to preserve the rule of law in the face of southern resistance to the civil rights movement. He was willing to confront his old law school associate, George Wallace. Although southern radicals have had their critics they also played a valuable role during the repressive years of the 1940s, 1950s and 1960s, when they kept alive the dream of a just South. This is especially true for James Dombrowski and Carl and Anne Braden. There was a significant minority of white southern students who took part in the civil rights and anti-war movements.

However, the challenges which produced southern liberal Democratic political leaders, such as Jimmy Carter of Georgia and Bill Clinton of Arkansas, also saw the revolution in voting in the South after 1968. Since the Civil War the vast majority of white southerners voted Democrat. Only in a few isolated areas, such as East Tennessee or northern Alabama which had supported the North during the Civil War, was it possible for a Republican to stand for election and be sure of winning. Truman, Kennedy, and even to some extent Johnson could rely on the instinctive white southern support for the Democratic party. Richard Nixon and Ronald Reagan changed that. The South is Republican, a fact underlined by the sweeping gains of the Republicans in the 1994 mid-term elections.

The Senator

Albert Gore Sr of Tennessee grew up on a farm and struggled during the Depression to gain an education. He taught in a small school where he lived with a coal miner and his family, whose poverty made a profound impression on him. He had wanted to enter politics since his school days and eventually, at the age of 29, he was elected as a pro-New Deal Democrat from the Fourth District of Tennessee in 1938. In 1952 he was elevated to the Senate, a post he held until his defeat in 1970. He liked to be known as a 'maverick' because he believed most Tennesseans were mavericks. In a long and distinguished career he never turned to the old tactic of race baiting (Gore, 1972).

Gore describes himself as a Populist – a movement at the turn of the century which he saw as 'an outstandingly liberal movement' and a lost opportunity in which African Americans and poor whites could have been united in their opposition to the reactionary forces that dominated the South. Gore saw Democratic party policies of the New Deal, Fair Deal, the Great Society and the party platform of George McGovern in 1972 as the eventual triumph of Populism. Although critical of some aspects of the New Deal, he became a self-confessed 'extravagant admirer' of FDR. He supported the liberal policies of Truman and opposed the 'Dixiecrat' movement led by Strom Thurmond. 'Fortunately, not enough Southerners were willing any longer to follow blindly this advance to the rear'. The significance of the Dixiecrats was the willingness of the Bourbon leaders to desert the Democratic party 'in order to maintain white supremacy' (Gore, 1972).

When the Supreme Court ruled in *Brown* in 1954 that separate but equal was unconstitutional and ordered the integration of schools, Gore admits that he was not one of the 'political "heroes"'. Although he had never indulged in race baiting, he had not been 'a torchbearer for racial equality in my first campaign for the Senate in Tennessee in 1952' (Gore, 1972). He had openly solicited the votes of black and poor whites on economic and social issues. He confronted Memphis 'Boss' Ed Crump, who had controlled the black vote in that city for many years. Gore knew that if African Americans had a free and independent vote then the Crump machine would be destroyed.

Following the Court ruling in *Brown*, Gore defended it and described himself as a moderate. The powerful Georgia Democrat Roy Harris, assistant to the state Governor Herman Talmadge, contended that, 'Moderation means gradualism and gradualism means race mixing'. Similar resistance was mounted in Tennessee by a White Citizens Council, a States Rights Council, a Federation for Constitutional Government, which included Vanderbilt University English Professor Donald Davidson, and the Tennessee Society to Maintain Segregation. Gore knew that moderation for most southern demagogues was nothing short of communism because even before the *Brown* ruling politicians in Georgia and Mississippi had anticipated the possibility of integration and in Georgia, for example, had tried to convert the public school system into a private system (Gore, 1972).

East Tennessee saw the worst violence against integration. The small town of Clinton in Anderson County had too few blacks to justify expenditure on a separate black high school and so they had been bussed to a segregated school in Knoxville. The efforts of local and state authorities to prepare for the integration of the local high school failed. Although there was much violence, the Citizens Council candidates were defeated in the Clinton elections. There were brave individuals who sought to uphold the law. The white pastor of the First Baptist Church, the Reverend Paul Turner, volunteered to take the black children to the school and was beaten for his action. His stand did not prevent the bombing of the school in 1958 (Greene, 1982).

Senator Gore admired the willingness of Governor Frank Clement to send National Guard troops into Clinton to ensure integration, but it was not only the Governor who was tested over implementing the *Brown* decision. Opposition was growing in the South with Citizens Councils 'formed to intimidate the Negro and keep the whites in line'. This was reflected in the attitudes of members of the House of Representatives and the Senate. The aim of the reactionary southerners was to label integration as 'subversive and unAmerican'. As part of this campaign, southern elected officials were asked to sign a Declaration of Constitutional Principles, popularly known as the Southern Manifesto. This 'bit of low doggerel', as Gore describes it, was the handiwork of Strom Thurmond of South Carolina. It was Thurmond who publicly challenged Gore in the Senate to add his name to the document. Gore refused. Later he explained: 'I regarded the manifesto (what an irritating and pretentious name!) as the most unvarnished piece of demagoguery I had ever encountered'. He was certain 'that nothing but tragedy and sorrow could come of this open defiance of the law, this cheap appeal to racism' (Gore, 1972).

Despite the popularity of actions by Faubus of Arkansas, Gore continued to pursue economic reform measures that would help the working class and poor, whether they were black or white. He voted for the 1957 Civil Rights Act because 'it did place Congress on the side of social justice and ... the mere passage of civil-rights legislation was itself worthy of note'. However, Gore supported segregationist Buford Ellington for Governor. Why? Gore was a party loyalist. More importantly, Gore had presidential ambitions and he needed Ellington and the Tennessee Democrats' support in the 1960 convention. This act of political expediency was not rewarded – Ellington preferred to back Lyndon Johnson.

During the 1960 campaign Gore worked closely with John Kennedy even though many southerners saw the Massachusetts senator as a dangerous liberal and disliked him because of his Catholic faith. After the election Gore acted as one of Kennedy's speech writers. Gore supported Kennedy's civil rights actions, especially the integration of the University of Mississippi, which the Tennessean hailed as the end of the interposition argument. However, Gore was not happy with Kennedy's tax-cutting policies, which the Tennessean believed helped only the rich.

Although Gore had many ideas in common with LBJ there were important differences. 'One was that I had grown stronger in

Populist leanings and had become an inveterate enemy of special privilege, while Johnson had become a bedfellow of big money, oil, and military brass'. It was Gore's Populism as much as his increasing opposition to the war in Vietnam that led to his disputes with Johnson. But despite these differences both southerners fought hard for the Medicare programme providing medical assistance for the elderly and Medicaid for the poor, and for federal aid for elementary and secondary education. Gore voted for the Voting Rights Act of 1965 and for its renewal in 1970, and the 1968 Open Housing Act (Gore, 1972).

Gore considered the 1968 presidential election 'a travesty on democracy' because all three candidates – Nixon, Humphrey and Wallace – supported the war in Vietnam. He campaigned for Humphrey as the best man to extricate America from the war. As he recalled, it was a period 'when false patriotism was prevalent, a time when frustration, bigotry, recrimination, fear, and littleness of spirit and mind spread across the land like waters from a flash flood'. Gore was only too aware that liberal Democrats were the target of Nixon's southern strategy and that they would be in 'the eye of the storm'. He believed Nixon was appealing to racism and regionalism in the South and the easy thing to do would have been to trim. Gore refused. He continued his attacks on the Vietnam War and he accepted the challenge of Nixon when in 1970 the President set out to appoint southern conservative judges to the Supreme Court. Gore voted against Clement F. Haynesworth and G. Harold Carswell, both of whom he believed were totally unfit for such a prestigious office. As Gore writes, 'It had become the litmus test of loyalty or disloyalty to the South, of white supremacy or civil rights for blacks with no room left for moderation or reason. When my name was called I voted a firm "No," and I felt good inside.' Carswell's nomination was for Gore the absolute proof of Nixon's 'anti-black Southern strategy' (Gore, 1972). His stance against the war and the judicial nominees won him support from radical students in Tennessee (*Libra*, 22 October 1970).

There is one blemish on Gore's progressive civil rights record. He opposed the 1964 Civil Rights Bill because it gave authority to 'unspecified, middle-rank functionaries in the Department of Health, Education and Welfare to withhold funding from schools that refused to follow its guide-lines on integration'. For Gore this was an arbitrary use of power. He believed cutting funding to a school system because one school failed to comply with HEW regulations was unjust (Gore, 1970). However genuine his fears of arbitrary powers may have been, he must have known that it was not merely the question of one school failing to follow the guidelines but rather entire state systems refusing to do so, as in the case of the Massive Resistance of Virginia.

Despite this blemish on his record, Albert Gore Sr remained true to his Populist views. Although defeated in 1970 by the Republican William Brock, whose campaign exploited racial fears and religious prejudice, Gore was proud of his long service in Congress. He articulated the liberal critique of New Right economic policy as early as 1972: 'it had always seemed to me perfectly logical that government should play an active role in the nation's business affairs, and I had never lost the faith in the government's ability to guarantee economic justice to all its people' (Gore, 1972).

The President

Jimmy Carter of Plains, Georgia, was fond of recalling his Populist background and his mother, Lillian, claimed that her father was a close friend of the Populist leaders Tom Watson and Bishop William D. Johnson of the AME Church. A Jimmy Carter biographer has commented: 'Lillian has painted her father with a golden brush' (Kaufman, 1993). Even if that is the case, Lillian's frequent and sincere claims to the contrary may have influenced the political career of her son when he was Governor of Georgia and later President of the United States. There is certainly little evidence that he was a Populist during the 1950s and 1960s when African Americans were struggling to achieve equality under the law.

Jimmy Carter has been called a racial paternalist who did not question segregation in Georgia. From 1959 to 1961 he was a member of the Americus and Sumter County Hospital Board and in the same years he was on the Carnegie Library Board and he accepted the segregationists' policies. During the years 1956 to 1962, when he served on the Sumter County Board of Education and was the chairman for 1962, he failed to initiate change in the school system. Carter's explanation, that he was guilty of naive unawareness, is questionable because he actively delayed construction of one school for blacks and never supported properly equipping the schools that were supposedly separate and equal. Certainly the school board did nothing to implement the *Brown* ruling of the Supreme Court (Glad, 1980).

Carter is also accused of failing to help a Christian inter-racial community in southwest Georgia known as Koininia. One of his neighbours, Jack Singletary, was threatened by nightriders and told not to attend the Plains Baptist Church because he had lived in the community for a short period. Herbert Birdsey of Macon who had sold supplies to the community had had his store bombed. Carter did not help the community although he did help in easing the boycott against Singletary. Carter did not take the lead in these matters. But he did not join the States Rights Council, Georgia's equivalent of the White Citizens Council. However, a biographer points out, 'If he had stood with some of his other friends against integration, he would have undermined his potential as a political leader for the entire state, and eventually for the nation' (Glad, 1980).

As a state senator from 1963 to 1966, he attacked special-interest groups and their influence in the state legislature. He 'stressed the importance of caring for the poor, the underprivileged, and the under represented in Government'. This experience in the legislature spurred him to seek the governorship in a campaign that even his own advisers would later regret. Carter opposed bussing to achieve racial integration, and he visited a segregated private school (Kaufman, 1993).

Not all features of this campaign are so negative and his later moderation as Governor was not so surprising. Undoubtedly Carter wanted to win the Wallace vote but he also knew that the biggest grievance in Georgia was the inequity of the tax system. He used the Populist language of 'freedom, opportunity and equal treatment' and promised to remove tax inequalities, to obey school desegregation orders as well as reform state government. One of his aides described it as 'stylistic' Populism. 'It was more an attempt to articulate the deeper feelings and frustrations of the small people – their suspicions of the urban centers, the rich, the big interests – than a fundamental challenge to the established centers of power' (Glad, 1980).

Although Carter did not trim the power of banks and big business in Georgia, he did declare at his inauguration as Governor that the days of segregation were over. He increased the number of black Georgia state employees from 4850 to 6684, he improved services for mentally handicapped people, and opened over 100 health centres. He made important symbolic gestures as well, such as hanging a portrait of Martin Luther King Jr in the state capitol.

His success as Governor and his long campaign for honesty in government had wide appeal and he was persuaded to seek the Democratic presidential nomination. Carter was helped by the Watergate scandal which led to the forced resignation of Richard Nixon. In the primaries, despite strong opposition from Jesse Jackson, Carter won the majority of the black vote even in states that he lost, such as Massachusetts. His candidacy and ultimate victory demonstrated that a southerner who had a popular appeal on economic issues and who was liberal on racial matters could be elected President without having to deny his southern origin.

Ironically, it was the African American legislators who made up the Black Caucus in Congress who were the most critical of Carter. His determination to control inflation led to bitter disputes within his own party but for black legislators it meant cutbacks in programmes that were designed to help the disadvantaged. Despite Carter's conservative attitude towards the economy he fulfilled many of his promises. During the campaign he promised to increase the number of minority appointments in the judiciary. Carter appointed more blacks and Hispanics to the federal judiciary than any President before him. The percentage of black federal judges increased from 4 per cent in 1977 to 9 per cent in 1981. He made sure that minority-owned companies had their fair share of federal contracts and that federal funds were deposited in banks owned by minorities. Unlike Nixon, and later Reagan and Bush, Carter gave additional power to the Justice Department over voting rights and strengthened the Equal Employment Opportunities Commission to help it fight job discrimination. He had two black women in his cabinet: Juanita Kreps, vice president of Duke University, accepted the post of Commerce Secretary; and Patricia Harris, the dean of Howard University Law School, Secretary of Housing and Urban Development. Andrew Young, the Atlanta congressman and former civil rights leader, was appointed ambassador to the United Nations.

When Carter was in the White House the Supreme Court heard the first challenge to the affirmative-action policy that had been encouraged by Richard Nixon. Because of previous discrimination, businesses and universities had set up special programmes which gave priority to minority candidates and universities retained a system of minority places. Marine veteran Allan Bakke challenged these programmes at the University of California at Davis because he had not been admitted to the medical school whereas African American and other minority candidates with lower scores had gained places. He won his case in the California Supreme Court and the regents of the University appealed to the US Supreme Court.

Whatever position Carter took on *Bakke v Regents of the University of California* was bound to cause him trouble. The Jewish community backed affirmative action where it set targets, but not where it provided quotas. Organised labour, another traditional group to support the Democratic party, was totally opposed to affirmative action, and the black community, which had given Carter 89 per cent of their votes, was totally committed to affirmative action and quotas. The advice he was given at first by the Attorney General gave no direct support to affirmative action. Following consultations the administration submitted a brief which strongly endorsed the controversial policy and the Supreme Court ruled five to four that affirmative action was constitutional but that the system of racial quotas as used by the University was unconstitutional. It was widely acknowledged in the African American community that the Justice Department's brief was 'one of the major contributions to the cause of civil rights' (Kaufman, 1993).

Although Carter may have exaggerated his integrationist sympathies before he was Governor of Georgia, it is clear that as Governor and as President of the United States he not only accepted rulings of the courts but took positive action to benefit minority groups, especially the black community. It is ironic that civil rights leaders such as Julian Bond, Hosea Williams and Ralph Abernathy refused to support the Georgian, Williams and Abernathy preferring to back Ronald Reagan. This division in the black vote is no more surprising than white southern Baptist voters rejecting Carter, a born-again Baptist from the South, in favour of Ronald Reagan, who was to become the first divorced President in the history of the country – running on a religious programme that emphasised the sanctity of the family.

Mayors, Congressmen and the Governor

The South has seen a major transformation in its politics which has increased its power on the national scene. The civil rights movement and the resistance to it, ironically, brought democracy to vast areas of the South which had only known one-party rule by the Democratic party upheld by flagrant anti-democratic devices which denied African Americans their right to exercise the franchise. The 1965 Voting Rights Act not only resulted in moderation by Democrats, with Senator Herman Talmadge of Georgia seeking the support of black voters, it also saw the emergence of a strong moderate Republican party, with governors such as Winthrop Rockefeller in Arkansas and Linwood Holton of Virginia. The latter state had been the centre of massive resistance to the *Brown* decision to integrate schools. However, by 1970 Holton in his inaugural address said: 'As Virginia has been the model for so much else in America in the past, let us now endeavor to make today's Virginia a model in race relations. Let us, as Lincoln said, insist upon an open society "with malice toward none charity for all."'

In the 11 states that had formed the Confederate States of America in defence of slavery, the black registered voters more than doubled from 1.5 million to 2.7 million between 1960 and 1966, and had nearly doubled again by 1980 to 4.3 million. The effect was not merely on national politics but was profound at a local level. By 1980 Dixie had 2600 elected black officials. This was helped by the Supreme Court in several rulings – *Gomillion v Lightfoot* (1960), *Baker v Carr* (1962) and *Gray v Sanders* (1963) – overturning gerrymandering devices used by whites to deprive blacks of representation. Tuskegee, Alabama, had its first black mayor in 1972. Birmingham, the site of some of the worst police violence, elected the African American Richard Arrington as Mayor. Atlanta, the commercial and cultural capital of the South, elected Maynard Jackson and former United Nations ambassador and civil rights leader Andrew Young as Mayor (Cooper and Terrill, 1991). The North Carolina city of Charlotte, the national centre of attention when the Supreme Court ruled in favour of bussing to achieve integration, elected a black mayor. The latter's election was dependent on white voters because blacks constituted only 25 per cent of the population.

John Lewis, who spoke at the Washington rally in 1963, was elected to Congress in the district previously held by Andrew Young.

Lewis defeated another major civil rights leader, Julian Bond. A black congresswoman from Texas came to national prominence as a member of the House Judiciary Committee impeachment hearings in the Watergate affair. Barbara Jordan, an African American and a former Texas judge, on 26 June 1972 told millions of Americans watching the proceedings on television that the phrase 'We the people' in the original Constitution had not included her or others of her race. But she added: 'My faith in the Constitution is whole, it is complete, it is total, and I am not going to sit here and be an idle spectator to the diminution, the subversion, the destruction of the Constitution' (Emery, 1994).

An African American had never been a Governor in the history of the United States; the highest state post held by a black person had been that of Lieutenant Governor Pinchback during Radical Republican rule in Louisiana after the Civil War. Virginia, the home of Robert E. Lee, commander of the Confederate forces, was the first state to elect an African American as Governor. In 1989, L. Douglas Wilder became the first black Governor in the history of the United States, defeating a conservative Republican in a campaign in which Wilder defended the right of women to choose an abortion if they so wished, although he was forced to modify his opposition to the death penalty.

The danger, predicted by LBJ when he signed the 1965 Voting Rights Act, is that the Democratic party is seen as the party for African Americans only, the view that southern whites had had of the Republican party for so many years. With the vast majority of African Americans voting for and standing for election for the Democratic party, the result has been racial polarisation along party lines. Historians of the South fear 'that the South's recently acquired two-party politics may become one party for blacks and one party for whites, a disquieting reminder of the past' (Cooper, 1991). Their fears have come true.

In addition to state offices, African Americans have representation in city government, as well as the state legislature, the federal Congress and the state and federal judiciary; they are also in the city and state police forces. The white state troopers who had been used by white officials to defy the rule of law are now all integrated. There is not just a white sheriff and his deputies but in many counties there are black sheriffs and their deputies. In Alabama the integration of the police force was brought about by a remarkable federal judge whose support of the law brought no reward from Richard Nixon and other Presidents who pursued a southern strategy.

The Judge – Frank Johnson

Frank Johnson was born in Winston County, northern Alabama, and grew up as a devout Baptist and Republican. The hill country had no enthusiasm for slavery and few supported the Confederacy. Its Republican politics was shaped by the Civil War experience. Although not poor themselves, the Johnsons lived in an area of Alabama where coal mining, not cotton, was the main business. Many of the miners were poor and he married Ruth Jenkins, an impoverished miner's daughter. While he was at the University of Alabama Law School at Tuscaloosa, a fellow student was George Wallace, future Governor. Johnson had accepted segregation as a young man because he said: 'I wasn't confronted with it like I would have been had I grown up down in the Black Belt, in Lowndes County or Macon County or someplace like that'. However, he had never accepted the prevailing belief of the majority of whites that blacks were racially inferior. His wife had openly challenged the system by being the first white woman to receive a graduate degree at the formerly all-black Alabama State College. As she stated, even in her youth 'I was known as a "nigger lover"' (Yarborough, 1981).

In 1955 President Eisenhower appointed Johnson to the Middle District Court in Alabama and Johnson moved to Montgomery with his family. He also served on the Fifth Circuit Court of Appeals that heard cases from all over the Deep South. What surprised many was his attitude and rulings on civil rights matters. During the 1955 Montgomery boycott Fred Gray, one of two black lawyers in the city, filed a case on behalf of Aurelia S. Browder and 11 other women challenging the city segregation ordinances that applied to transport. Frank Johnson was one of the three judges who would hear the case. Johnson and Justice Richard Rives in *Browder v Gayle* ruled in a two-to-one decision which attacked the *Plessy v Ferguson* decision of the Supreme Court of 1896. They argued 'that the separate but equal doctrine can no longer be followed as a correct statement of law'. Montgomery did not appreciate the liberal views of the judge.

'Behind his back and in the press, he and his rulings were subjected to vitriolic abuse; relations with certain employees cooled noticeably; and at times even his friends and employees were made to feel community resentment' (Yarborough, 1981).

Johnson was a judge and as such he did not need to pander to the baser instincts of the white voters. He found himself in a situation where he was confronted by politicians who realised that defying the courts was an easy way to win votes. It was not only his old law school friend George Wallace who was eagerly soliciting the segregationist vote. John Patterson, who had defeated Wallace in the 1958 Democratic primary, used the slogan 'law and order' as a means of attacking the law and the courts. Johnson was willing to confront Patterson and Wallace, who sought to impede the work of the Civil Rights Commission. The Commission was meeting in Alabama following the Civil Rights Act of 1957, seeking to find information about voting discrimination in the state. When Patterson and Wallace sought to defy the Commission and prevent them from gaining access to the records, Johnson issued orders requiring the officials to comply with a subpoena that necessitated officials to give evidence. Wallace continued in his defiance and Johnson cited him for contempt of court and threatened to jail him. Wallace, playing to the segregationist sentiment, was eventually tried and found not guilty. But Johnson was concerned that the show of defiance was threatening judicial authority. As a state judge, Wallace had made many public statements about his determination to defy the federal court but had secretly assisted the Commission. Johnson commented that 'this court refuses to allow its authority and dignity to be bent or swayed by such politically generated whirlwinds' (Yarborough, 1981).

Although not sympathetic to the Freedom Riders, Johnson insisted that Alabama African Americans should have the right to vote and to attend an integrated school. In 1963 Wallace, now Governor, was determined not only to keep the University of Alabama all white but to thwart efforts to desegregate city schools in the state. The major confrontation took place at Huntsville, where Governor Wallace had sent state troopers to surround the high school. The parents condemned Wallace's grandstanding and the Montgomery *Advertiser* lamented his actions and asserted: 'Alabama is not a banana republic'. Johnson was one of several federal judges who signed a restraining order against Wallace. Johnson thwarted

Wallace in his campaign and continued to issue orders enjoining universities and schools to obey the *Brown* decision. In November, Auburn University was ordered to admit Harold Franklin, an African American graduate student.

Johnson found himself in the national spotlight again with the march from Selma to Montgomery. The Freedom March was an opportunity for Wallace to play the race card yet again. For Martin Luther King Jr it was an opportunity to expose the denial of the vote for African Americans in the South. The violent beatings of the marchers by Sheriff Clark swept around the nation and led to national and international protests. Johnson issued an order to stop further marches. Wallace and King were party to an agreement that would allow a symbolic march in defiance of the court order. Eventually Johnson agreed with the NAACP Legal Defense Fund and approved a route for the marchers and required Wallace to provide protection. It was because the marchers were seeking the right to vote that persuaded Johnson that King's tactics were right (Yarborough, 1981).

However, Johnson was not an uncritical sympathiser. He was concerned about the wider implications of civil disobedience. He maintained: 'The philosophy that a person may – if his cause is labelled "civil rights" or "states rights" – determine for himself what laws and court decisions are morally right or wrong and either obey or refuse to obey them according to his own determination, is a philosophy that is foreign to our "rule-of-law" theory of government' (Yarborough, 1981).

Johnson remained in the firing line. He was the judge who presided over the trial of the murderers of Mrs Viola Liuzzo and he played a major part in ensuring that the jury would eventually convict the murderers. His struggle for justice and civil rights led to a sweeping attack in 1972 on the abuses that occurred in the state mental health institutions, which he denounced as 'human warehouses'. He ordered Governor Wallace to comply with strict standards for care and treatment of patients, set up human rights committees for each hospital and granted them sweeping powers to ensure the protection of patients. Also in 1972, in *Newman v Alabama*, Johnson ordered that the shocking neglect of prisoners' medical care should cease, he laid down minimum conditions for prisoners and set up human rights committees to ensure that his order was fulfilled.

Ignored by Richard Nixon, who was intent on pursuing a southern strategy which did not include liberal Republicans such as Johnson, it was Democrat Jimmy Carter who saw the merits of this remarkable judge. The FBI had suffered from its involvement in the Watergate break-ins and cover-up and desperately needed new leadership. Carter offered the post to Johnson. Owing to ill health and two operations, he asked Carter to withdraw his name from nomination. After he had recovered it was Carter who promoted him to the Fifth Circuit Court of Appeal. Ironically, in 1979 it was one of the politicians who had attacked the courts and Johnson's rulings, John Patterson, who praised his civil rights role and inducted Johnson into the Alabama Academy of Honor (Yarborough, 1981).

The Students

It was African American women and men who led the struggle for justice in the civil rights movement, especially students from the state-sponsored black colleges and universities. Their struggle inspired many young white southerners to challenge the myths that their parents had elaborately woven to ensure the rule of white supremacy. Just as much as the politicians and judges, these young white southerners were prepared to challenge the South, its traditions and more importantly to question the authority of their families, religious leaders and educators.

Judge Johnson's son was one such student. While at the University of Alabama, Johnny Johnson led the Young Democrats in 1968 and he and his fellow Democrats endorsed the campaign of Eugene McCarthy. George Wallace was campaigning with the aid of state officials when the Young Democrats passed a resolution that the state employees should return to their jobs and Wallace could stay away from the state as long as he wished.

However, Johnson Jr had the example and support of his mother and father, who faced constant controversy for their civil rights stand. Others had much greater challenges. They were all part of the longer tradition of southern radicals as represented by Carl and Anne Braden, James Dombrowski and Myles Horton. But these young southerners are barely mentioned by historians of radicalism.

Moreover, in a recent study of the movement the reader is assured that apart from 'islands' such as Austin, Texas, New Orleans, Louisiana, and Atlanta, Georgia, southerner students were not merely untouched by but were positively antagonistic to the radical movement against the war in Vietnam, the free speech movement, women's rights and gay rights. The author states: 'In 1968 two movies were popular: *The Graduate* was a hit in large liberal cities, while *The Green Berets* played to crowds in small-town America. Few southern universities witnessed demonstrations' (Anderson, 1995). White students not only participated in the civil rights movement but also many became activists in their opposition to the war in Vietnam, and extended their civil rights activity to include women, gays and any group they considered victims of repression.

The response of southern students to the struggle of African Americans for justice was just as complex as the response of their parents. The South was not solid. Students at the University of North Carolina at Chapel Hill participated in the movement and Ralph Allan was a member of SNCC. In 1961 white students at Presbyterian and Baptist seminaries were arrested for taking part in sit-ins in Louisville, Kentucky. White and black students participated in sit-in demonstrations in Nashville, Tennessee (*The Student Voice*, April and May 1961). A year before the students at the University of Tennessee at Knoxville had petitioned the trustees, asking them to integrate the University, and the board complied with the students' wishes. Myles Horton of the Highlander Folk School in Monteagle, Tennessee, organised a workshop on 'The Role of the Student in the Changing South'. The workshop, held on 11–13 November 1960, was attended by 80 students from black and white universities throughout the South.

Bob Zellner was typical of the white students who became involved in the civil rights movement. The son of a Methodist minister he was raised in Alabama and attended Huntington College in Montgomery, Alabama. In recalling the segregated society of his youth he commented: 'It was just the way things were. You didn't think about it. Sometimes when you are inside the system, you can't see it very well. But children are not born racists. They are taught to have racial attitudes' (Morrison and Morrison, 1987). His interest in and sympathy for the civil rights struggle resulted in the Ku Klux Klan burning crosses at the College. He refused to resign from the College, graduated, joined SNCC and found himself in jail when working on voter registration in McComb, Mississippi, and took part in a march to protest against the murder of a black SNCC worker. At first Zellner did not want to take part in the planned protest. He realised that the young black students were leading the first protest march in Mississippi since Reconstruction and that if they failed they would lose everything. He joined the march and was subjected to extreme violence.

Zellner was also at the Freedom March from Selma to Montgomery. As he recalled later: 'My parents supported me, but it was very alarming to my mother. She was always pleading with me to be careful.' She had good reason: Zellner's grandfather and uncle were members of the Ku Klux Klan and had threatened to murder him. Later he was present at the Danville, Virginia, protest in 1963, which resulted in the hospitalisation of hundreds of activists.

Ironically, just as more young southerners were prepared to challenge the southern power structure of white supremacy, black southerners became increasingly wary of cooperating with whites. During the Freedom Summer of 1964 many blacks in the movement resented the attitude of many of the white northern students. Although Zellner was excluded from the criticism because he was a southerner and 'just one of the niggers', it was decided to exclude whites from SNCC. As a charter member of the organisation and one who had happily taken beatings and imprisonment for the struggle, he was told he could remain on the staff, attend meetings but not vote. Zellner refused. He believed 'it was a mistake. It was playing into the hands of the enemy to have a formal exclusion of whites from SNCC.' Despite his personal disappointment he refused to be bitter (Morrison, 1987).

The emergence of Black Power came when a significant minority of southern white students were seeking to bridge the gap and were willing to take up the challenge. Although excluded from SNCC and CORE with the rising tide of black nationalism, these white southern students participated in or were influenced by the civil rights struggle and they continued the fight for reform. After leaving SNCC Zellner assisted Carl and Anne Braden and SCEF, working with white and black pulpwood cutters who had formed in 1967 the Gulfcoast Pulpwood Association, many of whose members earned less than $3000 a year. On 23 September 1971 in Laurel, Mississippi, Charles Evers, the African American Mayor of Fayette, Mississippi, and the independent candidate for Governor, addressed a rally organised by Zellner of workers who were involved in a four-year strike against the Masonite Corporation. The president of the Association was James Simmons of Forest Home, Alabama. Evers told the strikers, 'I've always known that the poor black and poor white would some day get together. Thank God, it's beginning here in Jones County.' White pulpwood worker Juston Pulliam agreed with Evers and Zellner: 'People are beginning to see that rich people are out for just one thing – more money. The only way to stop it is for all the poor people to get together, no matter what color their skin is. Black and white is brothers' (*New York Times*, 24 September 1971).

Some southern students, like those from eastern and northern universities, adopted the tactics of nonviolent disobedience to oppose the war in Vietnam. Virtually all college campuses in the South saw a remarkable amount of dissent and it was the work of these activists that has been largely ignored. Radical activism was a feature of many southern campuses in the South. This included underground newspapers, cooperatives, as well as educational and social reform. In Knoxville, Tennessee, between 1968 and 1980 there were several radical student and community papers, such as *Paperbag, Up-Country Revival, Libra, Bad News, Rhapsody* and the *Knoxville Gazette*. All of them reported on women's and gay liberation and radical activities in the South and the nation. Like students in the North and West, radical activists were in a minority but they played a significant role in many aspects of the movement in the history of 1960s and 1970s radicalism.

There were students who opposed the war in Vietnam. In 1966 University of Tennessee (UT) students set up the Vietnam Education Group and many of its members had been involved in the civil rights movement in Mississippi, Tennessee and Georgia. The majority of those involved in the anti-war demonstrations were from Tennessee and other southern states. For example, John Z. C. Thomas was a graduate student from Montgomery, Alabama, David W. Bowen was from Memphis, Tennessee, where in 1965 he ensured the integration of the city swimming pools, and Tom Wilson, from Mississippi, had defended the right of African Americans to attend Mississippi State University. Most of the 500 students who demonstrated against the visit of Lieutenant General Lewis Hershey, Director of the Selective Service, were Tennesseans. The protesters issued a statement not only attacking Johnson for betraying his promises of peace and a Great Society but also for failing to reform the Selective Service, which 'places an unjustly large burden of this war on the poor, the disadvantaged and the black man'. These students were joined by many more in a memorial service held in honour of Martin Luther King Jr after his assassination in Memphis in April 1968. When Ralph Abernathy led the Poor People's March on Washington through Knoxville, the students helped with the housing and feeding of the marchers.

The free speech movement that had swept through the University of California at Berkeley also affected universities in the South. The response of southern university administrators was the same as that in California. The president of Auburn University, Alabama, banned the anti-war activist, the Reverend William Sloane Coffin, who had been invited by the students. Tennessee banned the drugs advocate Dr Timothy Leary. Students and faculty at both universities sued for and won an open speaker policy.

The argument over speaker policy reflected the growing concern among senior administrators at the increasing radicalism on the campus. Efforts by students to establish a UT chapter of the Southern Student Organizing Committee (SSOC) were temporarily thwarted. However, a chapter was functioning by 1968 and SSOC, along with a 'hippie' group calling themselves the Big Oranges for a Democratic Society, led demonstrations against attempts by the university to enforce its *in loco parentis* policy.

Student power, the anti-war movement, and racial justice were common themes for students at UT and universities in other southern states. In the same year, Nixon ordered the invasion of Cambodia and was bitterly opposed, not only on northern and so-called liberal campuses, but throughout the South. And the killing of students at Kent State University in Ohio on 4 May 1970 saw student strikes sweep across the nation, including the South. At UT, led by Jimmie Baxter, the first black student president of a predominantly white university, 70 per cent of the students supported strike action following the Kent State killings. They protested also at the murder of six black people by the National Guard in Augusta, Georgia. At least 31 universities and colleges were hit by strikes. National Guardsmen, this time unarmed, removed student activists from the University of South Carolina campus and a 100-man police riot team quelled riots at the University of Alabama at Tuscaloosa. Classes were cancelled at Florida, Florida State and

Miami Universities. In North Carolina violent protests were held at Chapel Hill and Duke University and a strike at the University of Virginia was reported by the students as '80 per cent effective'.

Nixon and his staff were badly shaken by the protests and the President needed to be seen on a university campus. The evangelist Billy Graham had hired the football stadium at UT, Knoxville, for a revival meeting, despite doubts about such religious rallies being held on University property. Graham declared the meeting of 28 May 1970 a youth festival and invited Nixon to the campus. Most anti-war activists realised the dangers of this provocation but 1500 activists attended the rally carrying signs with the commandment 'Thou Shalt Not Kill'. Gus Hadorn, a student from Sweetwater, Tennessee, recalled, 'On that particular day, I saw a lot of people that had come to the Billy Graham Crusade with hate in their eyes' (*Esquire*, September 1970). After Nixon and his entourage and the national media circus had left town the police set about arresting students and faculty who had participated in the protest.

The faculty protested against the arrests but the UT lawyer announced that he was investigating faculty for misconduct and threatened to fire them. The student newspaper attacked the proposed witch-hunt, as did the faculty senate, and there were no dismissals. Dan Pomeroy on behalf of the history graduate students attacked the Board of Trustees' actions. He pointed out: 'As graduate students, we are intensely interested in working for excellence in this university and resent the fact that not only are the students denied an effective voice in working for that change, but that change in general is now suspect on this campus' (Riches, 1987).

These southern students in Knoxville, Jackson, Chapel Hill and even in Oxford, Mississippi, stood against the prevailing mores of the South and their families on issues of peace, racial equality, gay rights, the women's movement and the rights of the poor. Their story has been ignored by historians of the civil rights movement. They shared most of the aspirations of many radical students in America. The ripples on the pond set in motion by the civil rights struggle affected all parts and all persons of the nation.

7

RIPPLES FROM THE POND

The civil rights struggle was a coalition of African American men and women who, in cooperation with their white female and male supporters, sought to bring about the second Reconstruction that would assure black Americans that they were American citizens. It was the shared experiences of the struggle that influenced other civil rights groups of the 1960s and 1970s. It was the success of these groups which led to a backlash which continues to dominate the political discourse in the 1990s.

African American Women

Once African Americans refused to accept their segregated, inferior status the impact was widespread and the ripples were felt by all sectors of American society. In the movement, women were often treated as second-class citizens. It was black men who saw themselves as the leaders and it was white male politicians and press that focused on the role of these men, such as Martin Luther King Jr, Ralph Abernathy, John Lewis and Robert Moses. Black nationalism reinforced this secondary status for women. It was the conventional view of historians and sociologists that the black male had suffered the most from the institution of slavery. The male slave's leadership in a patriarchal society had always been denied because the institution of marriage was forbidden. The ultimate power always rested with the master not the slave. Black nationalists took particular exception to this view, as expressed in the 1965 report *Negro Family* authored by Daniel Patrick Moynihan. 'In essence the

Negro community,' according to Moynihan, 'has been forced into a matriarchal structure which, because it is out of line with the rest of American society, seriously retards the progress of the group as a whole and imposes a crushing burden on the Negro male and, in consequence, on a great many Negro women as well.' As Davis argues: 'The controversial finale of the Moynihan Report was a call to introduce male authority (meaning male supremacy of course!) into the Black family and the community at large' (Davis, 1994). Paula Giddings points out, 'The Moynihan Report was not so much racist as it was sexist' (Giddings, 1984).

It was not only white sociologists such as Moynihan who sought to reinforce or introduce patriarchy, but it was also the exponents of Black Power in the later sixties in SNCC and other organisations such as the Nation of Islam, or Black Muslims. Angela Davis was criticised by black cultural nationalist leader Ron Karenga in San Diego for taking an active role in organising a rally in 1967: 'A woman was supposed to "inspire" her man and educate his children'. She recalls that when she had a prominent role with SNCC in Los Angeles this caused resentment: 'By playing such a leading role in the organization, some of them insisted, we were aiding and abetting the enemy, who wanted to see Black men weak and unable to hold their own' (Davis, 1988).

Paula Giddings shows that Black Muslims 'in an era of male revolt' insisted that black women should be 'submissive' and that black men should not allow black women on the streets alone because Elijah Muhammad, the spiritual leader of the Muslims, maintained females are 'given to evil and sin while men are noble and given to righteousness'. She attacks the views of Imamu Amiri Baraka (LeRoy Jones), who had also demanded that black women should be submissive to the 'wiser' black man. According to Giddings, 'It was but a short step from this sort of thinking to advocate that women remain politically barefoot and literally pregnant' (Giddings, 1984). As Davis discovered during her work for SNCC in Los Angeles: 'It was a period in which one of the unfortunate hallmarks of some nationalist groups was their determination to push women into the background' (Davis, 1988).

When they first became involved in the civil rights movement African American women were not gender conscious but rather they were concerned with the struggle for justice and liberty for all – male and female. In these early years, women and men put their bodies (literally) on the line when they challenged the white supremacy of the South. When civil rights activists called for 'jail no bail' they did not suggest that this applied to men only and, as Cynthia Fleming argues, black women were impatient with the complaints of white women in 1964 that they were only doing menial tasks. Black SNCC staffer Cynthia Washington told Fleming that the grumbling of Casey Hayden did not make sense to her because she had her own project. 'What Casey and other white women seemed to want was an opportunity to prove that they could do something other than office work. I assumed that if they could do something else they'd probably be doing that' (Fleming, 1994).

It is this tradition of female participation combined with encouragement of education among black women, something that had been traditionally discouraged among white women, that led to tensions with the women's movement. Failure to understand the reasons for the relative success of black women faced with the double discrimination of being black and a woman meant that 'the women's movement and the Black movement failed to benefit from the valuable lessons inherent in that achievement. Consequently, the failure effectively to challenge Moynihan's solution, with all its implications, retarded both movements' (Giddings, 1984).

Black women's ambivalence about black male leadership was a source of difficulty. While they were willing, even eager, to criticise white leaders, it has been claimed that African American women deferred to the black ministers who led the movement, and even if they criticised male activists they were willing to accept their leadership. Anne Standley's explanation for this behaviour is that black women 'did not consider themselves oppressed by black men either in or out of the movement, and in some respects believed that black men were worse off than black women' (Crawford *et al.*, 1993). In these early years, women of colour were concerned about race, not gender. It was their experience in the movement and the growing rivalries with white women that made them much more conscious of gender issues.

The Women's Movement

As early as 1964 the white women in the civil rights movement, such as Casey Hayden and Mary King, questioned the role of male leadership in SNCC and they circulated a letter to women in SNCC and SDS arguing that there were parallels in the plight of women and the treatment of blacks and that both were the victims of a caste system. When women tried to raise the issue at an SDS conference in 1965 they were howled off the platform by the white male radicals. At the annual meeting in 1967 women were given another hostile reception when they tried to raise the issue of equality. But for women such as Mary King, 'civil rights issues are at the core of the women's movement'.

Influenced by the civil rights movement, Betty Freidan, Pauli Murray, Mary Eastwood and Kathryn Clarenbach established the National Organization for Women (NOW), demanding that Title VII of the Civil Rights Act outlawing discrimination against women should be enforced, that women should control the reproductive rights of contraception and abortion, and that there should be an Equal Rights Amendment. The last idea was first proposed in 1923 (Anderson, 1995). They described NOW as the 'NAACP for women' (Giddings, 1984).

In 1968, growing anger with male chauvinism in the anti-war movement encouraged women to hold their own peace demonstration and to bury 'Traditional Womanhood' in the Arlington Cemetery. They protested also at the Miss America pageant, declaring that it was degrading for women, that it was an all-white, racist event in which the winner went to Vietnam to entertain American troops. By 1969 the term 'women's liberation' was used throughout America. As Terry Anderson points out, women in Milwaukee were not allowed at a lunch counter in one restaurant because men required the faster service 'because they have important business to do'. Women were deemed unfit to run marathons, were prone to hysteria, and their best place was in the kitchen or bed. It is hardly surprising that in the same year Gayle Rubin was publishing a pamphlet about 'Woman as Nigger'. It was not until the 1970s that the women's liberation movement gathered mass support (Anderson, 1995).

Women organised support groups, held conferences, and sought to redefine themselves and their roles in society. The stress was on women's autonomy – 'the personal as political'. Women exposed the caste system that led to second-class citizenship. They attacked the teaching of history and renamed it herstory. They fought for an end to discrimination in hiring, not only in the professions but in blue-collar jobs and in the military. Although 40 per cent of women worked outside the home in 1970 they were confined largely to menial service work. In their struggle for equality they met fierce resistance from the Nixon administration, which in 1970 promised to enforce affirmative action over race but refused to consider the issue of gender.

The Equal Opportunities Commission was equally lax. It was not only in employment that women were denied equal pay for equal work. In many states women were considered in law unfit to handle their own finances. Male co-signers were required if they wanted to hire a car or buy a house. Women in Arizona were labelled criminals if they used obscene language; in law husbands could not be punished for raping their wives; in Kentucky only a man could get a divorce on the grounds of adultery; and in Rhode Island it was legal for a man to 'chastise' his wife. Many states refused single women the right to use contraception and they were denied the right of abortion even though in 1968 it was estimated that there were one million abortions, of which 1000 had resulted in the death of the woman.

Betty Freidan was the initial advocate of reform. She was suspicious of support from lesbian women, whom she dubbed the 'lavender menace' (Miller, 1995). It is therefore not surprising that the group who established Redstockings favoured separatism. 'Women radicals, therefore, turned the tables on radical men: They acted like men, confronting the culture, shocking the movement, shouting out for liberation, calling for separatism, and along the way they became radical women' (Anderson, 1995).

What were the gains of the movement? Legislation that had been passed by men denying women the right to work in the mines, or at hard manual labour, was rewritten. The military, which had excluded women as front-line fighters in the army, navy and air force, was forced to revise its rules. However, the Equal Rights Amendment failed in the growing backlash. There were disputes with church leaders and former civil rights activists over the issue of abortion. The Supreme Court had given the women's movement perhaps its greatest successes, especially in matters of reproduction. In 1965 the Supreme Court in *Griswold v Connecticut* legalised distribution of contraceptives to married women, and in *Eisenstadt v Baird* gave the same rights to all individuals. In 1973, in the case of *Roe v Wade*, the Court legalised abortion throughout the United

States, arguing that a woman's right to terminate a pregnancy was fundamental. Twenty years later feminists argued reproduction was 'socially gendered. Women are raped and coerced into sex.' Catherine MacKinnon argues that: 'Reproduction in the lives of women is a far larger and more diverse experience than the focus on abortion has permitted'. She maintains that:

> Because the social organization of reproduction is a major bulwark of women's social equality, any constitutional inter-pretation of a sex equality principle must prohibit laws, state policies, or official practices and acts that deprive women of reproductive control or punish women for their reproductive role or capacity. (Kauffman, 1993)

The Equal Rights Amendment (ERA), which was passed with overwhelming support in the Senate in 1972, was attacked by Phyllis Schafly, founder of the Stop ERA movement and a 'brilliant debater and organizer backed by well-financed right-wing groups'. She succeeded and the Amendment was never ratified. The NOW response to the Schafly onslaught was to water down 'feminist ideas to make them more palatable to those women who were desperately clinging to their pedestals' (Giddings, 1984). Other women spoke out in defence of the 'traditional' role of women and attacked the feminist movement. Anita Bryant, a singer, led the crusade against sexual liberation.

However, it was men who led the backlash. John Wilke not only opposed ERA but set up the National Right to Life group, which opposed abortion. It was Joseph Scheidler who wrote the text for the militant anti-abortion movement and Randall Terry who was a major leader of Operation Rescue, a militant anti-abortion group. Male fundamentalist preachers such as the Reverend Jerry Falwell attacked immorality in society which he claimed was partly due to women rebelling against their 'natural roles'. The New Right's assaults were laced with religious zealotry. Ronald Reagan did not hesitate to exploit the backlash. In this he had enthusiastic support from the male-dominated media and universities. Whereas in the 1970s and 1980s it had been difficult to challenge affirmative action on the grounds of race, white males felt no inhibitions in attacking affirmative action when it was seen to benefit females (Faludi, 1993).

It was race that also weakened the women's movement. Angela Davis was not the only one to attack racism shown by feminists (Davis, 1983). Although Aileen Hernandez, a black woman, took over the leadership of NOW from Betty Freidan, 'the perception of the women's movement in general, disturbed Black women' (Giddings, 1984). 'What drew me to politics was my love of women,' writes Cherríe Moraga, 'the agony I felt in observing the straight-jackets of poverty and repression I saw people in my own family in. But the deepest political tragedy I have experienced is how with such grace, such blind faith, this commitment to women in the feminist movement grew to be exclusive and reactionary. I call my white sisters on this' (Moraga and Anzalúda, 1983). This traditional hostility was not helped in that many black women saw the women's movement as exploiting the civil rights movement at a time when African Americans were finding it increasingly difficult to gain sympathy for their cause. In addition, it was feared that any advance for white women would be gained at the expense of black men and black women. For many black activists the women's movement was a white gender quarrel and blacks would be better off if they stayed out of it. Many black women did not like the shrill tone of the feminist movement. Ida Lewis said: 'If we speak of a liberation movement, as a Black woman I view my role from a Black perspective – the role of Black women is to continue the struggle in concert with Black men for the liberation and determination of Blacks' (Giddings, 1984).

For most white feminists the right to abortion was paramount. It was this demand that made many women of colour reluctant to join the feminist movement. White feminists were accused of ignoring medical history in the United States where contraception, abortion and sterilisation were seen by many in the medical profession and advocates of eugenics as the ideal way to prevent reproduction in ethnic groups or those they considered mental defectives. If they had been sensitive to the concerns of the people of colour, Davis argues, 'young white feminists might have been more receptive to the suggestion that their campaign for abortion rights include a vigorous condemnation of sterilization abuse, which had become more widespread than ever'. In 1972 the HEW Director of Population Affairs Office estimated that the federal government had funded between 100 000 and 200 000 sterilisations in that year alone (Davis, 1983).

Many of the disputes between black women and white feminists surfaced during the 1972 presidential campaign of the African American Shirley Chisholm. As the first black woman in Congress, Chisholm of New York symbolised the new politics of the 1970s. As an early member of NOW and the National Women's Political Caucus, it seemed as though she had certain constituencies at her command. Although her failure was partly due to lack of finance, disorganisation and lack of preparation, it also 'revealed the shortcomings of the Black and feminist movements, shortcomings that would be fundamentally damaging to both'. Betty Freidan and Gloria Steinem, both members of NOW and the Caucus, failed to give enthusiastic support to Chisholm's candidacy and only reluctantly came out in her favour after the two male candidates were not sound on women's issues. 'But the belated support for Chisholm was too slight to have any impact. The lesson that could be learned was that Black women also figured slightly in the priorities of the leaders of the women's movement' (Giddings, 1984).

It was not just white women who failed to support Chisholm, it was also black men. Black political leaders such as Julian Bond, Richard Hatcher, Mayor of Gary, Indiana, Jesse Jackson of Chicago, and Clarence Mitchell of Atlanta met with other men, such as Baraka, and they considered three options: to run 'favourite son' candidates in several states, to support George McGovern or to back a black candidate. None of those present at the Chicago meeting supported a black woman, Shirley Chisholm. Her defence of Angela Davis, in prison on charges of 'murder, kidnapping and conspiracy', did not win her support either. Ironically, given its extreme sexism, it was the male-dominated Black Panther party that was the major group in the black community which endorsed Chisholm's candidacy. 'She concluded that the failure of her campaign was due more to sexism than racism, and the realization was demoralizing'. In 1983 Chisholm did not seek re-election to the House of Representatives (Giddings, 1984).

Although the women's movement failed with ERA and it engendered a backlash, women did see improvements in their status in the United States. Women and African Americans were not the only ones to challenge traditional roles that had been imposed in a white-male-dominated culture. As women raised questions about sexuality and gender, those who rejected the dominant heterosexual society also sought to free themselves and assert their homosexuality and lesbianism. Rita Mae Brown, a lesbian feminist, asserted that she became a lesbian because 'the culture that I live in is violently anti-woman. How could I, a woman, participate in a culture that denies my humanity?... To give a man support and love before giving it to a sister is to support that culture, that power system' (Faderman, 1992). Just as the slogan in the African American community was 'Black Power', it soon became 'Gay Power' in the homosexual community.

Gay Liberation

Gay liberation was part of the wider sexual revolution which had dramatically transformed sex relations in the so-called 'straight' community. The arguments were that homosexuality was not only natural but also good. Many of those who wrote in defence of homosexuals pointed out that it had always existed and that often, historically, it had been the preferred relationship. It was important that people should have the freedom to choose their relationships and as a result of that free choice they should also be free to live openly gay lives. All acts between consenting adults should be legalised and the social discrimination faced by gays should end (Miller, 1991).

Just when gays were demanding equality and their civil rights, the New York police in June 1969 raided the Stonewall, a gay bar in Greenwich Village. Although this was not the first raid on a gay bar it was 'the first time in memory, gay men stood and fought back'. In the second raid the following night there were pitched battles between the police and men and women, and as the police charged into the crowd the crowd chanted 'Gay Power' (Anderson, 1995). A few weeks after the raid the underground newspaper *Rat* reported the formation of the Gay Liberation Front, which had a militant programme: 'We are a revolutionary homosexual group of men and women formed with the realization that complete sexual liberation for all people cannot come about unless existing social institutions are abolished' (Miller, 1991).

Although the Gay Liberation Front had its most active chapters in the large cities of the east and west coast, even in the smaller towns across the country men and women were prepared to come out of the closet. An underground newspaper, *Libra,* in Knoxville, Tennessee, in December 1970 and February 1971 published long articles supporting the goals of the Gay Liberation Front. Five years later another underground paper urged the gay community to vote Republican for mayor because the Democrat had harassed 'members of the counter culture' (*Longstreet Journal,* 29 October 1975).

In many southern towns there were gay bars which operated openly, unlike the earliest gay bar in Knoxville, which had always been very discreet. But the gay bar movement increased as a result of the New York raid. Over 50 different organisations were established to protest on behalf of the homosexual community. The subject of homosexuality was treated in journals such as *Time* magazine and at the first anniversary of the Stonewall raid 10 000 people paraded up New York's Sixth Avenue.

Despite this new-found self-confidence, gay men and women were – and are – subject to discrimination and the danger of random attack from the public and police. The medical profession in many instances continued to stigmatise homosexuality as a disease: it was not until 1973 that the American Psychiatric Association stopped listing homosexuality this way. All Christian churches rejected homosexuality as a sin. The American military had often been tolerant of gays, especially during World War II, although it was sometimes denied that lesbianism actually existed in the armed forces. There were occasional searches for 'homosexual addicts' but very few men or women were dismissed from the military because of their sexuality. Such tolerance did not last after the war and homosexuals were often dismissed as security risks (Faderman, 1992). More recently, President Bill Clinton failed to keep his pledge to remove restrictions on homosexuals in the armed forces, partly because of the bitter resistance of the African American General Colin Powell, head of the Joint Chiefs of Staff (Miller, 1995).

Such hostility from an African American is not surprising; after all, they were concerned about their own status in America and many were as intolerant of homosexuals as most white men. In the play *The Toilet* LeRoy Jones (Baraka) shares the negative response of black nationalists to homosexuality. A homosexual relationship between a black boy and a white boy is used to symbolise the wider conflict between the races in America. In the play black youths allow the white boy to leave but savagely beat the black youth. When interviewed Baraka said that his only regret was that the white youth was not also beaten. Any possibility of a link with the broader civil rights movement was generally resisted. However, it should be stressed that Martin Luther King Jr knew that a friend and adviser, Bayard Rustin, was homosexual and a former communist. King continued to work with and consider Rustin as his friend despite pressure from friends and supporters of black civil rights who were concerned that the media would use this knowledge to destroy the civil rights leader (Garrow, 1988). In their efforts to 'expose King for the clerical fraud and Marxist he is,' the FBI used wiretaps on the civil rights leader and his associates, and provided detailed background reports on them for the Kennedy White House. As early as August 1963 one memorandum had four pages of 'derogatory information' on Bayard Rustin. In addition, reports on Rustin and others were circulated to the media in an attempt to discredit King (O'Reilly, 1994). The FBI also gave information to Senator Strom Thurmond, who read the details of Rustin's arrest on a morals charge into the Congressional Record (Miller, 1995).

Just as in the civil rights and women's movements, there were divisions in the gay movement. Middle-class white men, concerned about the radicalism of the Gay Liberation Front, broke away and formed the Gay Activists Alliance, and the Gay Pride Rally in 1973 was marked by bitter in-fighting. However, there were notable examples of cooperation between lesbians and gay men. When singer and entertainer Anita Bryant launched her Save Our Children campaign against homosexuals, lesbians and gay men counter-attacked and even boycotted the Florida orange juice she advertised and forced the company to cancel her contract. In California in 1978 state congressman John Briggs wanted the state to stop hiring and to dismiss teachers who were homosexual. The New Alliance for Gay Equality ensured that the proposal was defeated. But despite this cooperation, which was mirrored in other cities, there were increasing tensions between lesbian feminists and gay men. For the feminists these gay men were as chauvinist as any straight men. 'Lesbian-feminists insisted that they were not the "ladies auxiliary of the gay movement." The slogan became: "We are angry, not gay"' (Miller, 1995). They did not support changes in the law which permitted promiscuity; they especially disliked the dominant–submissive roles that shaped male gay culture and in 1977 lesbian feminists held a separate event to commemorate the

Stonewall rally. As in the civil rights movement, there were separatists who advocated complete rejection of a society dominated by males, straight or gay. Many feminists withdrew into communes (Faderman, 1992). This communitarian movement had been a feature of sixties radicalism. For Jill Johnston, lesbians should concentrate on building a lesbian nation. 'If gay men created a community that seemed to mirror mainstream society, lesbians tried to forge one that was more utopian, more in line with counter-cultural values' (Miller, 1995).

The first cases of AIDS were reported in 1981, although originally it was thought to be a 'gay cancer'. The first article, by Larry Kramer, warning about the new disease was published the same year. At first the reaction was denial, and then when the test proved its existence, by the late 1980s 'with so little progress being made and the Reagan administration seeming so uncaring, the accommodation to the dailiness of AIDS gave way to a wave of anger and protest' (Miller, 1995).

The epidemic spread rapidly. In April 1983, 1300 were infected and the official figures had increased by 1985 to 8797, half of whom had died from the disease. As many as 50 or 60 per cent of the gay men in New York had tested HIV positive. 'But because, for so many homosexual men in the post-Stonewall period, gay identity and culture had been expressed almost entirely in sexual terms, the new disease cut to the very heart of gay liberation. It threatened an entire way of life.' The bathhouse, which had been a popular place for gay and bisexual men to meet, was criticised not only by straights but also by gay activists. The attacks on the bathhouses resulted in their closure. There was a similar decline in the gay bars (Miller, 1995).

Rather than socialise in bathhouses or bars, more and more gay men chose other activities, such as their separate churches, which included the gay Pentacostal churches founded in Oklahoma City, Houston, and Dayton, Ohio. In Washington, DC, black gay men established an evangelical church and gay Jews in San Francisco had a separate synagogue. The AIDS crisis also helped heal the rift between lesbians and gays. The change in focus of gay culture meant that lesbians did not feel so alienated. The result was closer cooperation between lesbians and gays. Just before the death of movie star Rock Hudson, Reagan proposed in his 1986 budget to cut AIDS research. This galvanised the homosexual community into becoming politically active.

While AIDS played a part in overcoming the separatism that had divided the gay community in the 1970s and helped make them politically active, the epidemic also gave powerful ammunition to conservative and religious groups, who 'were quick to take advantage of public concern with AIDS, equating homosexuality and disease' (Miller, 1995). Republican presidential hopeful and newspaper columnist Pat Buchanan led the assault on homosexuals. In 1983 he wrote 'The sexual revolution has begun to devour its children.... The poor homosexuals: they have declared war on nature and nature is exacting an awful retribution' (Miller, 1995). It was a theme he repeated at the Republican national convention in 1992, where he was supported by the conservative evangelist Pat Robertson. Ironically for these conservatives, the National Conservative Political Action Committee had been founded and directed by a gay man, Terry Dolan. This did not stop Dolan from working with the conservative congressman Phil Crane, who had stated in a fundraising letter, 'Our nation's moral fiber is being weakened by the growing homosexual movement and the fanatical ERA pushers many of whom publicly brag they are lesbians'. The founder of the American Conservative Union, Robert Bauman, lost his attempt at re-election to the House after being found guilty in 1980 of soliciting a male prostitute. His later defence of gay rights led to efforts to remove him from the board of the Union. It was increasingly difficult for homosexuals to be conservative because the New Right associated itself with the Moral Majority and its homophobic attitudes (Miller, 1995).

Native Americans

The challenge to segregation and inequality by African Americans had alarmed the same conservative forces that were dismayed at the way in which women and homosexuals challenged the traditional mores of society. A similar threat came with the increasing ethnic consciousness which was part of the reaction to the civil rights movement. The stress was now on the 'hyphenated Americans'. Scholars challenged the traditional view that America was a melting pot in which immigrants had been bound together by blood, history and shared ideals to create a new race – the American. Rather it was pointed out that ethnic groups had remained surprisingly distinctive, that the Irish, Polish, Russian and Italian Americans had kept much of their European culture. In short, the melting pot had only melted at the edges. And in this discovery of their roots, Americans rediscovered the Native Americans, and more importantly the Native Americans discovered themselves. They too were significantly influenced by the African Americans' struggle for justice. Just as the black Americans met resistance, so too would the red.

The National Congress of American Indians (NCAI), established in 1944, was the first pan-Indian movement and it has been suggested that it provided a solid foundation for further pan-Indian politics based on a sense of common racial and cultural ethnicity. The NCAI used the courts to obtain justice in the same way that the NAACP had done for the African American community. They sued state and federal governments over discrimination in employment, fishing rights, over issues involving schooling and the breaking of treaty rights. The successes of the NAACP persuaded NCAI members such as Vine Deloria Jr to go to law school. At a meeting with the head of the NAACP Legal Defense Fund, he saw the opportunity to establish a legal programme in the same way that African Americans had. 'I could see us piling case upon case, precedent upon precedent, until we had forged a new definition of Indian rights'. However, unlike NAACP, it was never the intention of NCIA to seek integration into American society, but rather to ensure Native American cultural integrity.

In 1958 NCIA was successful in preventing the Eisenhower administration from terminating reservation rights. They campaigned for industry and employment on the reservations and gained a pledge from John Kennedy for a programme which would develop the human and natural resources of the reservations. For other groups such as the United Native Americans, cultural centres, fishing and land rights, and education in Indian culture for the young were also the major issues.

As African Americans had had to fight against negative stereotypes of themselves, the same was true for Native Americans. Although hippies were willing to accept the noble savage figure, and to build communes trying to ape Hopi Indian ways, the majority of Americans saw the original inhabitants of their country either as savages to be slaughtered in Hollywood B movies, or as happy servants as portrayed by the television character Tonto in the serial *The Lone Ranger*. As one of them remarked, 'Even the name Indian is not ours. It was given to us by some dumb honky who got lost and thought he'd landed in India' (Anderson, 1995). Such was the contempt for Native Americans that in 1964 the tribes of California were offered 47 cents an acre for the land they had lost to the whites. The figure was arrived at based on the value of the land according to its 1851 market value!

Native Americans were angry about their status in such an affluent society. Half the 700 000 Native American population lived on the reservations, where life was short and hard. Poverty was endemic on the reservations, with unemployment levels ranging from 20 to 80 per cent and where life expectancy was 44 years compared with the national average of 64 in the 1970s. Diseases which no longer troubled most white Americans, such as tuberculosis, continued to kill thousands of Native Americans. Like African Americans between the ages of 16 and 25, Native Americans were prone to suffer from depression and this resulted in a high suicide rate. Housing and education, as for many black Americans, were substandard.

The increased militancy of the 1960s and 1970s was directed against the Bureau of Indian Affairs (BIA), most of whose members were white. The Bureau issued money, controlled education, and had enormous power over the reservations. 'To control Native Americans, officials erected a web of thousands of rules, regulations, laws and court decisions that governed only the tribe.... And Cherokee Robert Thomas declared that the BIA had created "the most complete colonial system in the world"' (Anderson, 1995). Those NCAI leaders who cooperated with the Bureau came under growing suspicion and were called 'Apples' – red on the outside but white on the inside. The same hostility to bourgeois leadership in the African American community was reflected in the term 'Oreo' to describe some black leaders. The name came from an American cookie made up of two chocolate biscuits with white cream in the centre. As black youth referred to some older blacks as 'Uncle Toms', so red youth referred to 'Uncle Tomahawks'.

Native Americans decided to fight back, and the civil rights movement and the student protests of the New Left meant that there were many Americans who were willing to listen. Just as civil rights workers used music to capture the nation's attention and boost their own morale, with songs 'We Shall Overcome', 'Eyes on the Prize', 'Freedom Is a Constant Struggle', and 'Over My Head I See Freedom in the Air' (Seeger and Reiser, 1989), the same was true for the Native American movement. Peter La Farge, a cowboy from Colorado who had been adopted by the Tewa Tribe of the Hopi nation, recorded songs protesting the abuse of Native Americans by whites in a 1968 Folkways recording entitled 'As Long As the Grass Shall Grow'. This was a phrase frequently used in treaties with the Indian nations by white folks, and just as frequently broken by them. Another popular folk singer was Buffy St Marie. Protest was not just left to the singers. In 1969 one NCAI member, Vine Deloria Jr, published *Custer Died For Your Sins*. In the following year Dee Brown published one of the most influential books on Native Americans, *Bury My Heart at Wounded Knee: An Indian History of the American West*.

In 1969, 14 men and women occupied the island of Alcatraz, which had been abandoned as a federal prison six years earlier. The Native Americans offered to buy the island for '$24 in glass beads and cloth', the amount that whites had paid for Manhattan. Their proposal was to turn the prison into a Native American museum and institute. They were refused. Two weeks later 80 returned and occupied the island and were fed by students in the San Francisco Bay area. The numbers grew steadily until several hundred were involved. Eventually over 10 000 Indians visited the island, which even had its own radio station, Radio Free Alcatraz, named after the American government propaganda station Radio Free Europe. Even popular magazines such as *Newsweek* and *Look* were aware of the significance of the Alcatraz occupation.

Red Power

Stokely Carmichael had called for Black Power and had received support from young African Americans in SNCC and the Black Panther party, and the same was true for Native Americans who called for Red Power and had separatist ideas – views strengthened because of the existence of reservations. The complaints against the paternalism and racism of the BIA fuelled a Red Power movement. Many tribes were involved in occupation of federal lands, violating state and federal fishing regulations, and in Maine members of the Passamaquoddy tribe even collected tolls on a busy highway which crossed their land. But the most militant group, the American Indian Movement (AIM), had had its origins in one of the few Native American city ghettos – in the Twin Cities of Minneapolis–St Paul. Faced with police harassment and racial discrimination, young Native Americans set up patrols to monitor the police. Founded by Chippewa Clyde Bellecourt in 1968, these patrols, with men dressed in red berets and jackets, led to a dramatic decline in arrests of Indians (Anderson, 1995). The Indian population in the local jails fell by 60 per cent. But AIM also sought to improve the housing, education and employment of Indians in the city. Such goals would be achieved, they believed, only if Indians in Minneapolis had pride in their heritage and had positive images about their people.

In the 1970s with the growth of Red Power it seemed that anything was possible and that a group such as AIM would benefit. Initially it did. From 1969 to 1970 they established 18 chapters and were no longer a ghetto organisation but also encompassed many still on the reservations. In 1971 they held their first national convention, where they stressed tribal nationhood, treaty violations and the need for positive images. The last issue meant attacks on the portrayal of Native Americans in history and art, the end of Indian mascots and criticism of the names of the National Football League team, the Washington Redskins, and the Atlanta Braves baseball team.

AIM, along with other Indian organisations, took part in the Trail of Broken Treaties to the BIA in Washington, DC. The name came from the removal by President Andrew Jackson of the Cherokee Indians from Georgia–North Carolina border, to what is now Oklahoma in a forced march that became known as the Trail of Tears. AIM activists occupied BIA offices because the Bureau had been working behind the scenes to undermine the effectiveness of the protest, which had considerable support. In searching the files AIM members claimed that if the bureaucrats, mostly white men, were dismissed then the budget could go directly to Indian families, giving them an income of $4000 a year. Although they had gained considerable publicity, the Nixon administration ignored their 20 demands. They were seen by many Indians as dangerous 'revolutionaries'. Mary Black-Rogers writes that Dan Raincloud, an Ojibwa shaman, was invited to a meeting of AIM in 1972 to give prayers to

Indians from 13 states who were preparing to march on Washington, DC, and he was upset at their failure to translate his prayers for the benefit of those from other tribes. He was later concerned at the disruption and destruction of property when they got to the national capital. He believed, 'AIM's militancy was not much favored: it was not doing things in the Indian Way' (Clifton, 1989).

According to Terry Anderson, AIM's last stand at Wounded Knee in 1973 'clearly demonstrated that nationally the movement was in demise'. Unlike the events at Alcatraz, other Indians did not rush to South Dakota and 'it appeared in 1973 that Red Power was on the wane.' His reason for interpreting the occupation as a failure is that only 300 members of AIM participated (Anderson, 1995). On the other hand, that number can be seen as significant. Dee Brown in his widely read Indian history had used the site of the 1890 massacre of the Sioux in South Dakota as part of the title of his book, and the murder of Big Foot's Sioux is the last chapter in his history. Brown also reported that: 'one estimate placed the final total of dead at very nearly three hundred of the original 350 men, women, and children' (Brown, 1991).

AIM not only confronted the BIA and poor policing on the reservation, they also challenged an elected tribal leader, Richard Wilson. In an attempt to win support from traditionalists, AIM proposed a new election for tribal chairman, but Wilson, who was thought of as an 'Apple', refused to quit and called in tribal police to protect BIA property. AIM supporters seized buildings, and Wilson, with the support of the BIA, closed off the reservation. John Mitchell, the United States Attorney General, ordered the arrest of anyone heading towards the reservation, using an anti-riot law which had been passed to curtail the activities of Rap Brown and the Black Panther party.

Despite the obvious divisions among Native Americans, others who had been deeply involved in the civil rights and anti-war movement offered their support. These included Angela Davis, the black communist, and William Kunstler, the legal representative for many radicals such as the Chicago Eight. There were also Hollywood personalities who had been anti-war activists, such as Jane Fonda and Marlon Brando. This was in addition to the widespread sympathy for Native Americans as reflected in public opinion polls.

AIM, like many other groups, was greatly influenced by the media. For television crews the sight of war-painted Indians, the sound of drums and the war chants all made for good television in the same way that any hippie anti-war demonstration invariably dominated the news. One government official dismissed the affair as 'guerrilla theater'. But Wounded Knee, like Kent State in 1970, was a drama that soon became deadly, with sporadic shooting between federal marshals and Indians which left two Indians dead and one marshal paralysed.

It has been suggested that the sixties generation had graduated and that students were interested in getting ahead in their careers in the same way as the fifties generation. 'The 1970s was becoming the Me Decade'. Perhaps this is a better description of the 1980s, but it is true that nationally, not at a state level, activism was on the wane. As Anderson points out: 'Even though surveys demonstrated that college students ranked Native Americans with homosexuals as the groups most oppressed in the nation, there was no outpouring of support, no mass marches, no bus brigades heading for Wounded Knee' (Anderson, 1995).

For women who were Native American and lesbian the prejudices of all the communities and especially their own were immense. Beth Brant, a 52-year-old Seneca lesbian poet captures the despair of being rejected by her own people. Her poem 'Cells' was written while she was in prison for possessing a dangerous weapon. It not only reflects the pain of imprisonment but also the anguish of rejection because of her sexuality and ethnicity. For the men of AIM, women like Beth Brant threatened their warrior ideal in the same way as African American lesbians were seen by black men as a threat to their manhood.

Although the search for ethnic identity had many positive benefits for those who were searching for a new liberal American sense of identity, the same search appealed to those who wanted a return to a golden age as depicted in Norman Rockwell's covers for the popular *Saturday Evening Post*. Often white ethnic movements were conservative, as in the case of the Boston coalition of Catholic Irish and Italians who set up ROAR, Restore our Alienated Rights. They 'conducted the ABC campaign: anti-abortion, anti-bussing, anti-Communism. In an ironic twist, the movement inspired popular participation that contributed to the rise of the New Right' (Anderson, 1995). It was this populism of the New Right that was the driving force behind the George Bush administration, and which has shaped much of the policy of Bill Clinton.

8

BUSH, CLINTON, WILLIE HORTON
AND AMERICAN POLITICS

It was the blue-collar voters who flocked into groups such as Restore Our Alienated Rights whom the Republicans were eager to win over from the Democratic party and in the process unravel the gains made by disadvantaged groups ever since the New Deal of Franklin Roosevelt. For fundamentalists, whether Catholic or Protestant, the anti-abortion, anti-communism and anti-bussing crusade had a national, not merely regional, appeal. According to Howard Zinn, former SNCC activist and anti-Vietnam War protester, this new mood of conservatism which emphasised national unity had been engineered by the 'uneasy club of business executives, generals and politicos'. The elite ensured that the disadvantaged turned their anger against one another: it was poor black students who were bussed into poor, white-neighbourhood schools that were already substandard, while the superior suburban schools remained segregated (Zinn, 1980). The spokesman of this new conservatism was the former congressman, Chief of the Central Intelligence Agency (CIA) and Vice President, George Bush.

Bush was willing to jettison his regional identity as a southerner and even a lot of his past beliefs to achieve his presidential ambition. Fearing that his Democratic opponents, and right-wing forces in the Republican party, would portray him as a 'wimp', Bush claimed to be a native of Texas and was always eager to demonstrate his skill with a gun, as well as forcing journalists into endless hours of early-morning jogging. A man who had supported the ERA, women's right to choose an abortion and federally funded contraceptive services, now opposed all these in order to win the support of the conservative Moral Majority and Jerry Falwell, its evangelist leader.

In addition, Bush and the Republicans were prepared to pursue the southern strategy but no longer merely to rely on the politics of euphemism. His campaign was shaped by Lee Atwater, a young conservative from South Carolina who had earlier used negative campaign tactics to defeat Bush when he sought the Republican nomination and who opposed Ronald Reagan as the exponent of 'voodoo economics'. Atwater used Bush's earlier support for gun control legislation to ensure his defeat. Now Atwater used similar tactics to ensure the success of the Vice President.

Willie Horton and the 1988 Campaign

Atwater used tactics that were familiar to southern Democratic party demagogues and that many analysts had hoped were a thing of the past. The issue was race. The use of the race card was not new in Republican politics in the South; its most ardent player was Jesse Helms of North Carolina (Furgurson, 1986). However, it was Atwater who used it in the national campaign to rescue George Bush from almost certain defeat. In the May Gallup poll Bush, at 38 per cent, was trailing his Democratic opponent, Michael Dukakis, the Governor of Massachusetts. The liberal Democrat had a 16 per cent lead. 'Three Democratic losers, George McGovern, Jimmy Carter, and Walter Mondale, had negative ratings of 27, 28, and 29 percent respectively in their unsuccessful campaigns of 1972, 1980 and 1984. Bush's negatives topped all of theirs' (Johnson, 1991). The Atwater campaign was designed to portray Michael Dukakis as an ultra-liberal and thereby to increase the Governor's negatives in the eyes of the electorate.

Thirty New Jersey voters who had supported Reagan in 1984 and who were thinking of returning to their traditional Democratic party allegiance were selected by a marketing firm and were asked a series of questions by the Bush campaigners which emphasised the supposedly ultra-liberal stands of the Governor. The group were unaware that they were participating in a survey organised by the Republican party. It was stressed that, as Governor, Dukakis had vetoed a bill requiring the pledge of allegiance in schools but did not inform them that this had happened in 1977. In addition, it was pointed out that the Democratic candidate was a member of the American Civil Liberties Union (ACLU) without explaining that the ACLU was a bipartisan organisation which had defended not only the rights of radicals and civil rights workers, but also the Ku Klux Klan's right of free speech. They also told the group that it was Dukakis who had approved the furlough programme for Massachusetts prisoners. In particular, he had given a weekend furlough to a black prisoner named Willie Horton who had then raped and murdered a white woman in Maryland. The group was also told that Dukakis was opposed to the death penalty. Half the selected group switched their allegiance to Bush.

Despite later denials, it was evident that the Bush campaign was shaped by Atwater. Bush continually contrasted his support for the pledge of allegiance with the veto that had been cast by his opponent. Dukakis was portrayed as an ultra-liberal and a member of ACLU. Many of these assaults on his Democratic opponent were made on visits to factories that made American flags or at American Legion meetings. Yet the most effective attack came with the linking of crime and race. Dukakis and the Democrats, unlike Bush and the Republicans, were portrayed as and perceived to be soft on crime. In America, where fear of crime was spreading as rapidly as racism, the linking of the two issues was ominous. 'Richard Nixon initiated the use of thinly veiled racial code words that hinted at violence. Ronald Reagan imitated the practice in 1980, and George Bush took it to an especially cynical level in 1988 with his Willie Horton advertisements' (Nightingale, 1993).

The Willie Horton television commercial was shot in black and white, and it depicted prisoners in a revolving door entering and leaving prison. Viewers were informed that hundreds of these men had escaped and were still free. In another commercial by a Bush support group, the face of Willie Horton filled the screens as viewers were told of the rape and murder of the Maryland woman. Ironically, national television's response was one of the few times that it was critical of the Bush campaign, but by repeating the first commercial in news bulletins and comment programmes it was giving the Vice President free advertising. Political commentators who had argued that negative campaigning was counterproductive were proved wrong. While it is true that 'in depicting Willie Horton as a symbol of Dukakis' alleged softness on crime, the Bush campaign fomented racial fears for political purposes and appealed to the worst elements of the American character' (Johnson, 1991), it is also true that it did much to win George Bush his one term as President of the United States.

Bush won the election in November by 53.4 per cent as opposed to 45.6 per cent for Dukakis. But the margin of victory was even greater in the South, where Bush carried the 11 former Confederate states by 58.3 per cent compared with his opponent's 40.9 per cent. Apart from Washington, DC, the ten states won by Dukakis were all in the north and this was despite the Democrats running their own southern strategy with Texan Lloyd Bentsen as vice presidential candidate. Although conceding racism was part of the Republican southern strategy, one analyst has asserted that it was not 'the factor'. He suggests that the regional disparity in white support for the Democratic party 'would have been lessened significantly had the public's attention in the campaign been focused on economic issues and not on highly charged social issues' (Lamis, 1990). However, the aim of the southern strategy was to focus on these social issues. It was no comfort to African American voters that Atwater, when dying of a brain tumour in 1990, made a deathbed apology for the Willie Horton campaign and its exploitation of Americans' racial fears. Ralph Abernathy, who had deserted the Democratic party to campaign for Ronald Reagan, returned to the fold and supported the presidential bid of Jesse Jackson in 1988 (Abernathy, 1989).

Rodney King and the Los Angeles Police Department

Bush exploited the fear of the majority of whites, 56 per cent in 1990, that African Americans were prone to violence although only 6 per cent of murders and 9 per cent of rapes in 1990 were the result of attacks by blacks on white victims. Although one-third of street muggings were committed by black men on white victims, it was the perception of the white community that 'mugging and black men were synonymous'. The use of violence by the police against black males has long been sanctioned by the white community – from the murder of Black Panther party members in Chicago, the use of live ammunition in riot control by police captain Frank Rizzo in Philadelphia in 1964, to the beating of Rodney King on a California motorway by members of the Los Angeles Police Department. 'The 1990 videotape of the beating of Rodney King in Los Angeles serves as another important reminder of the connection between racism and state repression in America' (Nightingale, 1993). The failure in the first trial to find the officers involved guilty of police brutality also reminded African Americans that the judicial system benefited those who were white when the victim was black. The ensuing race riot in Los Angeles in 1992 was partly motivated by the belief that African Americans could not get justice. It was also a result of the 40 per cent cuts of the Reagan/Bush administrations in community funding and social service programmes, 63 per cent cuts in job training, and an 82 per cent reduction in spending on subsidised housing. However, the riot 'was the catalyst forcing greater attention from President Bush and all Americans to the nation's widening economic and racial divisions' (Shull, 1993). It was tragic that it required a riot to make the President aware of such monumental problems.

George Bush and African Americans

At his inauguration Bush called for a kinder, gentler America in which 'We must hope to give them [our children] a sense of what it means to be a loyal friend, a loving parent, a citizen who leaves his home, his neighborhood and town better than he found it'. In this society shaped by public generosity the community would care for 'the homeless, lost and roaming' (Shull, 1993). That so many Americans were in such a parlous state after eight years of the Reagan revolution was a sad commentary on years of economic mismanagement.

It was not the poor who benefited under Bush but the savings and loan companies that took $8 billion dollars. It was the homeless who had been the victims of the corruption in the Department of Housing and Urban Development. Central to the scandal that unfolded in the first days of the Bush administration were the Reagan political appointees who had funnelled tens of millions of dollars to those developers who had appointed influential Republicans as consultants. Presiding over this corruption was Samuel R.

Pierce, a Wall Street lawyer who was Reagan's only black cabinet appointment. The beneficiaries were Republicans such as disgraced former office holder John N. Mitchell, Nixon's Attorney General. Mitchell made $75 000 for work on one project for the Department. Carla Hills, Bush's special trade representative, earned $138 000 for two projects (Johnson, 1991).

Bush not only faced the problems of mounting budget deficits but also a bitterly partisan Congress. Reagan vetoed the 1988 Civil Rights Restoration Act, designed to reverse the limitations the Supreme Court had imposed on four civil rights laws. The Act constituted a major step in ending federally funded discrimination as well as extending civil rights legislation to women, the elderly and the disabled. Reagan and his conservative supporters did everything they could to kill the Bill but eventually Democrats, with support from some Republicans, overrode the veto. Democrats in Congress proposed further legislation in 1990 which would reverse Supreme Court decisions which made it very difficult for a complainant to prove job discrimination under the 1866 law and the 1964 Civil Rights Act. The legislation not only provided for jury trials but shifted the burden of proof from the employee to the employer, and it would not just apply to African Americans but was extended to include gender, disability, religion and national origin.

Senate minority leader Robert Dole and Republican Senator Orrin Hatch of Utah led the opposition to the Bill as proposed by Edward Kennedy. At first Bush was not involved, but as opposition mounted within the administration, led by Vice President Dan Quayle, the position of President Bush was crucial if the Bill was to succeed or fail. Bush vetoed the legislation. 'The veto represented the first defeat of a major civil rights bill in the last quarter century.' In the same year he vetoed a 'quota bill' designed to aid Native Americans, claiming that it 'is so seriously flawed that it would create more problems than it solved'. Bush was attacked for caving in to the right wing of his party (Shull, 1993). Although Bush aides sought to limit the damage by claiming that they supported some legislation for African Americans, such assurances were not accepted by the black community and the failure to extend the scope of the anti-discrimination legislation angered many women.

The veto of a civil rights bill merely confirmed for most African Americans that the Bush administration was content to lead the resistance to black equality. The Civil Rights Division of the Justice

Department had supported the struggle for justice under Kennedy and Johnson. With Reagan the Division had been headed by Bradford Reynolds, who had consistently sought to narrow enforcement of civil rights laws. To replace Reynolds, George Bush nominated William Lucas, a leading conservative black Republican. Lucas has the dubious distinction of being 'the first black candidate for federal office rejected by the Senate after being formally nominated' (Shull, 1993).

Lucas had enthusiastic support from the right, which is not surprising because he opposed racial quotas, supported racially segregated private schools that sought tax exemption and even argued that the recent Supreme Court decisions had not impeded those seeking equal opportunity. Faced with such staunchly conservative views, African American Representative John Conyers of Michigan withdrew his endorsement of Lucas. Jesse Jackson and the Mayor of Detroit, Coleman Young, also refused to continue their support. Most liberal groups backed away from Lucas and only SCLC continued to support the nomination. Faced with this mounting opposition, Bush appointed Lucas to a post in the Justice Department which did not require a Senate confirmation (Shull, 1993).

Appointing a Judge

Bush followed the example of Reagan. His nominations to the Supreme Court were judges who would actively support the conservative agenda. The retirement of Thurgood Marshall left a vacancy and George Bush proposed a poorly qualified African American, Clarence Thomas, who has been described as 'the most controversial Supreme Court nomination in U.S. history' (Shull, 1993). For one African American commentator, 'Thomas has emerged as the high court's most aggressive advocate of rolling back the gains Marshall fought so hard for' (*Time*, 26 June 1995).

Thomas was a devout believer in the conservative agenda. He opposed affirmative action, although he was a beneficiary because this policy had helped him enter Yale Law School. Ironically, he also fills the quota of one black on the Supreme Court. The nomination helped Bush in his attacks on racial quotas. Thomas also rejected class action suits which enable large numbers of people to seek justice. He was a firm believer in black self-help. During his confirmation hearings in the Senate, Thomas was accused by Anita Hill, a fellow black conservative and law professor at Oklahoma, of sexual harassment. Having asserted he would never play the race card, Thomas immediately accused liberals and women's groups of 'lynching' him. Thomas was narrowly confirmed because African Americans and liberal Democrats were deeply divided over the issue. It may have been 'politically brilliant' for Bush to appoint a black conservative (Shull, 1993) but it cost him many votes from African Americans and women when he sought re-election.

Thomas followed the ultra-conservative judge Antonin Scalia and supported him in the first eight cases he heard. The Court's 1992 attack on school desegregation in *Freeman v Pitts*, weakening school desegregation orders, was later supported by Thomas. Wade Henderson, Washington director of the NAACP, suggested that 'if Thomas had been on the court at the time, he would have opposed the decision in *Brown v The Board of Education*'. This drastic assertion seems to be borne out in Thomas's concurring opinion in *Missouri v Jenkins*, of June 1995. A lower federal court had ruled that the state of Missouri was wrong in its funding of predominantly white, suburban 'magnet' schools in Kansas City because the test scores at the predominantly black inner-city schools were below the national average. It was these latter schools which should have had the funding. In attacking the judge's ruling Thomas argued that he had misconstrued Supreme Court decisions, including *Brown*, and as a result the judge had supported 'the theory that black students suffer from an unspecified psychological harm from segregation that retards their mental and educational development. This approach not only relies upon questionable social-science research rather than constitutional principle, but it also rests on the assumption of black inferiority.' Thurgood Marshall, the lawyer who had impressed the young African Americans seeking to integrate Little Rock High School, would have been astounded and angered at the idea that he had supported black inferiority or that he had used 'questionable social-science research' in his great triumph in the *Brown* case. It is not surprising that Thomas has been described as 'Uncle Tom Justice' (*Time*, 26 June 1995). Such was his conservatism that he opposed the Bush administration when it favoured a broadening of the Voting Rights Act. Clarence Thomas followed his white mentor

Scalia and voted in support of the majority against Bush (Shull, 1993).

The Women's Movement and the New Conservatism

Thomas, who held the quota for black justices on the Supreme Court, not only opposed civil rights laws for African Americans but was also very hostile towards women and homosexuals. The great triumph of the women's movement had been the court ruling in *Roe v Wade*, legalising abortion throughout the United States. In his desire to limit the right to abortion, Thomas was only following the most conservative members of the Supreme Court. As Jane Sherron De Hart points out, 'the egalitarian and humane society envisioned by the feminists' had not been created (Kerber and Sherron De Hart, 1991). The 1980s and the new political conservatism meant that women were forced to struggle even to hold on to what they had achieved. In his election George Bush had stressed what he and the Moral Majority believed were the values of the family. Bush opposed the ERA although previously he had supported it: 'I don't think that thing's gotten off; I don't really see much steam behind it now. I think we have existing laws to protect the rights of women ... and I don't think it's particularly needed at this point at all' (Shull, 1993).

Although the Supreme Court had not overturned *Roe*, it had limited the use of federal funds in such cases, a move which was particularly harsh for poor women and women of colour. In 1989 in the *Webster* decision the Court ruled that states did have the right to limit abortions. It was not only reproductive rights that were threatened by the courts and the Bush administration, however. Laws requiring equal opportunities for women in education and employment were not only weakened by the courts but also by the attacks of Reagan and Bush. Previous efforts to ensure gender equality in American higher education were undermined by the Bush administration through financial cuts. The Small Business Administration reduced its assistance to women's enterprises; schemes for job evaluation, important for equal pay demands, were not carried out; day centres for working women had little funding, as did shelters for battered women and legal aid centres (Kerber and Sherron De Hart, 1991). The only concession offered by George Bush to working women was a campaign promise to give $20 in tax concessions to the poorest families to help pay for day care. With the average weekly costs four times that amount it was not even a viable proposition.

Bush did not like to be reminded that he had previously supported the ERA or that he had as a congressman in 1970 co-sponsored a bill which set up a federal contraceptive programme. A campaign organiser reassured a *New York Times* reporter that in the Bush campaign, 'We're not running around and dealing with a lot of so-called women's issues' (Faludi, 1993). Rather, opposition to abortion and attacks on single mothers were always in the context of a campaign that stressed family values – white, middle-class families only.

In 1984 it had been George Bush's proud boast that he had 'kicked a little ass'. The 'ass' involved was that of Geraldine Ferraro, the vice presidential nominee for the Democratic party. Although all the evidence shows Ferraro did not hurt the Dukakis campaign and she encouraged many other women to seek office and to vote for the Democratic party, it has become received wisdom that Ferraro cost the Democrats the election. Certainly, New Right activists stressed issues of sexuality. Ferraro recalled, 'There are rumours about me being involved in lesbianism, about my having affairs, about me having an abortion' (Faludi, 1993). One of the short-term effects was a dramatic decline in the number of women seeking public office. This was reversed in 1992 when the number of women increased dramatically and several were successful in their election campaigns, even in Senate races in Illinois and California. Although dubbed 'the year of the woman' by the popular press and with much talk of the campaign to increase the number of women elected to Congress, the so-called Emily's List, it remains to be seen if the new feminism has made significant gains under Bill Clinton. Certainly Bush's vetoing civil rights legislation, because it would ensure gender equality, partly explains why he failed in his re-election bid in 1992. American women voters switched their votes to the Democratic party. The role of Hillary Clinton, a successful career woman, also played an important part in Clinton's success.

George Bush and the Gay Community

Neglect, certainly not benign, was a feature of the Bush admini-stration's attitude towards African Americans and women, but the same was not true for the homosexual community, who were singled out by the Republicans as the group that was destroying America. Homosexuals and lesbians, according to George Bush, were not 'normal' and throughout his administration, and especially at the Republican national convention in 1992, the homosexual community was subjected to fierce assaults in the name of family values. Bush supported Pat Buchanan, a conservative journalist, who at the convention declared 'religious war' against homosexuals. The Reverend Donald Wilmot, head of the American Family Association and Christian Leaders for Responsible Television, located in Tupelo, Mississippi, and the Californian Reverend Louis Sheldon, leader of the Traditional Values Coalition, worked closely with the Bush campaign. 'In these men's views, homosexuals – the new Communists – are taking over' (Signorile, 1993).

After the convention *Time* magazine wondered, 'After Willie Horton Are Gays Next?' (Miller, 1995). Although his Democratic opponent actively sought the gay vote, 'gay bashing' did not become a major theme of the Bush campaign. Perhaps this was due to opinion polls that showed that the rhetoric of the Republican convention had not been well received by most Americans. Although Bush and Dan Quayle stepped back from an all-out attack on the homosexual community, their example was not followed by others, and the vehemence of their assault gave encouragement to state groups to initiate action.

In Oregon the state voters were asked to vote on Ballot Measure 9, which was intended to insert into the state constitution that homosexuality was 'abnormal, wrong, unnatural and perverse'. The measure was proposed by the Oregon Citizens Alliance, a fundamentalist group supported by prominent Republican Pat Robertson and his Christian Coalition. The Alliance was following up a success in 1988 when they rescinded an executive order of the Governor which outlawed discrimination against gays in state employment. The campaign was marked by neo-Nazi attacks and some murders of homosexuals. Lesbians and gays managed to win the struggle but 42 per cent of Oregon voters favoured positive discrimination against the homosexual community. And despite the success of the gay community in Oregon, a similar measure which encouraged discrimination against gays was passed in Colorado. In that state, following the election success, violence against the gay community rose by 300 per cent (Signorile, 1993).

The failure to meet the needs of the homosexual community, especially the AIDS crisis, made homosexuals more militant. 'ACT UP and Queer Nation tactics (especially the naming, or "outing" of closet homosexuals), may have antagonized many, but they were symptomatic of gays' and lesbians' growing self-confidence and determination to stick up for themselves' (Miller, 1995). The witch-hunt against homosexuals in the military, which resulted in the dismissal of over 13 000 from 1982 to 1992, particularly angered gay activists. In 1991 Brian Ramey of the navy and air-force captain Greg Greeley were dismissed from the services. At the same time, the Pentagon spokesman, Assistant Secretary of Defense for Public Affairs, Pete Williams, who was alleged to be homosexual, was apparently not subject to the same military code. Gay groups decided that Williams should be dragged out of the closet (Signorile, 1993).

Civil Rights for the Disabled

However, the Bush administration was not always opposed to civil rights issues and the most notable exception was the 1990 Americans with Disabilities Act, signed by the President at a ceremony on the White House lawn. This legislation 'brought civil rights protections for people with disabilities to a level of parity with civil rights protections already enjoyed by racial minorities and women'. Why did Bush support such a proposal when he was prepared to veto legislation that benefited women, African Americans and Native Americans?

This legislation was designed to help rehabilitate the disabled and make them self-sufficient tax payers, a proposal that no conservative could oppose because so many disabled were Vietnam veterans. The legislation stressed employment rather than affirmative action or quotas, which Republicans had been attacking throughout the 1980s. Many disabled people, moreover, voted Republican, unlike African Americans, for example, who overwhelmingly voted for the Democratic party. 'The political strategy of playing upon racial resentments did not have to affect civil rights for people with disabilities who,' according to Edward Berkowitz, 'in many people's minds, personified the deserving poor, lived in the suburbs and not just the cities, and were the antithesis of the stereotypical, menacing members of the underclass' (Graham, 1994). The estimated 50 million disabled people formed the largest minority group in America. The resulting legislation linked disability with civil rights.

The Election Campaign of 1992

George Bush's support for disability civil rights laws may have been influenced by the fact that he was a World War II veteran. Certainly, throughout his presidency he had stressed his war record and he did so again when he sought re-election in 1992. This strategy was dictated partly because his opponent, Bill Clinton, the Governor of Arkansas, had opposed the war in Vietnam and during his days at Oxford University participated in anti-war demonstrations in London. For many liberals, Clinton demonstrated that the sixties generation could achieve power and help shape the world. In addition, his wife Hillary graduated top of her class at Yale Law School. She was a brilliant career woman who had strong political views and who had also opposed the war in Vietnam. It was her determination to shape policy that later made her vulnerable to attack from conservatives.

Clinton chose as his running mate the senator from Tennessee, Albert Gore Jr, who had served in the war. Superficially it seemed that the nomination of Clinton and the selection of Gore were a triumph of the new liberal South, of the sixties generation, and a reassertion of the liberal agenda first established by FDR and his successors. But during the campaign there were signs that the candidates also had a different agenda from many liberals of the 1960s. Gore, who had unsuccessfully sought the Democratic nomination in 1984, was certainly an intelligent and ardent environmentalist, but his wife was better known for her attacks on popular music, especially rap. In 1985 Tipper Gore was shocked by the lyrics of Prince's 'Darling Nikki' and she was instrumental in setting up the bipartisan group Parents' Music Resource Center, designed to warn parents of the dangers of 'porn rock'. Her husband also took part in a Senate investigation of the music industry.

The appeal of Albert Gore Jr to the Clinton campaign staff was his environmentalism and his ability to attract the Yuppie voter. In

1984 Gore had won the vacant Senate seat for Tennessee, despite the landslide victory of Ronald Reagan and the unswerving loyalty to Reagan shown by his Republican opponent. Gore's victory, winning over 60 per cent of the votes cast, was despite efforts by his opponent to portray him as a liberal, with close ties to Edward Kennedy and Walter Mondale. Gore replied: 'The old labels – liberal and conservative – have far less relevance to today's problems than the efforts to find solutions to these problems. There's no need to rely on outdated ideology as a crutch' (Lamis, 1990).

It was this appeal to the end of ideology that Clinton and Gore stressed in their election campaign in 1992. However, they also had to keep the support of those traditional groups that had made the Democrats the majority party in American politics, such as African Americans, blue-collar workers, women and the new politically active group – homosexuals. Clinton's election has been ascribed to this latter group, especially by conservative commentators, but the significance of the gay vote is difficult to judge. CNN exit polls estimated Clinton won 72 per cent of the gay vote while others put the figure closer to 90 per cent. But the significant factor was none of these groups but the quixotic campaign of Texas billionaire Ross Perot. Running on a populist campaign, Perot claimed to speak for working people who could not get their opinions through to the Washington bureaucrats. He won the support of many blue-collar Republican voters and helped to ensure Bush's defeat. It was these, the very voters whom Bill Clinton and Albert Gore had hoped would return to the Democrats, who preferred to vote for the independent candidate. Clinton won with only 43 per cent of the votes cast, but he had a massive electoral college landslide.

Clinton and African Americans

During the campaign, Clinton, as Governor of Arkansas, allowed the execution by lethal injection of Rickey Ray Rector, an African American prisoner, on 24 January 1992, even though the man, as a result of a failed attempt to commit suicide, was totally unaware of his crime. The legacy of Willie Horton hung over the election of 1992 and Clinton was not going to be seen as soft on crime. Clinton was aware that Nixon, Reagan and Bush had been successful in making law and order a race question. The Governor had also been careful to sideline the leading African American politician Jesse Jackson. After mounting criticism from civil rights activists Clinton campaigned for an African American woman as Senator for Illinois. In this he achieved not only endorsements from African Americans but underlined his support for women's issues.

Similarly, after his election he appointed a black feminist, Jocelyn Elders, as Surgeon General of the United States and many African Americans were given high-level posts in the administration, including Ron Brown as Secretary of Commerce. In addition, blacks were pleased with the new southern President when he extended the Voting Rights Act. Despite the Voting Rights Act of 1965, state registrars of voters had been reluctant to register African Americans, and the Justice Department under Reagan and Bush had done little to ensure its enforcement. Clinton avoided these state and federal complications by ensuring that registration to vote was completed with the registration of a car. However, states were still reluctant to introduce the new procedures.

Clinton's reputation for avoiding tough battles resulted in charges of unwillingness to stick by his decisions. When Jocelyn Elders gave advice on sex education that offended conservatives, Clinton asked for her resignation. Wishing to retain African American support, Clinton nominated Henry Foster, a leading obstetrician who had been praised by George Bush. The nomination combined the issues of race and abortion. The right-wing Christian Coalition immediately swung into action in their assault on Foster, who was charged with committing abortions – a legal operation. Foster did not help the President by underestimating the number of abortions he had done. Conservative Republicans, especially Phil Gramm of Texas, wanted the support of the Christian Coalition movement, and its new leader Ralph Read, in his bid for the Republican nomination in 1996. Moderate Republicans were concerned that a strong anti-abortion stance would alienate many pro-choice voters. Republican Bill Frist of Tennessee supported Foster's appointment and as he told *Time* reporters: "'I know he must have seen botched abortions, women coming in the hospital bleeding," said Frist, adding he was aware too of the segregation suffered by black doctors. "I'm the only person on that panel who knows what it was like in the South in the 1960s"' (*Time*, 15 May 1995). Despite the efforts of the administration and support of moderate Republicans, conservatives were able to prevent the nomination coming to a vote and Foster was not appointed.

Clinton and the Women's Movement

In 1992 Clinton was able to win the support of the majority of American women. His support for the pro-choice campaign meant that he continued to hold women's support despite Elders' resignation. The conservative response was to continue to emphasise 'family values' and the role of women as homemakers. After the massive success of the conservative Republicans in the mid-term elections of 1994, the attack on women and especially on a woman's right to choose an abortion became one of the major issues. Clinton continued to support the pro-choice movement and moderate Republicans, such as Arlen Specter of Pennsylvania, appealed in 1995 to Democrats to vote in the Republican primaries to stop the 'antiabortion crazies' from taking over the party. On the other hand, the Governor of California, Pete Wilson, campaigned with the majority of Republican hopefuls on a pro-life platform. Wilson was accused of having a 'multiple choice' abortion record. According to Roger Stone of Planned Parenthood and the National Abortion Rights Action League, 'He used to favor government funding for abortions for poor women, but doesn't any longer, and twice when he was Senator he cast the deciding vote restricting federal health-insurance plans from providing abortion coverage' (*Time*, 5 June 1995).

Clinton, Gays and the Military

As early as 1991, Bill Clinton promised that if elected President he would end the discrimination against homosexual men and women in the military. Although such a promise received widespread support in the gay community, it went relatively unnoticed during the election campaign. As soon as he was in the White House, Clinton wanted to follow the example of Harry Truman, who had ended racial discrimination in the military by executive order.

Clinton, as Commander in Chief, would do the same for homosexuals.

Clinton thought it would be just a stroke of the pen, but instead it became the main issue during his first days in office and his response to criticism was such that it lost him much support in the liberal as well as gay groups. Reed and his Christian Coalition, as well as other fundamentalists, launched an onslaught against the President. Colin Powell, the first black head of the Joint Chiefs of Staff, warned that homosexuals in the military would destroy military effectiveness and group morale. Ironically, it was exactly the same advice that General Eisenhower had given to President Truman about racial integration. Powell also had the support of the head of the Senate Armed Services Committee, Democrat Sam Nunn of Georgia. Robert Dole, a perennial presidential aspirant, also opposed the President.

Faced by mounting criticism, Clinton sought a way out so that he could concentrate on other issues. He announced that the ban on homosexuals would remain for six months. The dismissal of gays from the armed services would stop and new recruits were not to be asked about their sexual orientation. Meanwhile the military were asked to produce a code of sexual practice. William Schneider of the *New York Times* commented: 'I thought all along that the Willie Horton issue of the campaign would be gays and Clinton's support for gay rights. Well instead of happening in the campaign, it has come true now' (Miller, 1995).

The resulting compromise drawn up by Senator Nunn and General Powell was the 'Don't Ask, Don't Tell' proposal, which would allow homosexuals to remain in military service so long as their sexual preferences were kept private. Although this received a hostile reception from many activists, Barney Frank, one of the few openly gay members of the House of Representatives, realised that the compromise was the only one that would be accepted by the military and the President. Clinton was eager to get a settlement. Senator Nunn, however, was not happy with the proposal and did not want it left as an executive order that might be later amended and he pushed through an amendment to a defence appropriation which stipulated that 'persons who demonstrate a propensity or intent to engage in homosexual acts' were 'unacceptable risks' in the forces. In addition, the Secretary of Defense could reinstate the question about sexual orientation for new recruits and Clinton's proposal to end witch-hunts against gays in the military was not included in the amendment. Eager to be rid of the problem, Clinton signed the measure into law.

Ironically, the conservative Republican Barry Goldwater, who had been the party's candidate for President in 1964, in 1993 wrote in the Washington *National Post Weekly*, 'After 50 years in the military and politics, I am still amazed to see how upset people can get over nothing. Lifting the ban on gays in the military isn't exactly nothing, but it's pretty damned close'. After pointing out that he had flown more than 150 of America's fighter planes and bombers, the former senator from Arizona stated, 'I think it's high time to pull the curtain on this charade of policy' (Miller, 1995).

The failure to fulfil his promise to end discrimination in the military added to the growing resentment in the gay community to the Clinton administration. During his 1992 campaign Clinton promised to put into effect the 30 recommendations of the National Commission on AIDS that had been ignored by the Bush administration. The Governor of Arkansas pledged himself to another Manhattan project, which had produced the atomic bomb, but this would solve the AIDS crisis. On World AIDS Day, 1 December 1992, Clinton was attacked by a member of ACT UP and accused of doing nothing while members of the gay community died. 'One Year!! Slick Willie! The Republicans were right! We never should have trusted you' (Signorile, 1993).

EPILOGUE

Writing in 1892, Anna Julia Cooper, an African American woman, wrote: 'One muffled strain in the Silent South, a jarring chord and a vague and uncomprehended cadenza has been and still is the Negro. And of that muffled chord, the one mute and voiceless note has been the sadly expectant Black Woman' (Hopkins, 1988). The twentieth century, especially the years after the war, has seen the determination of Africans Americans to force white America to understand that cadenza, and the remarkable voice that African American women have found in their struggle for justice. So successful has that fight been that it gave encouragement to others, such as women, homosexuals and Native Americans, to take up their struggles against discrimination. In 1995 the white Southern Baptist Church apologised for its defence of slavery and its resistance to the civil rights struggle (*Time*, 3 July 1995). The Christian Coalition of conservative fundamentalists claims that it is reaching out to the black community. However, at a recent conference only two delegates were black (*Time*, 15 May 1995).

The 1980s and 1990s have seen the revival of the extreme right, such as the Aryan Nations, with demands for a 'white homeland' in the northwest and admiration of Hitler and its violent anti-Jewish and anti-black propaganda in the publication *Calling Our Nation*. The 1995 terrorist bombing in Oklahoma, allegedly the work of extreme right-wing forces, could unite the nation regardless of race because it killed so many without regard to race, religion, or gender. Certainly there is now no Otto Kerner, who warned Americans in 1968 that their nation was 'moving towards two societies, one black, one white – separate and unequal' (National Advisory Commission on Civil Disorders, 1968). The majority of white Americans have preferred to ignore the growing racial divide evident in the 1980s and 1990s. But if there were a Kerner, or even another Martin Luther King Jr, would most white Americans even bother to try to catch the muffled chord?

BIBLIOGRAPHY

Abernathy, Ralph David. *And the Walls Came Tumbling Down*. Harper and Row, New York, 1989.

Adams, Frank T. *James A. Dombrowski: An American Heretic, 1897–1983*. University of Tennessee Press, Knoxville, 1992.

Ambrose, S. *Eisenhower: The President*. Simon and Schuster, New York, 1984.

Ambrose, S. *Nixon*, 3 vols. Simon and Schuster, New York, 1989.

Anderson, Terry. *The Movement and the Sixties: Protest in America from Greensboro to Wounded Knee*. Oxford University Press, New York, 1995.

Aughey, A., G. Jones and W. T. M. Riches. *The Conservative Political Tradition in Britain and the United States*. Pinter Press, London, 1992.

Beals, Melba Pattillo. *Warriors Don't Cry*. Pocket Books, New York, 1994.

Bernstein, B. J., ed. *Politics and Policies of the Truman Administration*. Quadrangle Books, Chicago, 1970.

Bernstein, I. *Promises Kept: John F Kennedy's New Frontier*. Oxford University Press, New York, 1991.

Blum, J. M. *Years of Discord: American Politics and Society, 1961–1974*. W. W. Norton, New York, 1991.

Boyarsky, Bill. *Ronald Reagan: His Life and Rise to the Presidency*. Random House, New York, 1981.

Bracey Jr, J. H., August Meier and Elliott Rudwick. *The Afro-Americans: Selected Documents*. Allyn and Bacon, Boston, 1972.

Branch, Taylor. *Parting the Waters: Martin Luther King and the Civil Rights Movement, 1954–63*. Macmillan, London, 1989.

Brown, Dee. *Bury My Heart at Wounded Knee: An Indian History of the American West*. Vintage, London, 1991.

Burner, Eric R. *And Gently He Shall Lead Them: Robert Moses and Civil Rights*. New York University Press, New York, 1994.

Burns, James McGregor. *Roosevelt: The Soldier of Freedom*. Harcourt Brace Javanovich, New York, 1970.

Cannon, Lou. *President Reagan: The Role of a Lifetime.* Touchstone, New York, 1991.

Carson, Clayborne. *In Struggle: SNCC and the Black Awakening of the 1960s.* Harvard University Press, Cambridge, Mass., 1981.

Carson, Clayborne, ed. *The Student Voice, 1960–1963.* Meckler, Westport, Conn., 1990.

Carter, Jimmy. *Keeping Faith: Memoirs of a President.* Collins, London, 1992.

Chalmers, David M. *Hooded Americanism: The History of the Ku Klux Klan.* Quadrangle, Chicago, 1965.

Clifton, J. A., ed. *Being and Becoming Indian: Biographical Studies of North American Frontiers.* Dorsey Press, Chicago, 1989.

Cone, James H. *Martin and Malcolm and America: A Dream or a Nightmare.* HarperCollins, Glasgow, 1993.

Cooper, W. J. and Thomas Terrill. *The American South: A History.* Alfred Knopf, London, 1991.

Crawford, Vicki, Jacqueline Rouse and Barbara Woods. *Women in the Civil Rights Movement: Torchbearers and Trailblazers.* Indiana University Press, Bloomington, Indiana, 1993.

Dallek, Robert. *Ronald Reagan: The Politics of Symbolism.* Harvard University Press, Cambridge, Mass., 1984.

Dallek, Robert. *Lone Star Rising: Lyndon Johnson and His Times, 1908–1960.* Oxford University Press, New York, 1991.

Daniel, Pete. *Standing at the Crossroads: Southern Life in the Twentieth Century.* Hill and Wang, New York, 1986.

Davis, Angela. *Women, Race and Class.* Vintage, New York, 1983.

Davis, Angela. *An Autobiography.* Random House, New York, 1988.

Davis, Angela. 'Civil liberties and women's rights: twenty years on.' *Irish Journal of American Studies,* 1994, vol. 3, pp. 17–30.

Dawley, Alan. *Struggles for Justice: Social Responsibility and the Liberal State.* The Belknap Press of the Harvard University Press, Cambridge, Mass., 1991.

Diggins, John P. *The Proud Decades: America in War and Peace, 1941–1960.* W. W. Norton, New York, 1989.

Douglass, Frederick. *Life and Times of Frederick Douglass.* Collier Macmillan, London, 1962.

Duberman, Martin. *Paul Robeson.* Pan Books, New York, 1989.

Dyson, Michael E. *Making Malcolm: The Myth and Meaning of Malcolm X.* Oxford University Press, New York, 1995.

Eaton, C. *A History of the Old South.* Macmillan, New York, 1966.

Ely, James C. *The Crisis of Conservative Virginia: The Byrd Organization and the Politics of Massive Resistance.* University of Tennessee Press, Knoxville, 1976.

Emery, Fred. *Watergate: The Corruption and Fall of Richard Nixon.* Jonathan Cape, London, 1994.

Essien-Udom, E. U. *Black Nationalism: A Search for Identity in America.* Dell, New York, 1964.

Faderman, Lillian. *Old Girls and Twilight Lovers: A History of Lesbian Life in Twentieth Century America.* Penguin, London, 1992.

Fairclough, A. *To Redeem the Soul of America: The Southern Christian Leadership Conference and Martin Luther King, Jr.* University of Georgia Press, Athens, Georgia, 1987.

Faludi, Susan. *Backlash: The Undeclared War Against Women.* Chatto and Windus, London, 1993.

Fleming, Cynthia Griggs. 'Black women activists and the Student Non-violent Coordinating Committee: the case of Ruby Doris Smith Robinson.' *Irish Journal of American Studies,* 1994, vol. 3, pp. 31–54.

Foner, Eric. *Free Soil, Free Labor, Free Men: The Ideology of the Republican Party Before the Civil War.* Oxford University Press, New York, 1970.

Fraser, Tom. 'Two American presidents and Israel: studies in ambiguity.' *Irish Journal of American Studies,* 1994, vol. 3, pp. 93–113.

Furgurson, Ernest. *Hard Right: The Rise of Jesse Helms.* W. W. Norton, New York, 1986.

Garrow, David. *Bearing the Cross: Martin Luther King Jr. and the Southern Christian Leadership Conference.* Jonathan Cape, London, 1988.

Garson, Robert A. *The Democratic Party and the Politics of Sectionalism, 1941–48.* Louisiana State University Press, Baton Rouge, 1974.

Gates, Jr, Henry L. *Colored People.* Viking, London, 1995.

Giddings, Paula. *When and Where I Enter: The Impact of Black Women on Race and Sex in America.* Bantam, New York, 1984.

Glad, Betty. *Jimmy Carter: In Search of the Great White House.* W. W. Norton, New York, 1980.

Gore, Albert. *The Eye of the Storm: A People's Politics for the Seventies.* Herder and Herder, New York, 1970.

Gore, Albert. *Let the Glory Out: My South and its Politics.* Viking Press, New York, 1972.

Graham, Hugh Davis. *The Civil Rights Era: Origins and Development of a National Policy, 1960–1972.* Oxford University Press, New York, 1990.

Graham, Hugh Davis, ed. *Civil Rights in the United States.* Pennsylvania State University Press, University Park, 1994.

Green, James R. *Grass Roots Socialism: Radical Movements in the Southwest, 1895–1943.* Louisiana State University Press, Baton Rouge, 1978.

Greene, John R. *The Limits of Power: The Nixon and Ford Administrations.* Indiana University Press, Bloomington, 1992.

Greene, Lee S. *Lead Me On: Frank Goad Clement and Tennessee Politics.* University of Tennessee Press, Knoxville, 1982.

Grubbs, Donald H. *Cry From the Cotton: The Southern Tenant Farmers' Union and the New Deal.* University of North Carolina Press, Chapel Hill, 1971.

Halberstam, David. *The Fifties*. Fawcett Columbine, New York, 1993.

Hamby, A. L. *Beyond the New Deal: Harry S Truman and American Liberalism*. Columbia University Press, New York, 1973.

Hopkins, Pauline E. *Contending Forces. A Romance Illustrative of Negro Life North and South*. Oxford University Press, New York, 1988.

Howard, Gerald. *The Sixties*. Washington Square Press, New York, 1982.

Issel, William. *Social Change in the United States, 1945–1983*. Macmillan, Basingstoke, 1985.

Jackson, K. T. *The Ku Klux Klan in the City, 1915–1930*. Ivan R. Dee, Chicago, 1992.

Johnson, Haynes. *Sleepwalking Through History: America in the Reagan Years*. W. W. Norton, New York, 1991.

Johnson, Lyndon B. *The Vantage Point: Perspectives of the Presidency, 1963–1969*. Popular Library, New York, 1971.

Jordan, Winthrop. *White Over Black: American Attitudes Toward the Negro, 1550–1812*. University of North Carolina Press, Chapel Hill, 1968.

Kauffman, L. S. *American Feminist Thought at Century's End*. Blackwell, Cambridge, Mass., 1993.

Kaufman, Burton I. *The Presidency of James Earl Carter, Jr.* University of Kansas Press, Lawrence, 1993.

Kearns, Doris. *Lyndon Johnson and the American Dream*. Signet, New York, 1976.

Kerber, Linda and Jane Sherron De Hart, eds. *Women's America: Refocusing the Past*, 3rd ed. Oxford University Press, New York, 1991.

King Jr, Martin Luther. *Chaos or Community?* Hodder and Stoughton, London, 1967.

Klibaner, Irwin. *Conscience of a Troubled South: The Southern Conference Educational Fund, 1941–1966*. Carlson Publishing, New York, 1989.

Knight, Douglas M. *Street of Dreams: The Nature and Legacy of the 1960s*. Duke University Press, Durham, North Carolina, 1989.

Lamis, Alexander P. *The Two Party South*, 2nd ed. Oxford University Press, New York, 1990.

Lasky, M. J. *The Hungarian Revolution*. Martin Secker and Warburg, London, 1957.

Laue, James H. *Direct Action and Desegregation 1960–1962: Toward A Theory of the Rationalization of Protest*. Carlson Publishing, New York, 1989.

Lawson, Steven F. *Running For Freedom. Civil Rights and Black Politics in America Since 1941*. McGraw Hill, New York, 1991.

Lawson, Steven F. 'Mixing moderation with militancy: Lyndon Johnson and African American leadership.' In Robert Divine, ed. *The Johnson Years*. University Press of Kansas, Lawrence, 1994.

Loevy, Robert D. '"To write it in the books of law:" President Lyndon B Johnson and the Civil Rights Act of 1964.' In Bernard Firestone and Robert Vogt, eds. *Lyndon Baines Johnson and the Uses of Power*. Greenwood, New York, 1980.

Marable, Manning. *Race, Reform and Rebellion: The Second Reconstruction in Black America, 1945–1982*. Macmillan, London, 1984.

Matusow, A. J. *The Unravelling of America. A History of Liberalism in the 1960s*. Harper and Row, New York, 1986.

McAdam, Doug. *Freedom Summer*. Oxford University Press, New York, 1988.

McCoy, D. R. *The Presidency of Harry S. Truman*. University of Kansas Press, Lawrence, 1984.

McCoy, D. R. and Richard Donald. *Quest and Response. Minority Rights and the Truman Administration*. University Press of Kansas, Lawrence, 1973.

McCullough, David. *Truman*. Simon and Schuster, New York, 1992.

Meier, August and Elliott Rudwick. *From Plantation to Ghetto*. Hill and Wang, New York, 1970.

Meier, August and Elliott Rudwick. 'The Bus Boycott Movement Against Jim Crow Streetcars in the South.' In David Garrow, ed. *We Shall Overcome: The Civil Rights Movement in the United States in the 1950s and 1960s*. Carlson Publishing, New York, 1989.

Miller, Loren. *The Petitioners: The Story of the Supreme Court and the Negro*. Meridian, New York, 1967.

Miller, Merle. *Plain Speaking: Conversations with Harry S. Truman*. Victor Gollancz, London, 1974.

Miller, Neil. *Out of Our Past: Gay and Lesbian History from 1869 to the Present*. Vintage, London, 1995.

Miller, Timothy. *The Hippies and American Values*. University of Tennessee Press, Knoxville, 1991.

Moraga, C. and Gloria Anzalúda. *This Bridge Called My Back: Writing of Radical Women of Color*. Kitchen Table, Women of Color Press, New York, 1983.

Morris, Aldon. *The Origins of the Civil Rights Movement: Black Communities Organizing for Change*. Free Press, New York, 1984.

Morrison, J. and R. K. Morrison. *From Camelot to Kent State: The Sixties Experience in the Words of Those Who Lived It*. Times Books, New York, 1987.

Myrdal, Gunnar. *An American Dilemma*. McGraw Hill, Toronto, 1964.

National Advisory Commission on Civil Disorders. *Report*. Bantam Books, New York, 1968.

Navasky, Victor. *Kennedy Justice*. Atheneum, New York, 1971.

Nightingale, C. H. *On the Edge: A History of Poor Black Children and Their American Dreams*. Basic Books, New York, 1993.

Nixon, Richard. *The Memoirs of Richard Nixon*. Sidgewick and Jackson, London, 1978.

O'Reilly, Kenneth. *Black Americans: The FBI Files*. Carroll and Graf, New York, 1994.

Parish, Peter. *The American Civil War*. Eyre Metheun, London, 1975.

Pinkney, Alphonso. *Red Black and Green: Black Nationalism in the United States*. Cambridge University Press, London, 1976.

Quarles, Benjamin. *The Negro in the American Revolution.* University of North Carolina Press, Chapel Hill, 1961.

Raines, Howell. *My Soul is Rested: Movement Days in the Deep South Remembered.* Penguin, New York, 1977.

Ralph, James R. *Northern Protest: Martin Luther King Jr., Chicago, and the Civil Rights Movement.* Harvard University Press, London, 1993.

Redkey, Edwin S. *Black Exodus: Black Nationalism and Back to Africa Movement. 1890–1910.* Yale University Press, New Haven, 1969.

Reed, Merl E. *Seedtime of the Modern Civil Rights Movement: The President's Committee on Fair Employment Practice, 1941–1946.* Louisiana State University Press, Baton Rouge, 1991.

Riches, W. T. M. *The 'Turbulent Decade'. The United States in the 1960s.* Irish Association for American Studies, 1987.

Rudwick, Elliott. *Race Riot in East St Louis, July 2, 1917.* Southern Illinois University Press, Carbondale, Ill., 1964.

Rudwick, Elliott. *W. E. B. Du Bois. Propogandist of Negro Protest.* Atheneum, New York, 1968.

Schlesinger, Jr, Arthur. *Robert Kennedy and His Times.* Futura, London, 1979.

Seeger, Pete and Rob Reiser. *Everybody Says Freedom: A History of the Civil Rights Movement in Songs and Pictures.* W. W. Norton, New York, 1989.

Shull, Steven A. *A Kinder, Gentler Racism? The Reagan–Bush Civil Rights Legacy.* M. E. Sharpe, New York, 1993.

Signorile, Michelangelo. *Queer Nation: Sex, the Media and the Closets of Power.* Abacus, London, 1993.

Spencer, Jr, Samuel. *Booker T. Washington and the Negro's Place in American Life.* Little Brown, Boston, 1955.

Stein, Judith. *The World of Marcus Garvey: Race and Class in Modern Society.* Louisiana State University Press, Baton Rouge, 1986.

Stockman, David. *The Triumph of Politics: The Inside Story of the Reagan Administration.* Avon, New York, 1987.

Stokes, Melvyn and Rick Halpern, eds. *Race and Class in the American South Since 1890.* Berg, Oxford, 1994.

Stoper, Emily. *The Student Nonviolent Coordinating Committee: The Growth of Radicalism in a Civil Rights Organization.* Carlson, New York, 1989.

Thornton, J. Mills. 'Challenge and response in the Montgomery bus boycott of 1955–1956.' In David Garrow, ed. *The Walking City: The Montgomery Bus Boycott. 1955–1956.* Carlson, New York, 1989.

Truman, Harry S. *Memoirs: Years of Trial and Hope.* Doubleday, New York, 1956.

Tuttle, William. *Race Riot: Chicago in the Red Summer of 1919.* University of Illinois Press, Urbana, 1982.

Washington, James M. *A Testament of Hope: The Essential Writings and Speeches of Martin Luther King Jr.* HarperCollins, New York, 1991.

Watters, Pat. *Down To Now: Reflections on the Southern Civil Rights Movement.* Pantheon, New York, 1971.

Weisbrot, Robert. *Freedom Bound: A History of America's Civil Rights Movement.* W. W. Norton, New York, 1990.

West, Cornell. *Keeping Faith: Philosophy and Race in America.* Routledge, New York, 1993.

White, John. *Black Leadership in America, 1895–1968.* Longman, London, 1985.

Whitfield, Stephen A. *A Death in the Delta: The Story of Emmett Till.* Collier Macmillan, London, 1988.

Wiedner, Donald. *A History of Africa South of the Sahara.* Vintage Books, New York, 1962.

Wolters, D. *The New Negro on Campus: Black College Rebellions of the 1920s.* Princeton University Press, Princeton, New Jersey, 1975.

Wynn, Neil A. *The Afro–American and the Second World War.* Paul Eleck, London, 1976.

Yarborough, Tinsley. *Judge Frank Johnson and Human Rights in Alabama.* University of Alabama Press, Tuscaloosa, 1981.

Zilversmitt, H. *The First Emancipation: The Abolition of Slavery in the North.* University of Chicago Press, Chicago, 1967.

Zinn, Howard. *A People's History of the United States.* Harper and Row, New York, 1980.

INDEX